Inhalt *Business English Intensivtraining*

Seite

Hinweis:
Eine Liste der ID-Nummern finden Sie für die Audio-CD von:

- ***CD 1: Telefonieren*** auf Seite 35
- ***CD 2: Geschäftsreisen*** auf Seite 66
- ***CD 3: Meetings*** auf Seite 97
- ***CD 4: Verhandlungen*** auf Seite 128
- ***CD 5: Small Talk*** auf Seite 159

Vorwort

Dieses Audio-Intensivtraining macht Sie rasch und gezielt fit für die wichtigsten Businessgespräche mit internationalen Partnern. Auf fünf Audio-CDs mit ca. sechs Stunden Ton können Sie sich professionell vorbereiten auf die typischen Situationen, Inhalte und Abläufe von Geschäftsgesprächen. In unterhaltsamen, hörspielartigen Dialogen und abwechslungsreichen Kommunikationsübungen trainieren Sie punktgenau Hörverständnis, sprachliche Ausdrucksfähigkeit und Sicherheit. Eine amüsante Story, gesprochen von Mutterspachlern und BBC-Sprechern, steht für Lernerfolg und -spaß. Jedes der fünf Themen ist selbstständig und in sich abgeschlossen, so dass Sie sich auch ganz gezielt auf ein Thema vorbereiten können.

Dieses Intensivtraining beinhaltet folgende fünf Themen:

1. **Telefonieren:** Hier kann der Lerner alles, was er für die moderne Telekommunikation mit Englisch sprechenden Geschäftspartnern braucht, ganz gezielt trainieren. Die Dialoge behandeln die wichtigsten Telefonsituationen im Geschäfts- und Berufsalltag.

2. **Geschäftsreisen:** Hier kann sich jeder professionell auf die Geschäftsreise und die wichtigsten Gesprächssituationen vorbereiten – von der Buchung und Reisedurchführung bis zu Besprechungen und Konferenzen.

3. **Meetings:** Der Lerner kann hier gezielt auf die wichtigsten Gesprächsituationen bei Geschäftsbesprechungen, Konferenzen und Präsentationen trainieren. Die Dialoge behandeln die typischen Gesprächsinhalte und -abläufe von Meetings – von der Begrüßung und Vorstellung, der Besprechung der Tagesordnung bis zum Meinungsaustausch und dem Umgang mit Einwänden und Zwischenfragen.

4. **Verhandlungen:** Die Dialogszenen behandeln die wichtigsten Gesprächsinhalte und -abläufe von Verkaufs-, Vertrags- und Preisverhandlungen – von der Organisation und Durchführung bis zum Kundengespräch und dem erfolgreichen Abschluss.

5. **Small Talk:** Dieses Audiotraining macht den Lerner sprachlich fit für die gelungene Kontaktaufnahme und -pflege mit internationalen Geschäftspartnern. Die Dialoge behandeln typische berufsrelevante Kommunikationssituationen – von der Begrüßung, der Gesprächseröffnung und dem Small Talk auf Geschäftsessen, Empfängen, Meetings und Konferenzen bis zum erfolgreichen Networking.

Jedes dieser fünf Themen ist auch als Einzelprodukt unter dem Reihentitel *Kommunikationstrainer Business English* im Buchhandel erhältlich.

Welche englischen Sprachkenntnisse werden vorausgesetzt?

Dieses Intensivtraining setzt Vorkenntnisse in Englisch voraus und ist ideal für alle, die ihr Schulenglisch direkt für den Beruf auffrischen möchten.

Was bietet Ihnen das Begleitbuch?

Im Begleitbuch sind alle Dialoge jeweils mit der deutschen Übersetzung abgedruckt, die Kommunikationsübungen jeweils mit der richtigen Lösung. So können Sie alle Hörtexte mitlesen. Zusätzlich finden Sie hier den Fachwortschatz und die wichtigsten Redewendungen. Typisch amerikanische Ausdrücke werden gesondert gekennzeichnet (AE).

Wie Sie vorgehen sollten, um das beste Lernergebnis zu erzielen:

1. Hören Sie sich den Dialog aufmerksam an und konzentrieren Sie sich auf die Situation.
2. Hören Sie sich dann den Dialog ein zweites Mal an. Falls Sie eine Stelle nicht verstanden haben sollten, spielen Sie den Dialog noch einmal ab und achten Sie dabei besonders auf diese Stelle. Um die Satzbeispiele und Redewendungen zu vertiefen, empfiehlt es sich, den Hörtext einmal parallel im Begleitbuch mitzulesen.
3. Wiederholen Sie nun die Redewendungen und Satzbeispiele des Dialogs in den Begleitübungen. Um das Lernen möglichst abwechslungsreich und einprägsam zu gestalten, gibt es insgesamt fünf verschiedene Übungstypen.

Effektives Üben:

Je nach Übungsform …
- sprechen Sie die Satzbeispiele nach oder
- formulieren Sie sie nach Vorgabe um.
- beantworten Sie Fragen zum Wortschatz.
- beantworten Sie inhaltliche Fragen zum Dialog.
- werden Sie selbst aktiv und übernehmen eine Sprecherrolle.

Wir wünschen allen Lernern viel Erfolg mit dem Business English Intensivtraining!

Abkürzungen

AE amerikanisches Englisch
s.o. *someone,* jemand
j-m jemandem
coll *colloquial* Umgangssprache
BE britisches Englisch
s.th. *something,* etwas
j-n jemanden

Telefonieren / Inhalt

1 Answering the Telephone

▲ Here you learn how to answer the telephone, to introduce yourself and to exchange greetings.

James Stuart works for Oxford and Chambers in London, and Sarah Mayhew works for the same organisation in San Francisco. In their role as management consultants, they will be working closely together. This is the first time they speak.

J: = James Stuart; S: = Sarah Mayhew

J: James Stuart speaking.
S: Hi, James. This is Sarah Mayhew from San Francisco! I thought I'd take the chance to make contact with you.
J: Sarah! Good to speak to you. I see we're on the same project team. Looks like we'll be working together quite a bit.
S: We sure will. How are you doing so far? Are you settling in okay?
J: So far, so good. I'm still finding my way around. Like everything else here, I've been thrown in at the deep end!
S: That sounds like Oxford and Chambers, but it's the best way to learn! Where were you working before?
J: I spent two years working with Barkers in the City. Before that I was finishing off my MBA. How about you?
S: Actually, I'm also pretty new. I just started three months ago. After graduating, I spent a couple of years with Archers in L. A. I prefer this though. It's more my kind of thing.
J: We're both relative newcomers then.
S: Yes, and we'll be learning the ropes together!
J: Great to hear it. I'll speak to you soon. Bye for now.
S: Bye.

Ein Gespräch annehmen

▲ Sie erfahren hier, wie man ein Gespräch annimmt, sich vorstellt und sich verabschiedet.

James Stuart ist Angestellter bei Oxford und Chambers, einer großen Beratungsfirma. Sie hat ihren Sitz in London. Sarah Mayhew arbeitet bei dem gleichen Unternehmen in San Francisco. Als Managementberater werden sie eng zusammenarbeiten. Hier sprechen sie zum ersten Mal miteinander.

J: Hier spricht James Stuart.
S: Hallo, James. Hier Sarah Mayhew aus San Francisco! Ich dachte, ich nutze die Gelegenheit, um mit Ihnen Kontakt aufzunehmen.
J: Sarah! Gut, mit Ihnen zu reden. Ich habe gesehen, dass wir beide im gleichen Projektteam sind. Das sieht nach einer ziemlich engen Zusammenarbeit aus.
S: Ja, genau. Wie läuft's denn bis jetzt so bei Ihnen? Finden Sie sich soweit zurecht?
J: So weit, so gut. Ich bin noch dabei mich einzugewöhnen. Wie hier üblich, musste ich gleich zu Anfang richtig ran!
S: Ja, das klingt ganz nach Oxford und Chambers, aber so lernt man am schnellsten! Wo haben Sie denn vorher gearbeitet?
J: Ich war zwei Jahre bei Barkers in der City [= London]. Davor habe ich mein Diplom in Betriebswirtschaft gemacht. Und Sie?
S: Eigentlich bin ich auch ziemlich neu hier. Ich habe erst vor drei Monaten angefangen. Nach meiner Ausbildung war ich ein paar Jahre bei Archers in L. A. Hier gefällt es mir aber besser. Das ist mehr nach meinem Geschmack.
J: Dann sind wir ja beide relativ neu.
S: Eben, und so werden wir uns gemeinsam einarbeiten.
J: Gut, das freut mich. Wir sprechen uns bald wieder. Auf Wiederhören.
S: Tschüss.

Exercises

1 Repeat the following sentences.

1. I thought I'd take the chance to make contact with you.
2. Looks like we'll be working together.
3. I've been thrown in at the deep end!
4. We'll be learning the ropes together!
5. I'll speak to you soon.

2 Listen to the following expressions and choose the correct definition.

1. I thought I'd take the chance to make contact with you.
   To make contact. *Does this mean:* to get in touch *or:* to work closely together?
   To make contact *means:* to get in touch.

2. Like everything else here, I've been thrown in at the deep end!
   To be thrown in at the deep end. *Does this mean:* to be given a lot of work to do *or:* to be in a new post which is hard to do at first?
   To be thrown in at the deep end *means:* to be in a new post which is hard to do at first.

3. We'll be learning the ropes together!
   Learning the ropes. *Does this mean:* taking an IT course *or:* gaining an understanding of a job?
   Learning the ropes *means:* gaining an understanding of a job.

3 Listen to the following extract from the dialogue and pay close attention to what James says.

J: James Stuart speaking.
S: Hi, James. This is Sarah Mayhew from San Francisco! I thought I'd take the chance to make contact with you.
J: Sarah! Good to speak to you. I see we're on the same project team. Looks like we'll be working together quite a bit.
S: We sure will. How are you doing so far? Are you settling in okay?
J: So far, so good. I'm still finding my way around. Like everything else here, I've been thrown in at the deep end!

Answer the telephone, taking the role of James. You'll hear one answer as a model. Other solutions are, of course, possible.

1. Hi, James. This is Sarah Mayhew from San Francisco! I thought I'd take the chance to make contact with you.

   And now it is your turn. Tell Sarah that it is good to speak to her and to be working together.
   Sarah! Good to speak to you. I see we're on the same project team. Looks like we'll be working together quite a bit.

2. We sure will. How are you doing so far? Are you settling in okay?

   Now it is your turn again. Tell Sarah how you are getting on at work.
   So far, so good. I'm still finding my way around. Like everything else here, I've been thrown in at the deep end!

ⓘ As we have just heard, Sarah introduces herself to James at the beginning of the conversation by giving her first and last name. She then continues by calling him "James".
In Great Britain and the United States of America, it is normal, with a few exceptions, to use first names during telephone conversations with business colleagues. This informal usage also applies when you are speaking to a colleague for the first time!

Vocabulary

to answer (the telephone)	ein Gespräch annehmen
to introduce *oneself*	*sich* vorstellen
to exchange (greetings)	Grußformeln austauschen; sich begrüßen
to work for …	Angestellte(r) bei … sein; für *j-n* arbeiten
management consultant	Managementberater(in)
to work closely together	eng zusammenarbeiten
to take the chance to make contact with *s.o.*	die Gelegenheit nutzen, mit *j-m* Kontakt aufzunehmen
to be on the same project team	am gleichen Projekt tätig sein; im gleichen Projektteam sein
to settle in (okay)	sich (gut) zurechtfinden
So far, so good.	So weit, so gut.
to find *one's* way around	sich zurechtfinden
to be thrown in at the deep end	gleich zu Anfang richtig ranmüssen
to sound (like)	klingen (wie)
It's the best way to learn.	So lernt man am schnellsten.
to finish off	vollenden; zu Ende führen
MBA (Master of Business Administration)	Diplom in Betriebswirtschaftslehre
to be pretty new	ziemlich neu sein
after graduating	nach dem Abschluss
a couple of	einige; ein paar
It's more my kind of thing.	Es ist mehr nach meinem Geschmack.
We're both relative newcomers then.	Dann sind wir beide relativ neu.
to learn the ropes together	sich gemeinsam einarbeiten
exception	Ausnahme
to use first names	Vornamen benutzen
last name	Nachname
informal usage	informeller Gebrauch
to apply	*hier:* gelten

2 Exchanging contact details

▲ We will show you here how to exchange telephone numbers and email addresses, and how to spell out names.

James Stuart and Sarah Mayhew will be working together on a project team advising a large construction company on how to introduce e-commerce into the business. They need to exchange some contact details for the file. Sarah is the first one on James' list ...

J: = **James Stuart; S: = Sarah Mayhew**

J: Hi, Sarah. It's James here. I'm putting together the contact file for the Rashamon project. What are the best numbers to reach you on?
S: Hi there. I guess we're getting closer to start up! You have my direct line already. If it's busy, you can leave a message on my voicemail. If you need to call the main switchboard, it's 001 415 842 3200.

J: What about your mobile?
S: My cellphone number is 07714 642 883.
J: And your email address?
S: It's sarah dot mayhew at oxfordchambers dot com. That's Sarah with an 'h' by the way. Mayhew is m-a-y-h-e-w. I also have a pager number if nothing else works. It's 01239 847210.

J: Great, I've got all that now.
S: What about you? I don't have all your details yet.
J: My email is james dot stuart at oxfordchambers dot co dot uk. My surname is spelt the Scottish way. That's s-t-u-a-r-t. My mobile is 0970 332 559 and my pager is 08879 204936. I'll email you the contact list as soon as I have the details of the others.

S: We have six on the team, right?
J: Yes. There's Michel Grand from Paris, Ingrid Petersson from Stockholm, Sammy Lee from Hong

Persönliche Daten weitergeben

▲ Hier lernen Sie, wie man persönliche Daten sowie Telefonnummern und E-Mail-Adressen weitergibt und wie man Namen buchstabiert.

James Stuart und Sarah Mayhew werden zusammen in einem Projektteam arbeiten, das ein großes Bauunternehmen bei der Einführung des E-Business beraten soll. Sie müssen ihre Adressen austauschen. Sarah steht oben auf der Liste von James ...

J: Hallo, Sarah. Hier James. Ich stelle die Adressliste für das Rashamon-Projekt zusammen. Unter welchen Nummern kann man Sie am besten erreichen?
S: Hallo, James. Der Start rückt also immer näher! Meine Direktdurchwahl haben Sie ja schon. Falls besetzt ist, können Sie eine Nachricht auf Anrufbeantworter hinterlassen. Wenn Sie die Telefonzentrale anrufen müssen: Die Nummer ist 001 415 842 3200.
J: Und Ihr Handy?
S: Meine Handy-Nummer ist 07714 642 883.
J: Und Ihre E-Mail-Adresse?
S: Die ist sarah dot mayhew at oxfordchambers dot com (sarah.mayhew@oxfordchambers.com). Sarah übrigens mit 'h'. Mayhew schreibt sich m-a-y-h-e-w. Ich habe auch einen Piepser, falls alles andere nicht läuft. Die Nummer ist 01239 847210.
J: Gut, dann habe ich alles.
S: Und was ist mit Ihnen? Ihre Daten habe ich noch nicht alle.
J: Meine E-Mail-Adresse lautet james dot stuart at oxfordchambers dot co dot uk (james.stuart@oxfordchambers.co.uk). Meinen Nachnamen schreibt man auf die schottische Art, das ist s-t-u-a-r-t. Meine Handy-Nummer ist 0970 332 559 und mein Piepser hat die Nummer 08879 204936. Sobald ich die Angaben der anderen habe, maile ich Ihnen die Liste.
S: Wir arbeiten zu sechst am Projekt, nicht wahr?
J: Stimmt. Michel Grand aus Paris, Ingrid Petersson aus Stockholm, Sammy Lee aus Hong

Kong and Rodrigo Velasquez from Caracas.
S: A truly international team and a lot of expertise! I'm looking forward to working with you guys!
J: Yes. It will be great to get things started!

Kong und Rodrigo Velasquez aus Caracas.
S: Ein wirklich internationales Team mit viel Sachkenntnis. Ich freue mich auf die Zusammenarbeit mit Ihnen allen!
J: Ja. Es wird toll sein, endlich anzufangen!

Exercises

1 Listen to the following sentences and answer the questions using "*Yes, I have got* …".

1. *Have you got a cellphone number?*
   Yes, I have got a cellphone number.
2. *Have you got voicemail?*
   Yes, I have got voicemail.
3. *Have you got an email address?*
   Yes, I have got an email address.
4. *Have you got a pager number?*
   Yes, I have got a pager number.

2 Listen to the following extract from the dialogue and pay close attention to what Sarah says.

J: And your email address?
S: It's sarah dot mayhew at oxfordchambers dot com (sarah.mayhew@oxfordchambers.com). That's Sarah with an 'h' by the way. Mayhew is m-a-y-h-e-w. I also have a pager number if nothing else works. It's 01239 847210.
J: Great, I've got all that now.
S: What about you? I don't have all your details yet.
J: My email is james dot stuart at oxfordchambers dot co dot uk (james.stuart@oxfordchambers.co.uk). My surname is spelt the Scottish way. That's s-t-u-a-r-t. My mobile is 0970 332 559 and my pager is 08879 204936. I'll email you the contact list as soon as I have the details of the others.
S: We have six on the team, right?
J: Yes. There's Michel Grand from Paris, Ingrid Petersson from Stockholm, Sammy Lee from Hong Kong and Rodrigo Velasquez from Caracas.
S: A truly international team and a lot of expertise! I'm looking forward to working with you guys!

Now take the role of Sarah. You'll hear one answer as a model. Other solutions are, of course, possible.

1. Could you tell me your email address and how to spell your name?
   And now it is your turn. Tell James your email address and how to spell your name.
   It's sarah dot mayhew at oxfordchambers dot com (sarah.mayhew@oxfordchambers.com). That's Sarah with an 'h' by the way. Mayhew is m-a-y-h-e-w.
2. Great, I've got that all now.
   Now tell James that you do not have all the details.
   What about you? I don't have all your details yet.
3. There's Michel Grand from Paris, Ingrid Peterson from Stockholm, Sammy Lee from Hong Kong and Rodrigo Velasquez from Caracas.
   It's your turn again. Say that it is an international team and that you are looking forward to working with them.
   A truly international team and a lot of expertise! I'm looking forward to working with you guys!

3 Listen to the dialogue again, paying particular attention to ways of leaving messages, email addresses, and how to spell names. Then answer the following questions.

1. *If Sarah's office number is busy, where can a caller leave a message?*
   A caller can leave a message on her voicemail.
2. *What is James's email address?*
   James's email address is james dot stuart at oxfordchambers dot co dot uk.
3. *How is 'Stuart' spelt?*
   'Stuart' is spelt: s-t-u-a-r-t.

ℹ Telephone numbers are generally spoken as separate digits in English, for example: "three-oh-six-nine-eight-five" in British English or "three-zero-six-nine-eight-five" in American English, rather than "thirty, sixty-nine, eighty-five". In British English, if two digits are the same, the word "double" may be used, for example: "double four", whereas in American English, the number is spoken twice, for example, "four four".

Vocabulary

to advise	beraten
construction company	Bauunternehmen
to introduce (into)	einführen
to exchange contact details	persönliche Daten austauschen
file	Akte; Ordner; Datei
to put together	zusammenstellen
to reach *s.o.*	*j-n* erreichen
I guess we're getting closer to start up.	Ich glaube, der Start/Beginn rückt immer näher.
to leave a message on voicemail	eine Nachricht auf Anrufbeantworter hinterlassen
main switchboard	Telefonzentrale
mobile phone (BE)	Handy; Mobiltelefon
cellphone (AE)	Handy; Mobiltelefon
if nothing else works	falls alles andere nicht läuft
to spell (the Scottish way)	(auf schottische Art) buchstabieren
a truly international team	ein wirklich internationales Team
a lot of	viel
expertise	Sachkenntnis
to look forward to	sich freuen auf
separate digits	einzelne Ziffern
whereas	jedoch; wohingegen
rather than	eher als

3 Leaving a message

▲ The following dialogue will show you how to leave a message on a voicemail system.

Sarah Mayhew is calling James Stuart in London. The phone rings twice and is picked up by James' voicemail.

J: = James Stuart; S: = Sarah Mayhew

(James's recorded voice:)
Hello, you're through to the voicemail of James Stuart. I'm sorry, I can't take your call right now, but if you'd like to leave a message, I'll get back to you.

(Automated voice:)
To speak to an operator dial 0 or remain silent; to speak to another person dial their extension now; otherwise, please leave your message for extension 4-6-3 after the tone.

S: Hi, James. This is Sarah calling. It's Monday, October 23rd , 8 a.m. I need to speak to you urgently regarding the Rashamon project. Please call me back as soon as possible.
When James returns from his meeting, he tries calling Sarah …
(Voicemail:)
Hi. You are through to extension 3209. There's no one here right now, but I can take a message if you like …

J: Sarah, it's James returning your call. I just got your message and hope I'm not too late getting back to you. I've been tied up in a meeting all day. I'm here for another thirty minutes, but after that you'll have to try me on my mobile.
James hangs up and a few minutes later his telephone rings.
J: James Stuart speaking.
S: Hi, James. Finally we manage to speak to each other in real time! Thanks for returning my message earlier. I have some urgent news

Wie man eine Nachricht hinterlässt

▲ Hier lernen Sie, wie man eine Nachricht auf Anrufbeantworter hinterlässt.

Sarah Mayhew ruft James Stuart in London an. Das Telefon läutet zweimal, dann meldet sich James' Anrufbeantworter.

(Man hört die aufgenommene Stimme von James:)
Hallo. Sie sind mit dem Anrufbeantworter von James Stuart verbunden. Leider bin ich momentan nicht erreichbar, Sie können aber gerne eine Nachricht hinterlassen und ich rufe Sie zurück.
(Automatische Stimme:)
Um mit der Vermittlung verbunden zu werden, wählen Sie bitte 0 oder warten Sie; um mit einer anderen Person zu sprechen, wählen Sie jetzt ihre Durchwahlnummer; ansonsten hinterlassen Sie bitte Ihre Nachricht für die Durchwahlnummer 4-6-3 nach dem Signalton.
S: Hallo, James. Hier Sarah. Es ist Montag, 23. Oktober, 8 Uhr. Ich muss dringend mit Ihnen über das Rashamon-Projekt sprechen. Bitte rufen Sie mich so bald wie möglich zurück.
Als James von seinem Meeting zurückkommt, versucht er bei Sarah anzurufen …
(Man hört wieder eine aufgenommene Stimme:)
Hallo. Sie sind mit der Durchwahlnummer 3209 verbunden. Im Moment können wir Ihren Anruf nicht beantworten, aber Sie können eine Nachricht hinterlassen …
J: Sarah, hier James. Ich habe gerade Ihre Nachricht bekommen und hoffe, ich rufe nicht zu spät zurück. Ich wurde den ganzen Tag in einer Sitzung aufgehalten. Ich bleibe noch dreißig Minuten hier, danach bin ich über mein Handy zu erreichen.
James hängt auf und ein paar Minuten später läutet sein Telefon.
J: James Stuart am Apparat.
S: Hallo, James. Endlich können wir direkt miteinander reden! Danke, dass Sie mich zurückgerufen haben. Ich habe Neuigkeiten über

on the Rashamon project that I need to speak to you about. Have you got a moment?

J: I have about fifteen minutes before I need to leave. Fire away!

S: The client has requested a meeting with the whole team next week. It sounds like they might want to pull the project unless they can get some major changes agreed. Are you able to come over?

J: I'll need some time to re-schedule my appointments, but I'm sure it won't be a problem. This sounds quite urgent anyway. Have you spoken with the rest of the team?

S: Yes. Ingrid and Sammy can make it. I'm still waiting to hear from the others.

J: Okay, let me know how it goes. I'll start freeing up my diary now.

S: Great, I'll speak to you tomorrow. Bye.

J: Certainly. Bye.

das Rashamon-Projekt, über die wir dringend sprechen müssen. Haben Sie jetzt Zeit?

J: Ich habe fünfzehn Minuten, bevor ich wegmuss. Schießen Sie los!

S: Der Kunde hat um eine Sitzung mit dem ganzen Team in der nächsten Woche gebeten. Es hört sich so an, als könnten sie das ganze Projekt einstellen, falls wir uns nicht auf einige wichtige Änderungen einigen. Können Sie herkommen?

J: Ich brauche etwas Zeit, um meine Termine umzustellen, aber das wird sicher kein Problem sein. Das klingt alles sehr ernst. Haben Sie schon mit den anderen Teammitgliedern gesprochen?

S: Ja. Ingrid und Sammy haben Zeit. Auf die Anrufe der anderen warte ich noch.

J: Okay. Geben Sie mir bitte Bescheid, wie es weitergeht. Ich fange jetzt an, meine Termine umzustellen.

S: Alles klar. Dann hören wir morgen wieder voneinander. Tschüss.

J: Sicher. Tschüss.

Exercises

1 Repeat the following sentences.

1. Please call me back as soon as possible.
2. It's James returning your call.
3. Thanks for returning my message earlier.
4. I have about fifteen minutes before I need to leave.

2 Listen to the following expressions and choose the correct definition.

1. I need to speak to you urgently.
   To speak to somebody urgently. *Does this mean:* to speak to somebody as soon as possible *or:* to speak to somebody regarding a meeting?
   To speak to somebody urgently *means:*
   to speak to somebody as soon as possible.

2. I've been tied up in a meeting all day.
   To be tied up in a meeting. *Does this mean:* to be setting up a meeting *or:* to be busy at a meeting?
   To be tied up in a meeting *means:* to be busy at a meeting.

3. Finally we manage to speak to each other in real time!
   To speak to somebody in real time.
   Does this mean: to leave a message on somebody's voicemail *or:* to actually talk to somebody?
   To speak to somebody in real time *means:* to actually talk to somebody.

4. I'll start freeing up my diary.
   To free up one's diary. *Does this mean:* to clear one's diary of appointments *or:* adding addresses to one's diary?
   To free up one's diary *means:* to clear one's diary of appointments.

3 Listen to the following sentences and answer the questions using *"Yes, I'd like to …"*.

1. *Would you like to leave a message?*
   Yes, I'd like to leave a message.
2. *Would you like to speak to an operator?*
   Yes, I'd like to speak to an operator.
3. *Would you like to try me on my mobile?*
   Yes, I'd like to try you on your mobile.
4. *Would you like to come over?*
   Yes, I'd like to come over.

Vocabulary

to leave a message	eine Nachricht hinterlassen
voicemail	Anrufbeantworter
to pick up the phone	das Telefon abnehmen
operator	Vermittlung
to dial	wählen (*Telefon*)
to remain silent	still bleiben; warten
extension (number)	Durchwahl(-nummer)
otherwise	ansonsten
urgent; urgently	dringend; ernst
regarding	bezüglich
to return a call	zurückrufen
to be tied up (in, with)	beschäftigt sein (in, mit)
to speak to each other in real time	direkt miteinander reden
news	Neuigkeiten; das Neueste
Fire away!	Schießen Sie los!
to request a meeting	um eine Sitzung bitten
to pull the project (AE)	das Projekt einstellen
to get major changes agreed	einige wichtige Änderungen vereinbaren
to re-schedule *one's* appointments	*seine* Termine umstellen
to make it (to the meeting)	es schaffen, zum (Termin) zu kommen
to free up *one's* diary	*seine* Termine umstellen

4 The line is busy

▲ James Stuart learns a useful tip: how to use the call-back facility when the extension dialled is engaged …

James Stuart has been trying to call Jane Miller in the legal department. For the last fifteen minutes the telephone has been constantly engaged. Just as he is starting to get frustrated, David Walker, a colleague, passes by …

J: = James Stuart; D: = David Walker

J: I'll try one more time and then I'll have to leave it till later …
J: I can't get through to anyone today!
D: Hi, James. That was a heartfelt sigh! What's happening with you today?
J: Hello, David. Just ignore me. It's pre-project frustration. I keep trying to get hold of our legal department, but the number's always busy.
D: Just put it on call-back and let the technology do the work!
J: I have to confess, I haven't read the manual for this system yet. How do you do that?
D: It's simple. Dial the number you need again … … is it still engaged?
J: Oh yes!
D: Then press six and replace the receiver. When it is free, your phone will ring and tell you!
J: As simple as that! If it works, it's really quite handy.
D: It will, don't worry. Anyway, I popped by because your phone was always engaged! I wanted to ask if you're coming to the pub after work. Andrew's leaving today and we want to give him a good send-off!
J: Hang on, I'll just get this …
Hello, Jane Miller? It's James Stuart here from the Project Office. I need to speak to you about …
D: I'll catch you later … give me a ring.

Die Leitung ist besetzt

▲ James Stuart bekommt einen nützlichen Hinweis: Wie man den Rückrufmodus einschaltet, wenn die Durchwahlnummer besetzt ist …

James Stuart hat versucht, Jane Miller in der Rechtsabteilung zu erreichen. Während der letzten fünfzehn Minuten war das Telefon ständig besetzt. Gerade als Frustration aufkommt, kommt David Walker, ein Kollege, vorbei …

J: Ich versuch's noch ein Mal, dann muss ich es auf später verschieben …
J: Ich erreiche heute niemanden!
D: Hallo, James. Der Seufzer kam von Herzen! Was ist heute mit dir los?
J: Hallo, David. Beachte mich gar nicht! Das ist nur der Frust vor dem Projekt. Ich versuche ständig, unsere Rechtsabteilung zu erreichen, aber es ist immer besetzt.
D: Dann stell doch einfach auf Rückruf um und lass die Technik arbeiten!
J: Ich muss gestehen, ich habe das Handbuch für dieses System noch nicht gelesen. Wie funktioniert das denn?
D: Ganz einfach. Wähl die Nummer, die du brauchst, noch einmal ... ist sie immer noch besetzt?
J: Oh, ja.
D: Dann drück die Sechs und leg wieder auf. Sobald sie frei wird, klingelt's dann bei dir.
J: So einfach ist das! Wenn's klappt, ist das wirklich ziemlich praktisch.
D: Es funktioniert, keine Sorge. Übrigens bin ich eigentlich vorbeigekommen, weil dein Telefon immer besetzt war! Ich wollte dich fragen, ob du nach der Arbeit in die Kneipe kommst. Heute verlässt Andrew die Firma und wir wollen ihm einen netten Abschied bereiten.
J: Warte mal, ich geh eben dran …
Hallo, Jane Miller? Hier spricht James Stuart aus dem Projektbüro. Ich muss dringend mit Ihnen sprechen über … .
D: Ich hol dich später ab, ruf mich an.

Exercises

1 Listen to the following sentences and answer the questions using *"No, I won't …"* or: *"No, I haven't …"*.

1. *Will you try one more time?*
   No, I won't try one more time.
2. *Have you got hold of the legal department?*
   No, I haven't got hold of the legal department.
3. *Will you come to the pub after work?*
   No, I won't come to the pub after work.
4. *Have you put it on call-back?*
   No, I haven't put it on call-back.

2 Listen to the following extract from the dialogue and pay particular attention to what David says.

J: Hello, David. Just ignore me. It's pre-project frustration. I keep trying to get hold of our legal department, but the number's always busy.
D: Just put it on call-back and let the technology do the work!
J: I have to confess, I haven't read the manual for this system yet. How do you do that?
D: It's simple. Dial the number you need again … … is it still engaged?
J: Oh yes!
D: Then press six and replace the receiver. When it is free, your phone will ring and tell you!
J: As simple as that! If it works, it's really quite handy.

Now take the role of David. You'll hear one answer as a model. Other solutions are, of course, possible.

1. Hello, David. Just ignore me. It's pre-project frustration. I keep trying to get hold of our legal department, but the number's always busy.
   And now it is your turn. Tell James to put it on call-back and let the technology do the work.
   Just put it on call-back and let the technology do the work!

2. I have to confess, I haven't read the manual for this system yet. How do you do that?
   It's your turn again. Tell James to dial the number again and then ask if it is still engaged.
   It's simple. Dial the number you need again … is it still engaged?

3. Oh yes!
   And now tell James to press six and to replace the receiver. Say that when it is free, the phone will ring.
   Then press six and replace the receiver. When it is free, your phone will ring and tell you!

3 Listen to the dialogue again, paying particular attention to using a call-back facility when an extension number is engaged. Then answer the following questions.

1. *What can a caller do, if the number dialled is always busy?*
   A caller can put the number on call-back.
2. *What is the first stage of using call-back?*
   The first stage of using call-back is dialling the number you need again.
3. *What is the second stage of using call-back?*
   The second stage of using call-back is pressing six and replacing the receiver.

ℹ Making telephone calls to Britain or the US does not only mean conversing in a foreign language, you also have to get used to unfamiliar dialling tones:
– Short, rapid tones signify an engaged or busy line in Britain and the USA.
– In Britain two long tones, a pause, two long tones, a pause and so on signify a ringing phone.
– One long tone, a long pause, a long tone, a long pause and so on signify a ringing phone in the USA.
– One long, continuous tone signifies that the line is free in Britain and the USA.

Vocabulary

useful	brauchbar; nützlich
call-back facility	Rückrufmodus
to get frustrated	frustriert werden
to pass by	vorbeikommen
a heartfelt sigh	ein Seufzer, der von Herzen kommt
Just ignore me.	*etwa:* Beachte mich gar nicht.
frustration	Frustration
to get hold of	*hier:* erreichen
legal department	Rechtsabteilung
constantly	ständig
busy; engaged (BE)	besetzt
to confess	zugeben; gestehen
manual	Handbuch
to replace the receiver	den Hörer wieder auflegen
handy	praktisch
Don't worry.	*etwa:* Keine Sorge.
to pop by	vorbeikommen
a good send-off	ein netter Abschied
anyway	übrigens
Hang on.	Warte mal.
I'll catch you later.	*etwa:* Ich hol dich später ab.
dialling tone (BE)	Amtszeichen
dial tone (AE)	Amtszeichen
rapid	schnell
to signify	bedeuten
continuous	ununterbrochen

5 I need to speak to …

▲ Here we listen to James Stuart trying to reach Sammy Lee in Hong Kong …

James Stuart needs to speak to Sammy Lee in the Hong Kong office. They're meeting in New York in five days' time, but first there are some details to be covered …

O: = **Operator; J:** = **James Stuart;**
R: = **Ruth King** (secretary of Sammy Lee);
Sa: = **Sammy Lee**

O: Good afternoon, Oxford and Chambers. How may I help you?
J: Hello, is it possible to speak to Sammy Lee?
O: Who's calling please?
J: This is James Stuart from the London office.
O: One moment, Mr Stuart, I'll try to connect you.
O: I'm sorry, there's no answer at the moment. Shall I put you through to his secretary?
J: Yes, please, it's quite urgent.
R: Good afternoon, Mr Lee's office. Who's calling please?
J: This is James Stuart from the London office. I'm the coordinator for the Rashamon project. Is Mr Lee available, please?
R: He's somewhere in the building. I'm expecting him back in half an hour.
J: This is quite urgent. Would it be possible to put a call out for him?
R: Certainly. Just one moment.
R: Could Mr Lee please contact Ruth immediately for an urgent telephone call?
Sa: Ruth, it's Sammy. You paged me. Who is calling me?
R: It's James Stuart from London. He needs to speak to you urgently.
Sa: Tell him I'm on the way. Please ask him to hold on.
R: Certainly. Mr Stuart, Mr Lee will be here shortly, please hold the line.
J: Thank you. You've been most helpful.
R: You're welcome.

Ich muss mit … sprechen

▲ Hier hören wir, wie James versucht, Sammy Lee in Hong Kong zu erreichen.

James muss mit Sammy Lee vom Büro in Hong Kong reden. Sie treffen sich in fünf Tagen in New York, aber vorher müssen ein paar Einzelheiten geklärt werden …

O: Guten Tag. Sie sind mit Oxford und Chambers verbunden. Wie kann ich Ihnen helfen?
J: Guten Tag. Ist es möglich, mit Sammy Lee zu sprechen?
O: Wie ist Ihr Name, bitte?
J: Ich bin James Stuart aus dem Londoner Büro.
O: Kleinen Moment, Herr Stuart, ich versuche Sie zu verbinden.
O: Tut mir Leid, im Moment nimmt niemand ab. Soll ich Sie mit seiner Sekretärin verbinden?
J: Ja, bitte, es ist ziemlich dringend.
R: Guten Tag, dies ist das Vorzimmer von Herrn Lee. Ihr Name, bitte?
J: Hier James Stuart aus dem Londoner Büro. Ich bin der Koordinator des Rashamon-Projekts. Ist Herr Lee zu sprechen?
R: Er ist irgendwo im Haus unterwegs. Ich erwarte ihn in etwa einer halben Stunde zurück.
J: Es ist ziemlich dringend. Wäre es möglich, ihn auszurufen?
R: Selbstverständlich. Einen Moment bitte.
R: Herr Lee wird gebeten, sich wegen eines dringenden Telefonats sofort bei Ruth zu melden.
Sa: Ruth, hier Sammy. Sie haben mich ausgerufen. Wer ist am Telefon?
R: James Stuart aus London. Er muss dringend mit Ihnen sprechen.
Sa: Sagen Sie ihm, ich komme sofort. Er möchte warten.
R: Selbstverständlich. Herr Stuart, Herr Lee wird gleich hier sein. Bitte bleiben Sie am Apparat.
J: Vielen Dank. Sie haben mir sehr geholfen.
R: Gern geschehen.

Sa: James! Sammy Lee here.
J: Sammy, glad to speak to you. I have a couple of things to discuss before we meet next week …

Sa: James! Hier Sammy Lee.
J: Sammy, ich bin froh mit Ihnen zu reden. Ehe wir uns nächste Woche treffen, muss ich einiges mit Ihnen besprechen …

Exercises

1 Repeat the following sentences.

1. Shall I put you through to his secretary?
2. Is Mr Lee available, please?
3. Would it be possible to put a call out for him?
4. I have a couple of things to discuss.

2 Listen to the following expressions and choose the correct definition.

1. I'll try to connect you.
   To connect. *Does this mean:* to put somebody through on the telephone *or:* to return somebody's telephone call?
   To connect *means:* to put somebody through on the telephone.

2. Please contact Ruth immediately.
   To contact immediately. *Does this mean:* to get in touch quickly *or:* to work together closely?
   To contact immediately *means:* to get in touch quickly.

3. Please ask him to hold on.
   To hold on. *Does this mean:* to remain silent *or:* to wait for a while?
   To hold on *means:* to wait for a while.

4. Mr Lee will be here shortly.
   To be here shortly. *Does this mean:* to settle in here quickly *or:* to arrive here soon?
   To be here shortly *means:* to arrive here soon.

3 Listen to the dialogue again, paying particular attention to reaching somebody by telephone. Then answer the following questions.

1. *Who is James trying to reach?*
   James is trying to reach Sammy in Hong Kong.
2. *Does James need to speak to Sammy urgently?*
   Yes, James does need to speak to Sammy urgently.
3. *How does Ruth contact Sammy?*
   Ruth contacts Sammy by putting a call out for him on the loudspeaker.

Vocabulary

to reach	erreichen
to cover	*hier:* (Thema) besprechen; klären
to connect	verbinden
to put *s.o.* through to …	*j-n* mit … verbinden
coordinator	Koordinator
available	*hier:* zu sprechen, frei
to expect	erwarten
to put a call out for *s.o.* (loudspeaker)	*j-n* ausrufen (Lautsprecher)
to page *s.o.* (loudspeaker or pager)	*j-n* ausrufen (Lautsprecher oder Piepser)
to be on the way	(schon) auf dem Weg sein; gleich da sein
shortly	gleich; bald
Please hold the line.	Bleiben Sie bitte am Apparat. Warten Sie bitte.

6 Making contact

▲The problems of mobile telephones are universal! Here we listen in as James Stuart tries to use his phone...

James Stuart has just arrived in Manhattan. He's on his way to his hotel when he gets a call on his mobile ...

S: = Sarah Mayhew; J: = James Stuart; M: = Matthew Peters

S: James, it's Sarah. Where are you?
J: Sarah, I can hardly hear you. Wait a moment, I'll see if I can find somewhere quieter ...
S: Can you hear me now?
J: Yes, that's much better. I'm in the subway and a train just arrived.
S: We had an urgent call from London. Matthew Peters tried to call you but couldn't get through. He wants you to call him right away.
J: Perhaps it's a problem with the signal. I've had the phone switched on since landing. Did he say what it was about?
S: He mentioned Clearwater, something to do with one of your projects? He needs some urgent information before the end of business today. Something about a contract clause. He didn't go into much detail.
J: Oh boy! I bet I know what it is! I'll try and call him now. Thanks for letting me know.

S: No problem. I'll see you at three.
James finds a quiet spot and dials his London office.
J: Matthew, it's James. Sarah told me you needed me.
M: James, thank goodness for that. I've been trying to reach you for hours.
J: My flight arrived only ninety minutes ago; I switched my mobile on then. What did you need me for?
M: Of course, I completely forgot you were travelling! It's about Clearwater. They are claiming we haven't delivered everything as per the specification ...

Sich in Verbindung setzen

▲ Probleme mit Handys sind allgemein verbreitet! Hier hören wir, wie James versucht eine Information zu bekommen ...

James ist gerade in Manhattan gelandet. Auf dem Weg zum Hotel bekommt er einen Anruf auf seinem Handy ...

S: James, hier ist Sarah. Wo sind Sie?
J: Sarah, ich kann Sie kaum hören. Moment, ich suche eine ruhigere Stelle ...
S: Können Sie mich jetzt hören?
J: Ja, das ist viel besser. Ich bin in der U-Bahn und gerade ist ein Zug eingefahren.
S: Wir bekamen einen dringenden Anruf aus London. Matthew Peters hat versucht Sie anzurufen, kam aber nicht durch. Er bittet um sofortigen Rückruf.
J: Wahrscheinlich bin ich in einem Funkloch. Mein Handy ist eingeschaltet, seit ich gelandet bin. Hat er gesagt, um was es geht?
S: Er erwähnte Clearwater, etwas mit einem Ihrer Projekte? Vor Geschäftsschluss braucht er noch dringend Informationen. Etwas wegen einer Vertragsklausel. Mehr Einzelheiten nannte er nicht.
J: Oh, Mann! Ich wette, ich weiß, um was es geht! Ich versuche jetzt gleich ihn zu erreichen. Danke für die Nachricht.
S: Kein Problem. Bis um drei Uhr also.
James findet eine ruhige Stelle und wählt sein Büro in London an.
J: Matthew, hier James. Sarah hat mir mitgeteilt, dass Sie mich brauchen.
M: James, Gott sei Dank! Ich habe stundenlang versucht, Sie zu erreichen.
J: Ich bin erst vor neunzig Minuten gelandet. Dann habe ich mein Handy wieder eingeschaltet. Worum geht's denn?
M: Ach ja, ich habe vollkommen vergessen, dass Sie unterwegs waren! Es geht um Clearwater. Sie behaupten, wir haben nicht alles gemäß der Aufstellung geliefert.

(Garbled sounds come from his mobile)
J: Matthew? I don't know if you can hear me, but I think we've lost the signal again. I'll call you as soon as I can get to the office!

(James stops a passing taxi.)

(Unverständliche Geräusche aus seinem Handy)
J: Matthew? Ich weiß nicht, ob Sie mich hören können. Ich glaube aber, wir haben das Funksignal wieder verloren. Ich rufe Sie an, sobald ich im Büro bin!
(James hält ein vorbeifahrendes Taxi an.)

Exercises

1 Listen to the following expressions and choose the correct definition.

1. I bet I know what it is!
   I bet. *Does this mean:* I am not certain
   or: I am certain?
   I bet *means:* I am certain.

2. I've been trying to reach you for hours.
   For hours. *Does this mean:* for a long time
   or: for a short time?
   For hours *means:* for a long time.

3. I switched my mobile on then.
   To switch something on. *Does this mean:* to turn something off *or:* to turn something on?
   To switch something on *means:* to turn something on.

2 Listen to the following sentences and answer the questions using *"Yes, I can …"*.

1. *Can you find somewhere quieter?*
   Yes, I can find somewhere quieter.
2. *Can you call me before end of business today?*
   Yes, I can call you before end of business today.
3. *Can you let me know about the contract clause?*
   Yes, I can let you know about the contract clause.
4. *Can you phone me as soon as you get to the office?*
   Yes, I can phone you as soon as I get to the office.

3 Listen to the following extract from the dialogue and pay close attention to what James says.

S: James, it's Sarah. Where are you?
J: Sarah, I can hardly hear you. Wait a moment, I'll see if I can find somewhere quieter …
S: Can you hear me now?
J: Yes, that's much better. I'm in the subway and a train just arrived.
S: We had an urgent call from London. Matthew Peters tried to call you but couldn't get through. He wants you to call him right away.
J: Perhaps it's a problem with the signal. I've had the phone switched on since landing.

And now take the role of James. You will hear one answer as a model. Other solutions, of course, are possible.

1. James, it's Sarah. Where are you?
   Now it is your turn. Say that you can hardly hear Sarah and that you will try to find somewhere quieter.
   Sarah, I can hardly hear you. Wait a moment, I'll see if I can find somewhere quieter …

2. Can you hear me now?
   Answer by saying the line is much better and tell Sarah that you are in the subway and that a train just arrived.
   Yes, that's much better. I'm in the subway and a train just arrived.

3. We had an urgent call from London. Matthew Peters tried to call you but couldn't get through. He wants you to call him right away.

It's your turn again. Suggest that it is a problem with the signal and say that you have had the phone switched on since landing.
Perhaps it's a problem with the signal. I've had the phone switched on since landing.

Vocabulary

hardly	kaum	**end of business**	Geschäftsschluss
quiet	ruhig; leise	**contract clause**	Vertragsklausel
subway (AE)	U-Bahn	**to bet**	wetten
underground; tube (BE)	U-Bahn	**for hours**	stundenlang
		completely	vollkommen
to call *s.o.* right away	*j-n* sofort anrufen; zurückrufen	**to claim**	behaupten
		to deliver	liefern
switched on	eingeschaltet	**as per**	gemäß
to mention	erwähnen	**specification**	Angabe; Beschreibung

7 The telephone conference call

▲ Here we find out how to arrange a telephone conference call across several time differences …

The Rashamon team frequently need to discuss the progress of the project. For this, face-to-face meetings are not always convenient. James Stuart asks his administrator, Michael Allan, to set up a conference call …

J:= James Stuart; Mi: = Michael Allan; Ro: = Roseanne Day; Sa: = Sammy Lee; S: = Sarah Mayhew; Rod: = Rodrigo Velasquez

J: Michael, I need you to arrange a conference call for the Rashamon team … can you find a suitable time within the next two days?

Mi: Okay, I'll see what I can do.

(Michael goes off to make arrangements …)

Mi: I'll start with New York…. *(He dials Roseanne Day, Sarah Mayhew's secretary.)*

Ro: Hi, Roseanne here.

Mi: Roseanne, it's Michael, I need to book a conference call. Can you check Sarah's diary? It should be in the next couple of days.

Ro: Sarah's diary is clear on Thursday.

Mi: Good. So let's say mid-afternoon … can you schedule Sarah for two p.m. London time?

Ro: Hmm … that's about six a.m. here. Can you make it a little later …?

Mi: I need to consider Sammy Lee as well. Hong Kong's eight hours ahead of London, so that would be ten in the evening … okay let's say three p.m. London time, that's seven in the morning for Sarah, and eleven at night for Sammy. Rodrigo should be fine in Caracas, I think they're about three hours behind.

Die Telefonkonferenz

▲ Hier erfahren wir, wie man eine Telefonkonferenz unter Berücksichtigung verschiedener Zeitzonen organisiert …

Das Rashamon-Team muss oft über den Fortschritt des Projektes sprechen. Sich persönlich zu treffen ist nicht immer praktisch. James bittet seinen Assistenten Michael Allan, eine Telefonkonferenz zu arrangieren …

J: Michael, Sie müssen bitte für mich eine Telefonkonferenz organisieren. Suchen Sie einen geeigneten Zeitpunkt innerhalb der nächsten zwei Tage?

Mi: In Ordnung. Ich werde sehen, was ich machen kann.

(Michael geht weg, um die Konferenz zu organisieren …)

Mi: Ich fange mit New York an … *(Er wählt Roseanne Day an, die Sekretärin von Sarah.)*

Ro: Hallo, hier Roseanne.

Mi: Roseanne, hier Michael. Ich muss eine Telefonkonferenz buchen. Können Sie in Sarahs Kalender nachschlagen? Die Konferenz sollte innerhalb der nächsten Tage stattfinden.

Ro: In Sarahs Kalender ist der Donnerstag frei.

Mi: Gut, dann sagen wir gegen Mitte des Nachmittages … können Sie Sarah den Termin für zwei Uhr Londoner Zeit eintragen?

Ro: Hm … das ist ungefähr sechs Uhr morgens hier. Können Sie ihn ein bisschen später legen …?

Mi: Ich muss auch an Sammy Lee denken. Hong Kong ist London acht Stunden voraus, dann ist es dort zehn Uhr abends … okay, sagen wir drei Uhr nachmittags Londoner Zeit; das ist dann sieben Uhr morgens bei Sarah und elf Uhr abends bei Sammy. Für Rodrigo in Caracas dürfte das kein Problem sein: Ich glaube, sie sind ungefähr drei Stunden zurück.

Ro: That's right. OK. It's in her diary now …

Michael continues until he has set up the call for all members of the team.
Two days later the team are gathered around their respective phones …

J: Hello, everyone, thanks for making the time. We'll be as quick as possible as I'm aware it's not an ideal time for everyone!

Sa: Hi, team. I'm speaking to you from a warm Hong Kong evening! I hope you're all fine.

S: Hi, everybody! I've just been for my early morning run on the beach! San Francisco is looking good today!

(The rest of the team give their greetings and the meeting gets started.)

J: Sorry Rodrigo, there was a bit of an echo there. Would you mind repeating that?

Rod: Sure. I said in order to finalize Stage Two we need to get an agreement on software; there's still too much uncertainty …

The meeting continues.

Ro: Das stimmt. In Ordnung. Der Termin steht jetzt in ihrem Kalender …

Michael macht weiter, bis er die Telefonkonferenz für alle Mitglieder des Teams organisiert hat.
Zwei Tage später warten die Teammitglieder neben ihren Telefonapparaten …

J: Hallo, allerseits, danke, dass Sie sich die Zeit nehmen. Wir machen so schnell wie möglich, weil mir bewusst ist, dass dieser Zeitpunkt nicht für alle ideal ist!

Sa: Hallo, Team. Ich rufe an einem warmen Abend aus Hong Kong an! Ich hoffe es geht Ihnen allen gut.

S: Hallo, allerseits. Ich komme gerade von meinem morgendlichen Strandlauf! San Francisco sieht heute herrlich aus!

(Die übrigen Teammitglieder begrüßen sich und dann geht's los mit dem Meeting.)

J: Entschuldigung Rodrigo, da war so etwas wie ein Echo. Würden Sie das bitte wiederholen?

Rod: Sicher. Ich sagte, um die zweite Phase zum Abschluss zu bringen, müssen wir eine Einigung über die Software erzielen, es gibt immer noch zu viel Unsicherheit …

Das Meeting wird fortgesetzt.

Exercises

1 Repeat the following sentences.

1. Can you find a suitable time within the next two days?
2. Can you schedule Sarah for two p.m. London time?
3. Thanks for making the time.
4. I'm aware it's not an ideal time for everyone.
5. Would you mind repeating that?

2 Listen to the following sentences and respond to the questions using *"No, I don't mind …"*.

1. *Do you mind arranging a conference call for me?*
   No, I don't mind arranging a conference call for you.
2. *Do you mind checking Sarah's diary?*
   No, I don't mind checking Sarah's diary.
3. *Do you mind making it a little later?*
   No, I don't mind making it a little later.

3 Listen to the dialogue again, paying particular attention to arranging a telephone conference call across several time differences. Then answer the following questions.

1. *Who does James ask to set up a conference call?*
   James asks Michael to set up a conference call.
2. *When is Sarah's diary clear?*
   Sarah's diary is clear on Thursday.
3. *Why must Rodrigo repeat what he has said?*
   Rodrigo must repeat what he has said because there is an echo on the line.

> ℹ Telephone conferences are an economic and efficient way to exchange ideas with several people at different places at the same time.
> Before setting up a telephone conference call, make sure you are aware of the time differences from country to country! "Ahead of" and "behind" are used to express these differences, for example: "Germany is six hours ahead of New York, and the UK is eight hours behind Hong Kong."

Vocabulary

telephone conference call	Telefonkonferenz
time difference	Zeitunterschied
frequently	häufig
progress	Fortschritt
face-to-face	persönlich
convenient	günstig; praktisch
administrator	*hier:* Assistent
to set up	organisieren
suitable	geeignet; passend
to book	buchen
diary	(Termin-)Kalender
to schedule	ansetzen; planen
about six a.m. / p.m.	ungefähr sechs Uhr morgens / nachmittags (abends)
to consider	bedenken; denken an; in Betracht ziehen
three hours behind	drei Stunden hinterher, zurück
to gather around	sich versammeln; *hier:* warten neben
I'm aware (that) …	Es ist mir bewusst, (dass) …
echo	Echo; Widerhall
Would you mind repeating that?	Würden Sie das bitte wiederholen?
to finalize	zum Abschluss bringen
to get an agreement	eine Einigung erzielen
uncertainty	Unsicherheit
eight hours ahead	acht Stunden voraus

8 Automated telephone systems

▲ We often find ourselves connected to automated answering systems when calling companies. Here we listen to Sarah Mayhew calling her bank in England, but it isn't as easy as it should be …

Voice Recognition Systems are used by many companies to handle calls from customers. Sarah Mayhew has an account at a London bank which she opened when she was working there several years ago. She would now like to close her account and transfer the money …

VRS: = Voice Recognition System;
S: = Sarah Mayhew; G: = Gerry Baxter

VRS: Welcome to Brindley's Banking Service. Please press or dial zero on your telephone now. *(Sarah presses 0.)* For automated services, say one after the tone; for credit cards, say two; for all other services, say nine after the tone.
S: One.
VRS: Speak your sixteen-digit card number, four digits at a time. First group of four digits, please …
S: Four-nine-one-six.
VRS: Second group of four digits, please …
(The system continues to ask until Sarah has given all sixteen numbers.)
VRS: Please speak your four-digit PIN number after the tone.
S: Two-three-two-seven.
VRS: Thank you. For a balance enquiry, say one after the tone; for credit card enquiries, say two after the tone; for all other enquiries, say nine after the tone.
S: Nine.
VRS: Thank you. We will shortly be connecting you to an operator.
G: Hello, you're through to Brindley's Bank Customer Services. Gerry speaking. How may I help you?
S: Hi, I need to close my account. Would you be able to help me?

Automatische Telefonsysteme

▲ Oft werden wir mit automatischen Telefonsystemen verbunden, wenn wir Firmen anrufen. Hier hören wir zu, wie Sarah versucht ihre Bank in England anzurufen … aber das ist nicht so einfach, wie es sein sollte …

Viele Konzerne verwenden Spracherkennungssysteme (VRS), um die Anrufe ihrer Kunden zu beantworten. Sarah Mayhew hat ein Konto bei einer Londoner Bank, das sie eröffnete, als sie vor einigen Jahren dort arbeitete. Nun möchte sie das Konto schließen und ihr Geld überweisen lassen …

VRS: Willkommen bei Brindleys Bankservice. Bitte drücken Sie oder wählen Sie die Null auf Ihrem Telefon. *(Sahra drückt die 0.)* Für automatische Dienste sagen Sie eins nach dem Ton; für Kreditkarten sagen Sie zwei; für alle anderen Dienste sagen Sie neun nach dem Ton.
S: Eins.
VRS: Sprechen Sie Ihre sechszehn-stellige Kartenzahl, in vier-stelligen Gruppen. Erste Gruppe, bitte …
S: Vier-neun-eins-sechs.
VRS: Zweite vier-stellige Zahlengruppe, bitte …
(Das System fragt weiter, bis Sarah alle sechzehn Nummern angegeben hat.)
VRS: Bitte sprechen Sie Ihre vier-stellige PIN-Nummer nach dem Ton.
S: Zwei-drei-zwei-sieben.
VRS: Danke schön. Für eine Kontostandabfrage sagen Sie eins nach dem Ton; für Kreditkartenanfragen sagen Sie zwei nach dem Ton; für alle anderen Fragen sagen Sie neun nach dem Ton.
S: Neun.
VRS: Danke schön. Sie werden gleich mit einem Mitarbeiter verbunden.
G: Hallo, Sie sind mit Brindleys Bank Kundendienst verbunden. Mein Name ist Gerry. Wie kann ich Ihnen helfen?
S: Hallo, ich möchte mein Konto schließen. Können Sie mir helfen?

G: No, but I'll connect you to the department which can …

VRS: You're through to Account Maintenance. To arrange a direct debit, say one after the tone; to transfer money between accounts, say three after the tone; for all other enquiries, say five after the tone; to speak to an operator, say nine after the tone.

S: Nine.

VRS: We're sorry. All our operators are busy at the moment. Please call back later. Remember your call is important to us.

S: It obviously isn't that important!

(Sarah slams the phone down.)

G: Nein, aber ich verbinde Sie mit der Abteilung, die Ihnen weiterhelfen kann …

VRS: Sie sind jetzt bei der Kontoverwaltung. Um eine Einzugsermächtigung zu erteilen, sagen Sie bitte eins nach dem Ton; um Geld zwischen Konten zu überweisen, sagen Sie drei nach dem Ton; für alle anderen Dienste sagen Sie fünf nach dem Ton; um mit einem Angestellten verbunden zu werden, sagen Sie neun nach dem Ton.

S: Neun.

VRS: Es tut uns Leid. Im Moment sind alle Leitungen belegt. Bitte rufen Sie später noch einmal an. Und nicht vergessen: Ihr Anruf ist uns sehr wichtig!

S: So wichtig scheint er ja nicht zu sein!

(Sarah knallt den Hörer auf.)

Exercises

1 Listen to the following expressions and choose the correct definition.

1. For automated services, say one after the tone.
   Automated. *Does this mean:* operated by computer *or:* paged by loudspeaker?
   Automated *means:* operated by computer.
2. For credit card enquiries, say two after the tone.
   Enquiries. *Does this mean:* news *or:* questions?
   Enquiries *means:* questions.
3. To transfer money between accounts, say three after the tone.
   To transfer something. *Does this mean:* to try to get hold of something *or:* to move something from one place to another?
   To transfer something *means:* to move something from one place to another.

2 Listen to the following sentences and respond to the instructions using *"Do I …?"*.

1. *Please press zero on your telephone now.*
   Do I press zero on my telephone now?
2. *Say nine after the tone.*
   Do I say nine after the tone?
3. *Speak your sixteen-digit card number.*
   Do I speak my sixteen-digit card number?

3 Listen to the dialogue again, paying particular attention to being connected by an automated answering service. Then answer the following questions.

1. *Why is Sarah calling her bank?*
   Sarah is calling her bank to close her account.
2. *Who or what does Gerry connect Sarah to?*
   Gerry connects Sarah to Account Maintenance.
3. *Why can't Sarah speak to an operator?*
   Sarah can't speak to an operator because they are all busy.

Vocabulary

automated telephone system	automatisches Telefonsystem
VRS (Voice Recognition System)	Spracherkennungssystem
to handle a call	einen Anruf beantworten
(bank) account	(Bank-)Konto
to transfer money	Geld überweisen (lassen)
digit; sixteen-digit number	Ziffer; sechszehnstellige Zahl
PIN (Personal Identification Number)	PIN-Nummer
balance (of account)	Kontostand
enquiry	Anfrage
customer services	Kundendienst
to close an account	ein Konto schließen
department	Abteilung
Account Maintenance	Kontoverwaltung
direct debit	Einzugsermächtigung
It obviously isn't that important!	*etwa:* So wichtig scheint es ja nicht zu sein!
to slam the phone down	den Hörer aufknallen

9 The video conference

▲ New technology should make communication easier. Here we listen in as the Rashamon team get to grips with their first video conference …

Sarah Mayhew is going over the technical details with her secretary, Roseanne Day, who has set up the conference. There is a television screen at one end of the table and a control box in the middle.

S: = Sarah Mayhew; Ro: = Roseanne Day; J: = James Stuart; I: = Ingrid Petersson; Sa: = Sammy Lee; Rod: = Rodrigo Velasquez

S: I haven't done a video conference before. What's the format?

Ro: You sit here next to the control box. The camera is on top of the TV. As I turn the television on … you should now be able to see yourself on the screen …

S: Yes, that definitely looks like me!

Ro: During the call you need to make sure you speak clearly into this microphone on the control box here. There will be a slight time lag between you speaking and the others hearing you, so you need to allow for that. So, don't all speak at once!

S: OK, let's see if the others are all there yet … *(As Sarah presses the button, the others appear in different areas of the screen.)*

S: Welcome everyone. Thanks for attending. Can you all see and hear me clearly?

J: Sarah, I can hear you, but I can't see you. I'll get the technician in again …

S: OK, as long as you can hear me, we might as well start. I'll kick off with an update on the US side of the project. Can you guys follow with your reviews?

I: Sarah, I don't know if you can hear me, but I'm not sure we have a connection here …

Die Videokonferenz

▲ Neue Technik sollte die Kommunikation erleichtern. Hier erfahren wir, wie das Rashamon-Team seine erste Videokonferenz angeht …

Sarah Mayhew geht die technischen Einzelheiten mit ihrer Sekretärin Roseanne Day durch, die die Konferenz organisiert hat. An einem Ende des Tisches steht ein Fernsehschirm, in der Mitte ein Kontrollkasten.

S: Dies ist meine erste Videokonferenz. Wie läuft das?

Ro: Sie sitzen hier neben dem Kontrollkasten. Die Kamera ist oben auf dem Fernseher. Wenn ich den Fernsehapparat jetzt einschalte … sollten Sie sich selbst auf dem Bildschirm sehen können …

S: Ja, das sieht mir sehr ähnlich!

Ro: Während des Anrufs sollten Sie deutlich ins Mikrofon hier auf dem Schaltkasten sprechen. Es gibt eine kleine Zeitverzögerung, wenn Sie reden, bis die anderen Sie hören, darauf müssen Sie achten. Also, nicht alle auf einmal reden!

S: In Ordnung, wollen wir mal sehen, ob die anderen schon da sind … *(Sarah drückt auf den Knopf, und die anderen erscheinen auf dem Bildschirm.)*

S: Ein herzliches Willkommen an alle. Danke, dass Sie teilnehmen. Können Sie mich alle deutlich sehen und hören?

J: Sarah, ich kann Sie hören, aber nicht sehen. Ich hole nochmal den Techniker …

S: O.K., wenn Sie mich hören, können wir anfangen. Ich werde mit einem Bericht über den neuesten Stand der US-Beteiligung am Projekt beginnen. Können Sie danach mit Ihren Berichten weitermachen?

I: Sarah, ich weiß nicht, ob Sie mich hören können, aber ich bin nicht sicher, ob wir hier eine Verbindung haben …

S: Ingrid, I can see and hear you …
I: If you can hear me, I'm going to disconnect and dial again …
J: Sarah, I don't think we've got Ingrid yet. She may be having some technical difficulties.

S: Can everyone else hear me?
(Sarah is greeted with silence apart from James' response.)
S: James. I'm not getting a response from anyone else. I think we're going to have to re-schedule this, until we have everything working.
(Suddenly everything bursts into life.)
I: At last, everything seems to be working here! Can you all hear me now?
Sa: Hi, there! Hong Kong is back on line.

Rod: Ah, it seems to be working. We had a small technical hitch. Shall we get started?

(They all start talking at once.)

S: Ingrid, ich kann Sie sehen und hören …
I: Falls Sie mich hören: Ich schalte aus und wähle nochmals …
J: Sarah, ich glaube nicht, dass wir schon eine Verbindung zu Ingrid haben. Sie scheint technische Schwierigkeiten zu haben.
S: Können mich alle anderen hören?
(Sarah bekommt außer von James keine Reaktion.)
S: James, es meldet sich sonst keiner. Ich meine, wir müssen dies verschieben, bis alles läuft.

(Plötzlich wird alles lebendig.)
I: Es scheint jetzt endlich zu funktionieren. Hören Sie mich jetzt alle?
Sa: Hallo, da drüben! Die Verbindung mit Hong Kong steht wieder!
Rod: Es scheint jetzt alles zu laufen. Wir hatten ein kleines technisches Problem. Wollen wir anfangen?
(Alle reden gleichzeitig los.)

Exercises

1 Repeat the following sentences.

1. I haven't done a video conference before. What's the format?
2. I'm going to disconnect and dial again.
3. I think we're going to have to re-schedule this.
4. We had a small technical hitch.

2 Listen to the following extract from the dialogue.

S: Welcome everyone. Thanks for attending. Can you all see and hear me clearly?
J: Sarah, I can hear you, but I can't see you. I'll get the technician in again …
S: OK, as long as you can hear me, we might as well start. I'll kick off with an update on the US side of the project. Can you guys follow with your reviews?
I: Sarah, I don't know if you can hear me, but I'm not sure we have a connection here …
S: Ingrid, I can see and hear you.
I: If you can hear me, I'm going to disconnect and dial again …
J: Sarah, I don't think we've got Ingrid yet. She may be having some technical difficulties.
S: Can everyone else hear me?

Now take the role of Sarah. Again, you will hear one answer as a model. Other solutions are, of course, also possible.

1. Sarah, I can hear you, but I can't see you. I'll get the technician in again …
   And now it is your turn. Say that as long as they can hear you, you can start with an update on the US side of the project.

OK, as long as you can hear me, we might as well start. I'll kick off with an update on the US side of the project.

2. Sarah, I don't know if you can hear me, but I'm not sure we have a connection here …
   Tell Ingrid that you can see and hear her.
   Ingrid, I can see and hear you.

3. Sarah, I don't think we've got Ingrid yet. She may be having some technical difficulties.
   It's your turn again. Ask if everyone else can hear you.
   Can everyone else hear me?

3 Listen to the dialogue again, paying particular attention to setting up a video conference and being connected to other participants. Then answer the following questions.

1. *In which way does James have trouble being connected at first?*
   James has trouble being connected at first, because he can hear Sarah, but he cannot see her.
2. *What kind of difficulties does Ingrid have at first?*
   Ingrid has technical difficulties at first.
3. *Who else apart from Sarah, James and Ingrid takes part in the video conference?*
   Apart from Sarah, James and Ingrid, Sammy and Rodrigo take part in the video conference.

Vocabulary

to get to grips with *s.th.*	*eine Sache* angehen, in den Griff kriegen
to go over *s.th.*	*etwas* durchgehen
technical details	technische Angaben
television screen	Fernsehschirm
control box	Kontrollkasten
to be on top of	oben drauf sein
What's the format?	*etwa:* Wie läuft das?
to turn on	einschalten
That definitely looks like me!	*etwa:* Das sieht mir sehr ähnlich!
during the call	während des Anrufes
to make sure	sicherstellen
slight	klein
to speak clearly	deutlich sprechen
time lag	Zeitverschiebung
You need to allow for that.	*etwa:* Du musst darauf aufpassen.
to attend (a conference)	an (einer Konferenz) teilnehmen
technician	Techniker
as long as	solange wie
to kick off	anfangen
Can you guys follow with your reviews? (AE)	*etwa:* Können Sie hinterher mit Ihren Berichten weitermachen?
to disconnect	ausschalten; trennen
technical difficulties	technische Schwierigkeiten
to re-schedule	verschieben
technical hitch	technisches Problem

10 The WAP telephone

▲ Here we listen in as Ben Andrews, an American colleague and a close friend of James Stuart, explains the benefits of WAP telephones to him.

James is given another new work tool, but first he needs to understand how to use it.

J: = James Stuart; B:= Ben Andrews

J: Ben, what does WAP stand for?

B: It means Wireless Application Protocol. As you can imagine, WAP sounds a bit friendlier! It's a messaging service for digital cellphones. It allows you to see Internet content in special text format on WAP-enabled phones …

J: STOP! Sometimes "techies" make life more complicated than it needs to be! Why all the acronyms?

B: Are you including me in that statement? Anyway, you know I prefer abbreviations!

J: True enough. I have a few of my own I could use on you!

B: I'm sure you do! Anyway, back to business … apart from being able to receive text messages, it also gives you access to the Internet …

J: … so I can check the cricket scores and see how my shares are doing?

B: Hmm, as a side benefit perhaps, although the main benefit is, of course, for business purposes!

J: OK, serious hat on now! Does it give me full access to the Internet?

B: Yes, but only if the web page has been written for it. There are more pages in this new format, but you won't be able to access everything yet.

J: What's the downside?

B: The technology is still slow. Downloading a web page takes forever, but this is improving all the time.

Das WAP-Telefon

▲ Hier hören wir zu, wie Ben Andrews, ein amerikanischer Kollege und ein guter Freund von James Stuart, ihm die Vorteile des WAP-Telefons erklärt.

James Stuart bekommt ein neues Arbeitswerkzeug, aber zuerst muss er lernen, wie es funktioniert.

J: Ben, was bedeutet eigentlich WAP?

B: Es steht für Wireless Application Protocol, d.h. etwa „drahtloses Anwendungsprotokoll". Wie du dir vorstellen kannst, klingt WAP etwas freundlicher! Das ist ein Nachrichtenservice für Handys. Er ermöglicht dir, Internetseiten in einem besonderen Textformat auf WAP-Telefonen zu lesen …

J: STOP! Manchmal machen Technikfreaks das Leben noch komplizierter, als es ist! Warum die ganzen Akronyme?

B: Schließt du mich in diese Behauptung mit ein? Du weißt, ich ziehe Abkürzungen vor!

J: Das ist wahr. Ich habe ein paar eigene, die ich auf dich anwenden könnte!

B: Davon bin ich überzeugt. Nun, zurück zum Geschäft … außer dass du Textnachrichten empfangen kannst, hast du auch Zugang zum Internet …

J: … damit ich den Stand des Kricketspiels prüfen und nachschauen kann, wie sich meine Aktien machen?

B: Hm … als Nebeneffekt vielleicht, obwohl der Hauptvorteil natürlich im geschäftlichen Bereich liegt!

J: O.K., jetzt mal im Ernst! Habe ich dann vollen Internetzugang?

B: Ja, aber nur zu Webseiten, die dafür gestaltet sind. Es gibt schon mehr Seiten in diesem neuen Format, aber alles kannst du doch noch nicht öffnen.

J: Und die Nachteile?

B: Die Technik ist noch langsam. Eine Webseite herunterzuladen dauert ewig, aber das wird immer besser.

J: So, I have another new tool in my briefcase. Is it all ready to go?
B: Yes, it's got a SIM card in it, so you can start using it today.
J: A SIM card?
B: Yes, that's a small card that slots into your cellphone. It contains details about your service level and the service provider. The phone won't work without it.
J: Oh, I see.
B: Here is the manual that goes with the phone. Why don't you read it and if you have any further questions, just ask me.
J: You can rest assured, I will have more questions!
(Their conversation takes a more sociable turn …)

J: Also, dann habe ich noch ein neues Werkzeug in meiner Aktentasche. Ist es startklar?
B: Ja, die SIM-Karte ist schon drin; du kannst es also ab heute benutzen.
J: Eine SIM-Karte?
B: Ja, das ist eine kleine Karte, die in deinem Handy steckt. Sie enthält Informationen über deinen Servicevertrag und deinen Internetdienst. Ohne sie funktioniert das Telefon nicht.
J: Aha. Ich verstehe.
B: Hier ist das Handbuch fürs Telefon. Lies es durch und falls du weitere Fragen hast, frag mich einfach.
J: Du kannst dich darauf verlassen, ich werde noch Fragen haben!
(Das Gespräch nimmt eine Wendung zu geselligeren Themen …)

Exercises

1 Repeat the following sentences.

1. WAP stands for Wireless Application Protocol.
2. It's a messaging service for digital mobile phones.
3. Apart from receiving text messages, it also gives you access to the Internet.
4. Here is the manual that goes with the phone.

2 Listen to the following expressions and choose the correct definition.

1. It allows you to see Internet content in special text format.
   Format. *Does this mean:* update *or:* appearance?
   Format *means:* appearance.
2. What's the downside?
   Downside. *Does this mean:* disadvantage *or:* frustration?
   Downside *means:* disadvantage.
3. Downloading a web page takes forever.
   To take forever. *Does this mean:* to handle a call *or:* to take a long time?
   To take forever *means:* to take a long time.

3 Listen to the following extract from the dialogue. Pay particular attention to what Ben says.

J: So, I have another new tool in my briefcase. Is it all ready to go?
B: Yes, it's got a SIM card in it, so you can start using it today.
J: A SIM card?
B: Yes, that's a small card that slots into your cellphone. It contains details about your service level and the service provider. The phone won't work without it.
J: Oh, I see.
B: Here is the manual that goes with the phone. Why don't you read it and if you have any other questions, just ask me.
J: You can rest assured I will have more questions!

Now take the role of Ben. You'll hear one answer as a model. Other solutions are also possible.

1. So, I have another new tool in my briefcase. Is it all ready to go?

And now it is your turn. Answer that the mobile has got a SIM card in it and James can start using it.
Yes, it's got a SIM card in it, so you can start using it today.

2. A SIM card?
Answer that it is a small card containing details about James' service level and provider.
Yes, that's a small card that slots into your cellphone. It contains details about your service level and service provider.

3. Oh, I see.
Your turn again. Tell James about the mobile manual, suggest that he reads it and offer to answer any further questions.
Here is the manual that goes with the phone. Why don't you read it and if you have any further questions, just ask me.

ⓘ Mobile phones are becoming more and more versatile – and ever smaller. As well as mobile phones with Internet access, there are now portable mobile phones available with in-built miniature TV screens, which provide up to 200 minutes of television viewing time!
What will the next telecommunications fad be?

Vocabulary

a close friend	ein enger Freund
WAP (Wireless Application Protocol)	*etwa:* drahtloses Anwendungsprotokoll
content	Inhalt
enabled	berechtigt
techie	*etwa:* Technikfreak
complicated	kompliziert
abbreviation	Abkürzung
Are you including me in that statement?	Schließt du mich in diese Behauptung mit ein?
access to the Internet	Internetzugang
cricket score	Ergebnis des Kricketspiels
shares	Aktien
side benefit	Nebenvorteil; Nebeneffekt
main benefit	Hauptvorteil
purpose	Zweck
Serious hat on now!	Jetzt werde ich ernst! Mal im Ernst!
web page	Webseite
downside	Nachteil
to download	herunterladen
to take forever	ewig dauern
to improve	besser werden; verbessern
tool	Werkzeug
briefcase	Aktentasche
SIM (Subscriber Identity Module); SIM card	SIM; SIM-Karte
to slot	hineinstecken
to contain	enthalten
service level	Servicevertrag
service provider	Internetdienst
further questions	weitere Fragen
You can rest assured.	Du kannst dich darauf verlassen.
versatile	vielseitig verwendbar
fad	Trend

Liste der ID-Nummern für CD 1: Telefonieren

Inhalt der CD	ID-Nummer:
Vorspann	1
Dialogue 1	2
Exercises	3–5
Dialogue 2	6
Exercises	7–9
Dialogue 3	10
Exercises	11–13
Dialogue 4	14
Exercises	15–17
Dialogue 5	18
Exercises	19–21
Dialogue 6	22
Exercises	23–25
Dialogue 7	26
Exercises	27–29
Dialogue 8	30
Exercises	31–33
Dialogue 9	34
Exercises	35–37
Dialogue 10	38
Exercises	39–41

Geschäftsreisen / Inhalt

1 Making a telephone call to arrange a meeting

▲ You will hear how John Bryant makes a phone call, asks for information and arranges an appointment to meet Tony McNamara.

John Bryant is the product manager at Galaxy Pax UK, a company which makes biodegradable packaging. His company wants to put their product – Earth Pax – onto the US market with the help of an American company, EZ Pack. They have already made contact, and now John Bryant wants to go to the US for a meeting with Tony McNamara, the project manager at EZ Pack. He phones EZ Pack to make arrangements.

SC: = Sarah Coen (secretary of Tony McNamara); JB: = John Bryant; TM: =Tony McNamara

SC: *EZ Pack*, Chicago. Good morning. My name's Sarah Coen. How may I help you?
JB: Hello. I'm John Bryant from *Galaxy Pax UK*. Could I speak to Mr McNamara, please?
SC: Just one moment, please. I'll put you through.
(Please hold the line …)
SC: Mr Bryant? I'm afraid Mr McNamara's at a meeting right now. Can I take a message, or should I ask him to call you back?
JB: I'll try again later. When would be a good time to phone?
SC: In about an hour, I guess.
JB: Yes. Fine. I'll try again then. Thanks.
SC: You're welcome. Thank you for calling. Goodbye.

An hour later John Bryant calls again. He finally speaks to Tony McNamara. You will hear how they make an appointment and how they arrange their meeting and discuss further details.

Telefonisch eine Verabredung treffen

▲ Sie hören, wie John Bryant ein Telefonat führt, Informationen einholt und einen Termin für ein Treffen mit Tony McNamara vereinbart.

John Bryant ist Produktmanager bei der Firma Galaxy Pax UK, die biologisch abbaubare Verpackungen herstellt. Seine Firma möchte ihr Produkt Earth Pax mit Hilfe der amerikanischen Firma EZ Pack auf den US-amerikanischen Markt bringen. Ein erster Kontakt ist bereits hergestellt, und nun will John Bryant in die USA fliegen und den Projektmanager von EZ Pack, Tony McNamara, treffen. Er ruft bei EZ Pack an, um die nötigen Vereinbarungen zu treffen.

SC: *EZ Pack*, Chicago, guten Morgen. Sie sprechen mit Sarah Coen. Was kann ich für Sie tun?
JB: Guten Tag, hier ist John Bryant von *Galaxy Pax UK*. Könnte ich bitte Mr. McNamara sprechen?
SC: Einen Augenblick bitte, ich verbinde.
(Bitte bleiben Sie am Apparat …)
SC: Mr. Bryant? Es tut mir Leid. Mr. McNamara ist gerade in einer Besprechung. Kann ich etwas ausrichten, oder soll er Sie zurückrufen?
JB: Ich probiere es später noch einmal. Wann wäre es denn am besten?
SC: In ungefähr einer Stunde, denke ich.
JB: Okay. Gut. Ich probiere es dann nachher noch einmal. Vielen Dank.
SC: Bitte sehr. Vielen Dank für Ihren Anruf. Auf Wiederhören.

Eine Stunde später ruft John Bryant noch einmal an. Dieses Mal erreicht er Tony McNamara. Sie hören, wie die beiden einen Termin für ihr Treffen vereinbaren und weitere Einzelheiten besprechen.

SC: *EZ Pack*, Chicago. Good morning. My name's Sarah Coen. How may I help you?
JB: Hello, it's John Bryant here again, from *Galaxy Pax UK*. I phoned about an hour ago.
SC: Oh, yes. Hello, Mr Bryant. Mr McNamara's expecting your call. Could you hold the line, please, while I put you through?
JB: Thanks.
(Please hold the line ...)
TM: Hello, John? How are you? It's good to hear you!
JB: Hello, Tony. I'm fine, thanks. Tony, I'm calling to see if we could arrange to meet in Chicago, perhaps in the next two weeks? Would that be possible?
TM: That's a great idea! It's about time we discussed things face to face. I'll just check my diary. ... How about next Tuesday – that's the 14th of March?
JB: That would be fine by me.
TM: Great! If you could get here on Monday, we could meet up in the evening and have dinner together. I know a great little restaurant. You'll just love it! What do you think? Then on Tuesday we can get down to business.
JB: Good idea. I look forward to it. I'll make all the flight and hotel arrangements and get back to you to confirm.
TM: If you let us know when you're arriving, we can arrange to have you picked up at the airport.
JB: Great. I'll let you know.
TM: Sure. It was nice talking to you. I look forward to meeting you.
JB: I'm looking forward to it, too. Bye, Tony, and thanks.
TM: Don't mention it. Bye now, John.

SC: *EZ Pack*, Chicago, guten Morgen. Sie sprechen mit Sarah Coen. Was kann ich für Sie tun?
JB: Hallo, hier ist nochmal John Bryant von *Galaxy Pax UK*. Ich hatte vor etwa einer Stunde schon einmal angerufen.
SC: Ja, natürlich. Hallo, Mr. Bryant. Mr. McNamara erwartet Ihren Anruf bereits. Bleiben Sie bitte am Apparat, ich verbinde Sie.
JB: Danke.
(Bitte bleiben Sie am Apparat ...)
TM: Hallo, John? Wie geht es Ihnen? Schön, von Ihnen zu hören.
JB: Hallo, Tony. Mir geht es gut, danke. Tony, ich rufe an, weil ich fragen wollte, ob wir uns in Chicago treffen könnten – vielleicht in den nächsten zwei Wochen? Würde Ihnen das passen?
TM: Das ist eine glänzende Idee! Es wird wirklich Zeit, dass wir uns einmal persönlich über alles unterhalten. Ich schaue nur kurz in meinen Terminkalender. ... Wie wäre es kommenden Dienstag – das ist der 14. März?
JB: Ja, das würde mir ausgezeichnet passen.
TM: Wunderbar! Wenn es Ihnen möglich wäre, am Montag hierher zu fliegen, könnten wir uns abends treffen und zusammen essen gehen. Ich kenne da ein tolles kleines Restaurant, das Ihnen bestimmt gefällt! Was halten Sie davon? Und am Dienstag können wir dann das Geschäftliche besprechen.
JB: Eine gute Idee. Ich freue mich. Ich kümmere mich um den Flug und das Hotel und melde mich dann wieder bei Ihnen.
TM: Wenn Sie uns mitteilen, wann Sie ankommen, lassen wir Sie gerne am Flughafen abholen.
JB: Wunderbar. Ich gebe Ihnen Bescheid.
TM: Schön. Es war nett, mit Ihnen zu sprechen. Ich freue mich darauf, Sie persönlich kennen zu lernen.
JB: Ich freue mich auch. Auf Wiederhören, Tony, und vielen Dank.
TM: Keine Ursache. Bis dann, John.

Exercises

1 Please listen to the following sentences and repeat them.

1. Just one moment, please. I'll put you through.
2. Should I ask him to call you back?
3. When would be a good time to phone?

2 Please listen to the following questions and form new questions using "*Would you mind …?*".

1. *Will you be trying again later?*
   Would you mind trying again later?
2. *Will you be checking your diary?*
   Would you mind checking your diary?
3. *We could meet up in the evening and have dinner together.*
   Would you mind meeting up in the evening and having dinner together?

3 Please listen to the following extract from the dialogue and pay close attention to what Sarah says.

JB: Hello. I'm John Bryant from *Galaxy Pax UK*. Could I speak to Mr McNamara, please?

SC: Just one moment, please. I'll put you through.
(Please hold the line …)

SC: Mr Bryant? I'm afraid Mr McNamara's at a meeting right now. Can I take a message, or should I ask him to call you back?

JB: I'll try again later. When would be a good time to phone?

SC: In about an hour, I guess.

Now it's your turn. Please take the role of Sarah. You'll hear one answer as a model. Other solutions are, of course, also possible.

1. Hello. I'm John Bryant from *Galaxy Pax UK*. Could I speak to Mr McNamara, please?
   Tell John Bryant that you'll put him through.
   Just one moment, please. I'll put you through.

2. I'll try again later. When would be a good time to phone?
   Tell John Bryant to call back in about an hour.
   In about an hour, I guess.

ⓘ Making telephone calls in Britain or the US does not only mean conversing in a foreign language, you also have to get used to unfamiliar dialling tones:
– Short, rapid tones signify an engaged or busy line in Britain and the USA.
– In Britain two long tones, a pause, two long tones, a pause and so on signify a ringing phone.
– One long tone, a long pause, a long tone, a long pause and so on signify a ringing phone in the USA.
– One long, continuous tone signifies that the line is free in Britain and the USA.

Vocabulary

biodegradable packaging	biologisch abbaubare Verpackung(en)
to make arrangements	Vereinbarungen (*hier:* eine Verabredung) treffen
I'm afraid …	ich befürchte …
I guess …	ich schätze …
I'll put you through.	Ich verbinde Sie.
Please hold the line!	Bitte warten Sie!; Bitte bleiben Sie am Apparat!
It's about time …	Es ist höchste Zeit …
to meet up	sich treffen
to pick up	abholen
I'm looking forward to it.	Ich freue mich darauf.
Don't mention it.	Nicht der Rede wert.

2 Making travel arrangements

▲ Here we learn what arrangements need to be made for a business trip.

John Bryant is making travel arrangements with his secretary, Sue Brown. They talk about visas and flight tickets.

JB: = John Bryant; SB: = Sue Brown; AE: = Airline employee

JB: Sue? I'd like you to arrange a few things for my trip to the States. You've been to the States before. Do I need a visa?

SB: No, not for a short business trip, John. You just fill out a visa waiver form on the flight.

JB: And what about money?

SB: I'd recommend taking your credit cards. They're even more useful in the US than here. You can also take traveller's cheques. They're as good as cash in the States. You can even buy things in supermarkets with traveller's cheques.

JB: One other thing. I'll need a car. The people from *EZ* are picking me up from the airport, but I think I'd like a car. I want to be independent and look around the area a bit.

SB: I'll see if I can hire a car for you when I book your flight. What sort of car did you have in mind?

JB: Oh, just something small – not one of those huge American cars.

SB: What about your hotel, John?

JB: Could you arrange somewhere not too far from the office?

SB: Consider it done!

JB: Thank you.

Sue phones the airline to book a ticket.

AE: Good morning, *UK Airlines*. How can I help you?

SB: Good morning. I'm calling from *Galaxy Pax UK*. I'd like to book a flight to America for a Mr Bryant.

Flug und Hotel buchen

▲ Hier erfahren Sie, wie man eine Geschäftsreise organisiert.

John Bryant organisiert die Geschäftsreise mit seiner Sekretärin, Sue Brown. Sie sprechen über Visum und Flugtickets.

JB: Sue? Ich möchte, dass Sie ein paar Dinge für meine Geschäftsreise in die Staaten erledigen. Sie waren doch schon dort. Brauche ich ein Visum?

SB: Nein, nicht für eine kurze Geschäftsreise. Sie müssen nur im Flugzeug ein Einreiseformular ausfüllen.

JB: Und was ist mit Geld?

SB: Ich würde Ihnen empfehlen, Ihre Kreditkarten mitzunehmen. Die sind in Amerika noch nützlicher als hier. Sie können auch Reiseschecks mitnehmen. Die werden in den Staaten wie Bargeld angenommen. Man kann sogar im Supermarkt mit Reiseschecks bezahlen.

JB: Noch etwas. Ich brauche ein Auto. Die Leute von *EZ* holen mich am Flughafen ab, aber ich möchte trotzdem einen Wagen. Ich will unabhängig sein und mir auch ein bisschen die Gegend anschauen.

SB: Ich werde versuchen, mit dem Flug zusammen gleich einen Mietwagen zu buchen. Was für ein Auto haben Sie sich denn vorgestellt?

JB: Ach, irgend einen Kleinwagen – bloß keinen so riesigen amerikanischen Schlitten.

SB: Was ist mit Ihrem Hotel, John?

JB: Vielleicht finden Sie etwas in der Nähe des Büros von *EZ Pack*?

SB: So gut wie erledigt!

JB: Danke.

Sue ruft bei der Fluggesellschaft an, um den Flug zu buchen.

AE: *UK Airlines*, guten Morgen. Was kann ich für Sie tun?

SB: Guten Morgen. Hier ist die Firma *Galaxy Pax UK*. Ich möchte für einen Mr. Bryant einen Flug in die USA buchen.

AE: Certainly, madam. Where and when does he want to travel?
SB: To Chicago on the 13th of March in business class, please.
AE: Okay. Just one moment, please. …
AE: Hello? There is a flight which arrives at Chicago at five in the afternoon. It leaves London at three in the afternoon.
SB: Fine. Would you book a return ticket please?
AE: I'll just take some details. What is Mr Bryant's first name?
SB: John.
AE: And … when would he like to return?
SB: Two weeks later – on the 27th of March.
AE: How would you like to pay?
SB: I'll give you our account details. Will you send the ticket to us?
AE: That isn't necessary. Mr Bryant can pick up the ticket at the airport.
SB: Thank you.
AE: So that's a flight to Chicago on Monday the 13th of March for Mr John Bryant, travelling business class.
SB: That's right.
AE: We'll fax you the details of the flight as soon as possible – could you let me have your fax number, please?
SB: Certainly. It's 0208 421 3772.
AE: OK, I've got that.
SB: One more thing. Mr Bryant would also like to hire a car for his two weeks in Chicago. Is it possible to do that through you?
AE: Yes, certainly. We have a partner car hire firm here – *Ready Wheels*. We can arrange that. Can you tell me what car you'd like?
SB: Well, Mr Bryant would like …

AE: Gerne. Wohin und wann möchte er fliegen?
SB: Nach Chicago, und zwar am 13. März. Business-Class, bitte.
AE: Okay. Einen Augenblick bitte. …
AE: Hören Sie? Wir haben einen Flug, der um 17 Uhr in Chicago ankommt. Abflug in London 15 Uhr.
SB: Sehr gut. Würden Sie bitte einen Hin- und Rückflug buchen.
AE: Ich brauche nur noch einige Informationen. Wie heißt Mr. Bryant mit Vornamen?
SB: John.
AE: Und … wann möchte er zurückfliegen?
SB: Zwei Wochen später … am 27. März.
AE: Und wie möchten Sie zahlen?
SB: Ich gebe Ihnen unsere Kontoverbindung. Schicken Sie uns das Ticket dann zu?
AE: Das ist nicht nötig. Mr. Bryant kann das Ticket am Flughafen abholen.
SB: Danke.
AE: Das wäre also ein Flug nach Chicaco am Montag, den 13. März, für Mr. John Bryant. Business-Class.
SB: Genau.
AE: Wir faxen Ihnen die Details so bald wie möglich. Geben Sie mir bitte Ihre Faxnummer?
SB: Selbstverständlich. Die ist 0208 421 3772.
AE: Okay, habe ich notiert.
SB: Noch eine Frage: Mr. Bryant möchte für die zwei Wochen in Chicago ein Auto mieten. Können wir das auch über Sie machen?
AE: Aber selbstverständlich. Wir arbeiten mit einer Mietwagenfirma zusammen – *Ready Wheels*. Das können wir organisieren. Was für einen Wagen hätten Sie denn gerne?
SB: Also, Mr. Bryant möchte einen …

Exercises

1 Please listen to the following sentences and then repeat them.

1. I'd like you to arrange a few things for my trip.
2. I'd recommend taking your credit cards.
3. I'd like to book a flight to America.

2 Please listen to the following questions and form new sentences using *"I'd like you to …"*.

1. *Can you arrange a few things for my trip?*
   I'd like you to arrange a few things for my trip.

2. *Can you hire a car for me?*
   I'd like you to hire a car for me.
3. *Can you fax me the flight details?*
   I'd like you to fax me the flight details.

2 Please listen to the following sentences and say whether they are true or false.

1. *For his trip to the States John needs a visa.*
   This sentence is false: For a short business trip John doesn't need a visa.
2. *Traveller's cheques are as good as cash in the States.*
   This sentence is true. You can even buy things in supermarkets with traveller's cheques.
3. *Sue wants to book a flight to New York.*
   This sentence is false: Sue books a flight to Chicago.

ℹ It is important to remember that people don't carry a lot of money with them. As a visitor, traveller's cheques are accepted at most places – even at supermarkets. The most important thing is to have a credit card. If you want to hire a car, you will always be asked for a credit card. If you want to pay cash people think that you've just robbed a bank!

Vocabulary

to fill out a form	ein Formular ausfüllen
visa waiver form	Einreiseformular
What about money?	*etwa:* Wie sieht's mit Geld aus?
one other thing	noch etwas
to pick up	abholen
independent	unabhängig
What sort of car did you have in mind?	An was für ein Auto dachten Sie?
Consider it done!	Betrachten Sie es als erledigt!; So gut wie erledigt!
huge	riesig
How can I help you?	Was kann ich für Sie tun?
to book a return ticket	einen Hin- und Rückflug buchen
account details	*hier:* Kontoverbindung
That isn't necessary.	Das ist nicht nötig.
as soon as possible	so bald wie möglich
Could you let me have …, please?	Könnten Sie mir bitte … geben?
car hire firm	Mietwagenfirma
We can arrange that.	Das können wir organisieren.

3 At the airport

▲ Here we listen as John Bryant checks in at the airport, finds his way to the bar and discovers there is a delay.

John Bryant is at London airport. He checks in and waits at the airport bar for his flight. The flight is delayed, so he has to contact his colleagues in the States, who wanted to pick him up from the airport.

CA: = Check-in agent; JB:= John Bryant; BK: = Barkeeper; L: = Lisa

CA: Good afternoon, sir. Can I have your passport and ticket, please?
JB: Yes, just a second – here you are.
CA: How many pieces of luggage are you checking in?
JB: Two suitcases to check in and one piece of hand luggage.
CA: I need to ask you for security reasons whether you packed all the bags yourself?
JB: Yes, I did.
CA: Are you taking anything with you that another person has given you and have you left your luggage unattended at any time?
JB: No.
CA: Here's your passport and your boarding card, sir. This is your seat number in the business class section – it's a non-smoking flight. The gate number will be announced later. Boarding time is two fifteen.
JB: Thank you very much.
CA: Have a nice flight.
John Bryant goes to the bar where he meets a fellow traveller, Lisa, an American.

BK: What can I get you?
JB: I'll have a whisky and soda, please. Oh, and a packet of peanuts, please.
BK: Coming right up.
L: I see you like the same drink as me!
JB: Oh, yes – I'm always a bit nervous before a flight.
L: Don't like flying, huh?

Am Flughafen

▲ Hier hören wir, wie John Bryant eincheckt, sich an die Bar setzt und erfährt, dass sein Flug Verspätung hat.

John Bryant ist am Londoner Flughafen. Er checkt ein und wartet an der Bar, dass seine Maschine aufgerufen wird. Weil der Flug Verspätung hat, muss er seine Kollegen in den USA verständigen, die ihn am Flughafen abholen wollten.

CA: Guten Tag. Ihren Reisepass und Ihr Ticket, bitte.
JB: Ja, einen Moment. Hier ist alles.
CA: Wie viele Gepäckstücke haben Sie?
JB: Zwei Koffer zum Aufgeben und ein Stück Handgepäck.
CA: Aus Gründen der Sicherheit muss ich Sie fragen, ob Sie alles selbst eingepackt haben.
JB: Ja, das habe ich.
CA: Haben Sie irgendetwas dabei, das Ihnen eine fremde Person mitgegeben hat, oder haben Sie Ihr Gepäck irgendwann unbeaufsichtigt stehen lassen?
JB: Nein.
CA: Hier Ihr Pass und Ihre Bordkarte. Das ist Ihre Sitzplatznummer in der Business-Class. Es ist ein Nichtraucherflug. Die Nummer des Flugsteigs wird später über Lautsprecher bekannt gegeben. Boardingtime ist vierzehn Uhr fünfzehn.
JB: Vielen Dank.
CA: Guten Flug.
John geht zur Bar, wo er mit Lisa ins Gespräch kommt, einer Amerikanerin, die ebenfalls auf ihre Maschine wartet.
BK: Was darf ich Ihnen bringen?
JB: Einen Whisky Soda, bitte. Oh, und ein Päckchen Erdnüsse.
BK: Sofort.
L: Ich sehe, Sie haben denselben Drink wie ich!
JB: Oh, ja. Ich bin immer ein bisschen nervös vor einem Flug.
L: Sie fliegen nicht gern?

JB: Not really, but a boat takes too long!
L: Where are you heading for?
JB: Chicago, on business.
L: Chicago's a great place. You'll enjoy it.

JB: If time allows! How about you?

L: I'm going home to New York. I was here on business, too. Six days. It's my first time in Britain – I just loved it here in London. I was lucky – I had time to go out and see some of the sights, and in the evenings we went to Indian or Chinese restaurants, and I even took in a movie and went to a West End theatre. Have you been to the States before?

JB: Unfortunately not. …
L: Oh, is that your flight there on the board? It seems like there's a delay.

JB: Oh, God, yes, it is. Two hours! Oh, no, and they're picking me up from the airport!

L: Oh, that's too bad! Well, I guess you'll have to let them know.
JB: Well, there's nothing I can do about it. I'll just have to phone them.
L: I have to wait a while, too. Shall we have another drink?
JB: Good idea – the same again?
L: Yep!
JB: Look, here's my card, in case you come to London again.
L: Oh, I have one, too – here it is. Look me up if you do business in The Big Apple!

Bryant talks on his mobile. It is hard for him to hear what is being said.
JB: Hello? It's John Bryant here.
Yes, that's right. Look, my flight has been delayed. I'll be arriving about two hours later than expected. … Will that be a problem? … Sorry? I didn't get that … That's kind of you, but … I could always take a taxi … Could you say that again? … It's very noisy here … Well, thanks a lot. I hope it's not too

JB: Nein, aber mit dem Schiff dauert es zu lange!
L: Wohin geht denn die Reise?
JB: Nach Chicago. Geschäftlich.
L: Chicago ist eine tolle Stadt. Es wird Ihnen gefallen.
JB: Ich hoffe, dass mir genügend Zeit bleibt. Und wohin fliegen Sie?
L: Ich fliege heim nach New York. Ich war auch geschäftlich hier. Sechs Tage. Ich bin zum ersten Mal in Großbritannien gewesen – London hat mir außerordentlich gut gefallen. Ich hatte auch Glück, da ich Zeit hatte, mir einige Sehenswürdigkeiten anzuschauen, und abends waren wir Chinesisch oder Indisch essen, und ich war sogar im Kino und in einem Theater im West End. Waren Sie schon einmal in den Staaten?
JB: Leider noch nicht.
L: Oh, ist das dort auf der Anzeigetafel nicht Ihr Flug? Die Maschine scheint Verspätung zu haben.
JB: Ach du lieber Himmel, ja. Zwei Stunden! Oh nein! Und ich werde doch am Flughafen abgeholt!
L: Wie ärgerlich! Nun, es wird Ihnen nichts übrig bleiben als dort Bescheid zu geben.
JB: Ja, ich kann es schließlich nicht ändern. Ich werde sie wohl anrufen müssen.
L: Ich muss auch noch eine Zeitlang warten. Wollen wir noch was trinken?
JB: Ja, gute Idee – noch mal das Gleiche?
L: Jawohl!
JB: Hier – meine Visitenkarte, falls Sie mal wieder nach London kommen.
L: Oh, ich habe meine auch dabei – hier, bitte. Melden Sie sich, wenn Sie mal in New York zu tun haben.
Bryant telefoniert per Handy. Er hat Probleme, seinen Gesprächspartner zu verstehen.
JB: Hallo? Hier ist John Bryant.
Ja, das ist richtig. Hören Sie, mein Flug hat Verspätung. Ich werde circa zwei Stunden später ankommen als geplant … Ist das ein Problem? … Entschuldigung, ich habe Sie nicht verstanden … Das ist sehr nett von Ihnen, aber … Ich kann selbstverständlich ein Taxi nehmen … Könnten Sie das bitte noch einmal

much trouble … Great. Well, I look forward to seeing you then. Thanks a lot. Bye.

sagen? Es ist furchtbar laut hier … Okay. Besten Dank. Ich hoffe, es macht nicht zu viele Umstände … Prima. Also ich freue mich darauf, Sie zu sehen. Vielen Dank. Bis dann.

Exercises

1 Please listen to the following sentences and form new sentences using *"I'd like a …"*.

1. *I'll have a whisky and soda, please.*
   I'd like a whisky and soda, please.
2. *I'll have a packet of peanuts, please.*
   I'd like a packet of peanuts, please,
3. *Here's your passport and your boarding card.*
   I'd like your passport and your boarding card.

2 Please listen to the following extract from the dialogue and pay close attention to what John says.

JB: Hello? It's John Bryant here.
JB: Yes, that's right. Look, my flight has been delayed. I'll be arriving about two hours later than expected
JB: Will that be a problem?
JB: Sorry? I didn't get that.

And now it's your turn! Please continue the role of John. You'll hear one answer as a model. Other solutions are, of course, possible.

1. Hello? It's John Bryant here.
   Say that your flight has been delayed.
   Look, my flight has been delayed.
2. *Now say that you'll be arriving about two hours later.*
   I'll be arriving about two hours later than expected. Will that be a problem?
3. *Say that you didn't understand what she said.*
   Sorry? I didn't get that.

3 Please listen to the dialogue again, paying particular attention to checking in at an airport. Then answer the following questions.

1. *How many pieces of luggage is John checking in?*
   John is checking in two suitcases and one piece of hand luggage.
2. *Has John left his luggage unattended at any time?*
   No, John has not left his luggage unattended at any time.
3. *Where will John be sitting during the flight?*
   John will be sitting in the business class section during the flight.

Vocabulary

just a second	einen Augenblick
pieces of luggage	Gepäckstücke
suitcase	Koffer
hand luggage	Handgepäck
for security reasons	aus Sicherheitsgründen
unattended	ohne Aufsicht
passport	Reisepass
boarding card	Bordkarte
non-smoking flight	Nichtraucherflug
gate	Flugsteig
to announce *s.th.*	*etwas* durchsagen; bekannt geben
here you are	hier ist es; bitte sehr
coming right up	sofort
Where are you heading for?	Wohin fahren Sie?; Wohin geht die Reise?
That's too bad! *(coll.)*	Wie ärgerlich!
in case	falls
Look me up!	Melden Sie sich bei mir!
The Big Apple	New York (von den Amerikanern liebevoll "The Big Apple" genannt)
mobile, mobile phone (BE)	Handy; Mobiltelefon
cell, cellphone (AE)	Handy; Mobiltelefon
Sorry? I didn't get that.	Bitte? Das habe ich nicht verstanden.
I hope it's not too much trouble.	Ich hoffe, es macht nicht zu viele Umstände.

4 Arriving in Chicago

▲ We follow John Bryant as he arrives at Chicago airport and goes through immigration. We also learn how he deals with his missing baggage.

JB: = John Bryant; IO:= Immigration officer; CA: = Check-in agent; CO: = Customs officer

JB: Hello, here's my passport. .
IO: Thank you. *(Looks at the passport.).* Are you here on business or vacation?
JB: Business, just for a few days.
IO: Where will you be staying?
JB: At the *Regal Hotel.*
IO: Keep this form in your passport. *(Handing passport back.).* Next!

John Bryant is collecting his luggage. One of his two suitcases has not arrived, so he goes to the lost luggage office.
JB: Excuse me, but one of my suitcases hasn't arrived.
CA: What was your flight number, sir?
JB: UK709, from London.
CA: Can I see the baggage receipt, please?
JB: Yes, here it is. It's a very important suitcase. It's got all my documents in it.
CA: I'll need you to describe your bag. Can you identify what type it is from this chart?

JB: Yes, it looks like this one. *(Pointing.)* It's quite large, dark grey, with wheels and a handle.

CA: Thank you, I'll put a trace on it right away. If you could just complete this form and give us your address in Chicago. As soon as we find it, we'll get it back to you – probably tomorrow.
JB: Good. Thank you. *(Slightly relieved)* It's like the advertisement: breakfast in London, dinner in New York, but luggage in Hong Kong!

CA: *(Not really amused.)* All right, Mr Bryant. We'll do what we can. Goodbye.
JB: Hmm. Goodbye.
John Bryant goes through Customs.

Ankunft in Chicago

▲ Wir begleiten John Bryant bei seiner Ankunft am Chicagoer Flughafen durch die Passkontrolle. Wir erfahren auch, was er wegen seines verlorenen Gepäcks unternimmt.

JB: Guten Tag, hier ist mein Pass.
IO: Danke. *(Er wirft einen Blick in seinen Pass.)* Sind Sie geschäftlich hier oder im Urlaub?
JB: Geschäftlich. Ich bleibe nur ein paar Tage.
IO: Wo werden Sie wohnen?
JB: Im *Hotel Regal.*
IO: Behalten Sie dieses Formular in Ihrem Reisepass. (*Er gibt ihm den Pass zurück.*) Der Nächste bitte!
John Bryant holt sein Gepäck. Einer seiner beiden Koffer ist nicht auf dem Förderband, deshalb wendet er sich an die Gepäckermittlung.
JB: Entschuldigung, aber einer meiner Koffer ist nicht angekommen.
CA: Wie war denn die Flugnummer?
JB: UK709 aus London.
CA: Kann ich bitte den Gepäckschein sehen?
JB: Ja. Hier, bitte. Der Koffer ist sehr wichtig. Alle meine Unterlagen sind darin.
CA: Bitte beschreiben Sie Ihren Koffer. Können Sie anhand dieser Abbildungen den Typ bestimmen?
JB: Ja. Er sieht ungefähr so aus wie dieser. *(Er zeigt auf einen der abgebildeten Koffer.)* Ziemlich groß, dunkelgrau, mit Rädern und einem Handgriff.
CA: Danke. Wir werden der Sache sofort nachgehen. Wenn Sie bitte dieses Formular ausfüllen und Ihre Adresse in Chicago angeben. Sobald wir ihn gefunden haben, bekommen Sie ihn gebracht. Wahrscheinlich morgen.
JB: Gut. Danke. *(Etwas erleichtert.)* Das ist wie in der Werbeanzeige: Frühstück in London – Abendessen in New York – Gepäck in Hongkong!
CA: *(Nicht wirklich amüsiert.)* Ja, Mr. Bryant. Wir tun unser Bestes. Auf Wiedersehen.
JB: Hm. Auf Wiedersehen.
John Bryant geht durch die Zollkontrolle.

CO: Welcome to Chicago, sir. I have a few questions. Did you visit a ranch or farm before you came here, or are you planning on visiting a ranch or farm here?

JB: No. I'm here on business. Why do you ask?

CO: We have to eliminate the danger of foot and mouth disease that you have in Europe.

JB: Oh, I see.

CO: And do you have anything to declare?

JB: Well, I have a few presents. A bottle of malt whisky and some English chocolate.

CO: Any other foodstuffs?

JB: Oh, yes. I've got some English cheese – Stilton.

CO: Oh. Well, I'm afraid you're not allowed to bring dairy products into the country.

JB: Oh, I didn't know that.

CO: Well, you're not allowed to bring in dairy products, meats, fruit or vegetables. Those are our restrictions. The chocolate and the whisky are okay. Would you take your suitcase to the gate on the left, please.

JB: Will I be fined?

CO: No sir, they'll just inspect your case, confiscate your cheese and check whether you have anything else – but next time try to be more careful!

JB: Thank you.

CO: Have a nice day!

JB: Er … yes, thanks.

CO: Herzlich willkommen in Chicago, Sir. Ich muß ein paar Fragen stellen. Haben Sie vor Ihrer Anreise eine Ranch oder einen Bauernhof besucht, oder haben Sie die Absicht, hier eine Ranch oder einen Bauernhof zu besuchen?

JB: Nein, ich bin hier aus geschäftlichen Gründen.

CO: Wir müssen das Risiko der Maul- und Klauenseuche eliminieren, die es bei Ihnen in Europa gibt.

JB: Ja, verstehe.

CO: Und haben Sie etwas zu verzollen?

JB: Also, ich habe einige Geschenke dabei. Eine Flasche Malt-Whisky und ein bisschen englische Schokolade.

CO: Noch irgendwelche Lebensmittel?

JB: Ach so, auch etwas englischen Käse – Stilton.

CO: Oh, es tut mir leid, aber Sie dürfen keine Milch- und Molkereiprodukte einführen.

JB: Oh, das wusste ich nicht.

CO: Ja, Sie dürfen weder Milch- und Molkereiprodukte noch Fleisch, Obst oder Gemüse einführen. So sind die Bestimmungen. Die Schokolade und der Whisky sind kein Problem. Bitte bringen Sie Ihren Koffer zum Tor hier links.

JB: Muss ich Strafe zahlen?

CO: Nein, Sir. Man wird dort nur Ihren Koffer inspizieren, den Käse beschlagnahmen und kontrollieren, ob Sie noch etwas anderes dabei haben. Aber sind Sie beim nächsten Mal bitte vorsichtiger!

JB: Danke.

CO: Einen schönen Tag noch.

JB: Th … ja, danke.

Exercises

1 Please listen to the following sentences and then repeat them.

1. Where will you be staying?
2. One of my suitcases hasn't arrived.
3. It's got all my documents in it.

2 Please listen to the following extract of the dialogue and pay close attention to what John says.

CA: What was your flight number, sir?

JB: UK709, from London.

CA: Can I see the baggage receipt, please?

JB: Yes, here it is. It's a very important suitcase. It's got all my documents in it.

CA: I'll need you to describe your bag. Can you identify what type it is from this chart?

JB: Yes, it looks like this one. (*Pointing.*) It's quite large, dark grey, with wheels and a handle.

Now it is your turn: Listen again and then take the role of John. You`ll hear one answer as a model. Other solutions are, of course, also possible.

1. What was your flight number, sir?
   Tell her that it was UK709 from London.
   UK709, from London.
2. Can I see the baggage receipt, please?
   Give her the receipt and tell her that's a very important suitcase with all the documents.
   Yes, here it is. It's a very important suitcase. It's got all my documents in it.
3. I'll need you to describe your bag. Can you identify what type it is from this chart?
   Tell her that the missing suitcase looks like this one and that it's quite large, dark grey with wheels and a handle.
   Yes, it looks like this one. It's quite large, dark grey, with wheels and a handle.

3 Please listen to the following sentences and then decide whether they are true or false.

1. *John will be staying at the Royal Hotel.*
   This sentence is false. John will be staying at the *Regal Hotel.*
2. *The missing suitcase is quite small and dark blue.*
   This sentence is false. The missing suitcase is quite large and dark grey.
3. *John couldn`t describe his suitcase.*
   This sentence is false. John could describe his suitcase and identify from the chart what type it was.

ℹ If you want to ask for permission, it is always a good idea to use one of the following expressions:
– **Could you ..., please?** ... as e.g. in: *Could you call me back, please?*
– **Would you ..., please?** ... as e.g. in: *Would you wait a minute, please?*
– **I wonder if ...** ... as e.g. in: *I wonder if you could help me, please.* Or:
– **Do you mind if ...?** as e.g. in: *Do you mind if we take a short break?*
And don't forget the magic word "please"!

Vocabulary

Are you here on business or on vacation?	Sind Sie geschäftlich hier oder im Urlaub?
lost luggage office	Gepäckermittlung
baggage receipt	Gepäckschein
to describe *s.th.*	*etwas* beschreiben
handle	Griff
I'll put a trace on it.	Ich werde der Sache nachgehen.
right away	sofort
to complete a form	ein Formular ausfüllen
We'll get it back for you.	Wir werden es Ihnen zurückbringen.
advertisement	Anzeige; Werbung
We'll do what we can.	Wir werden unser Bestes tun.
foot and mouth disease	Maul- und Klauenseuche
Do you have anything to declare?	Haben Sie etwas zu verzollen?
dairy products	Milch- und Molkereiprodukte
restriction	(Einfuhr-) Beschränkung
fined	bestraft; mit einer Geldbuße belegt
to inspect	inspizieren; untersuchen
to check	kontrollieren
to confiscate	beschlagnahmen
Next time try to be more careful!	Versuchen Sie, in Zukunft vorsichtiger zu sein!

5 Arriving at the hotel

▲ Here we listen in as John Bryant chats to Neil Cosby who has come to meet him at the airport and take him to his hotel.

John Bryant is picked up from the airport. He is met by one of the firm's staff and taken to his hotel, where he checks in.

NC: = Neil Cosby; JB: = John Bryant; R: = Receptionist

NC: John Bryant?
JB: Yes, that's me. Are you from *EZ Pack*?
NC: That's right, Mr Bryant. Welcome to Chicago. I'm Neil Cosby. Did you have a good flight? I heard about the delay.
JB: The flight was fine, apart from the delay. Thanks for picking me up. I'm sorry I was a bit late coming through, but one of my suitcases didn't turn up.
NC: Oh, you don't say! What are they going to do?
JB: They're sending it to my hotel – when – or if – they find it!
NC: Right. I'm sure you'll get it in the morning. Was there anything in it you need right now?
JB: Not tonight. But I do have some important documents for the meeting in it. I should have kept them in my hand luggage.
NC: Oh, that's too bad. We can phone the airport later to check, if you like.
JB: That might be a good idea.
NC: Okay. I'll take you to your hotel now and you can freshen up.

John Bryant checks in at the hotel reception.
R: Good evening. How can I help you?
JB: My name is John Bryant. I believe there's a room booked for me.
R: Ah, yes. Mr Bryant. Welcome to the *Regal Hotel*. Could you fill out this form, please,

Ankunft im Hotel

▲ Hier hören wir in das Gespräch hinein, das John Bryant mit Neil Cosby führt, der ihn am Flughafen abholt und zu seinem Hotel bringt.

John Bryant wird vom Flughafen abgeholt. Er wird von einem Mitarbeiter der Firma erwartet und zu seinem Hotel gebracht, wo er sich anmeldet.

NC: John Bryant?
JB: Ja, das bin ich. Sind Sie von *EZ Pack*?
NC: Genau, Mr. Bryant. Herzlich willkommen in Chicago. Mein Name ist Neil Cosby. Hatten Sie einen guten Flug? Ich habe von der Verspätung gehört.
JB: Der Flug war in Ordnung, abgesehen von der Verspätung. Danke fürs Abholen. Es tut mir Leid, dass ich jetzt erst hier bin, aber einer meiner Koffer ist nicht mitgekommen.
NC: Oh nein! Was geschieht denn jetzt weiter?
JB: Ich bekomme ihn ins Hotel gebracht, sobald – oder falls – er gefunden wird!
NC: Gut. Ich bin sicher, Sie haben ihn morgen früh wieder. Ist irgendetwas drin, was Sie im Moment brauchen?
JB: Nicht heute Abend. Aber ich habe ein paar wichtige Unterlagen für das morgige Meeting drin. Ich hätte sie besser ins Handgepäck tun sollen.
NC: Tja, das ist nicht so gut. Wir können ja später den Flughafen anrufen, um zu hören, ob es schon etwas Neues gibt.
JB: Das ist sicher eine gute Idee.
NC: Okay. Jetzt bringe ich Sie erstmal zu Ihrem Hotel, dort können Sie sich etwas frisch machen.

Bryant meldet sich an der Hotelrezeption an.
R: Guten Abend. Was kann ich für Sie tun?
JB: Mein Name ist John Bryant. Ich glaube, für mich wurde ein Zimmer reserviert.
R: Ah, ja. Mr. Bryant. Willkommen im *Hotel Regal*. Würden Sie bitte dieses Formular

Mr Bryant? You have room 112 – it's on the first floor – that's the ground floor to you! Here's your key …

JB: Thank you. And … here's the form. Oh, yes – is there Internet access in the room? I need to check my mail.

R: Yes, Mr Bryant. You can plug in your laptop and just surf away!

JB: One other thing. Do you have a map and some information about Chicago?

R: Yes, we do – just over there – there's an information desk with brochures and maps. Help yourself.

JB: Thanks.

R: You're welcome. Enjoy your stay, Mr Bryant.

ausfüllen, Mr. Bryant. Sie haben Zimmer 112 – das ist im Erdgeschoss – für Sie ist das *groundfloor*. Hier ist Ihr Schlüssel.

JB: Danke. Und … hier ist das Anmeldeformular. Ach ja – hat das Zimmer Internet-Zugang? Ich muss nachsehen, ob neue E-Mails für mich da sind.

R: Selbstverständlich, Mr. Bryant. Sie können Ihren Laptop einstecken und sofort lossurfen!

JB: Noch etwas. Haben Sie einen Stadtplan und ein paar Informationen über Chicago?

R: Aber ja. Gleich dort drüben. Da ist ein Ständer mit Broschüren und Stadtplänen. Bitte bedienen Sie sich.

JB: Danke.

R: Nichts zu danken. Angenehmen Aufenthalt, Mr. Bryant.

Exercises

1 Please listen to the following sentences and then repeat them.

1. Did you have a good flight?
2. One of my suitcases didn't turn up.
3. We can phone the airport later to check, if you like.

2 Please listen to the following sentences and form new sentences using *"We managed to …"*.

1. *We can phone the airport.*
   We managed to phone the airport.
2. *We're sending your suitcase to your hotel.*
   We managed to send your suitcase to your hotel.
3. *We pick you up at the airport.*
   We managed to pick you up at the airport.

3 Please listen to the dialogue again, paying particular attention to being met at an airport. Then answer the following questions.

1. *Who meets John at the airport?*
   Neil meets John at the airport.
2. *Where is the airport going to send the suitcase?*
   The airport is going to send the suitcase to the hotel.
3. *What else does John want from the receptionist?*
   John asks her for some information about Chicago and a map of the city.

ℹ The way floors in American buildings are numbered may be strange for Europeans. The numbering begins with the groundfloor which is the first floor in the USA. The first digit of a three-digit room number always stands for the floor. So room number 112 is on the groundfloor.

Vocabulary

the firm's staff	Mitarbeiter der Firma
right now	im Augenblick
That's too bad!	Das ist nicht so gut!
to freshen up	sich frisch machen
parking lot (AE)	Parkplatz
in an hour or so	in etwa einer Stunde
It's good to have you here!	Schön, dass Sie hier bei uns sind!
first floor	(AE) Erdgeschoss; (BE) erster Stock
ground floor (BE)	Erdgeschoss
Here you are!	Bitte schön!
internet access	Internet-Zugang
to plug in	anschließen
No problem at all!	Überhaupt kein Problem!
Help yourself.	Bitte bedienen Sie sich.

6 Making a complaint

▲ Here we learn about making a complaint if the hotel room is not up to standard.

John Bryant looks around his hotel room. The light bulb in his room suddenly goes out. He phones the reception to get it replaced.

R: = Receptionist; JB:= John Bryant

R: Reception. How can I help you?
JB: Oh. My name is Bryant. Room 112. I have a problem. The light bulb in my room seems to have gone. Can you send someone to replace it, please?

R: Oh, we'll see to it right away. I'll call the janitor.
JB: Thanks. I haven't got much time.
R: Don't worry, Mr Bryant. He'll be right up.
This time John Bryant tries to take a shower, but the water doesn't get warm. He goes and phones Reception again.
R: Reception. How can I help you?
JB: It's Bryant from room 112 again. Nothing seems to work here! This is going to cause me a delay!

R: What's the problem, Mr Bryant?
JB: There's no hot water – it's more or less cold. I have to take a shower and get ready to go out with my business partners. This is no good! Please do something about it right now!

Eine Beschwerde vorbringen

▲ Hier erfahren wir, wie man sich beschwert, wenn das Hotelzimmer nicht in Ordnung ist.

John Bryant schaut sich in seinem Hotelzimmer um. Plötzlich erlischt eine Glühbirne in seinem Zimmer. Er ruft die Rezeption an, um die Glühbirne ersetzen zu lassen.

R: Rezeption. Was kann ich für Sie tun?
JB: Hier spricht Bryant, Zimmer 112. Ich habe ein Problem. Die Glühbirne in meinem Zimmer scheint den Geist aufgegeben zu haben. Können Sie bitte jemand schicken, der das in Ordnung bringt?
R: Oh, selbstverständlich. Ich kümmere mich gleich darum. Ich rufe den Hausmeister an.
JB: Danke. Ich habe nicht viel Zeit.
R: Keine Sorge, Mr. Bryant. Er kommt sofort.
Nun möchte John Bryant duschen, aber das Wasser wird nicht warm. Er ruft wieder bei der Rezeption an.
R: Rezeption. Was kann ich für Sie tun?
JB: Noch einmal Bryant von Zimmer 112. Hier scheint ja überhaupt nichts zu funktionieren! Ich werde nie pünktlich fertig, wenn das so weiter geht!
R: Wo liegt das Problem, Mr. Bryant?
JB: Ich habe kein warmes Wasser – es ist praktisch kalt. Ich muss duschen und mich zum Essen mit Geschäftsfreunden fertig machen. So etwas darf einfach nicht vorkommen! Ich erwarte, dass Sie sofort etwas unternehmen!

R: We've been having problems with the hot water on the first floor for a while now – I thought it was fixed. I'll send the janitor up to take a look. If he can't do anything, we'll have to move you to another room. Would that be all right?

JB: Yes. YES! I just need to shower and get ready. I'm tired, I'm jet-lagged, I have to go out with my business colleagues and I'm beginning to get angry.

R: I understand, Mr Bryant. I'm terribly sorry. This doesn't normally happen.

JB: I certainly hope not! I think I'll have to speak to the manager tomorrow.

R: Of course. In the meantime may I send you up a bottle of champagne with the compliments of the house? Please accept my apologies for all the problems, Mr Bryant.

JB: Well … okay. That's nice of you. I'm sorry I was so angry – it was a long journey. It looks like I'm having a bad start to my trip here!

R: That's all right, Mr Bryant. We'll get everything in order for you.

R: Wir haben seit einiger Zeit Ärger mit dem warmen Wasser im Erdgeschoss, aber ich dachte, das wäre inzwischen geregelt. Ich schicke Ihnen den Hausmeister, dass der sich die Sache ansieht. Wenn er es nicht richten kann, müssen wir Ihnen ein anderes Zimmer geben. Wäre Ihnen das recht?

JB: Ja. JA! Aber ich muss duschen und mich fertig machen. Ich bin müde. Ich leide unter Jetlag. Ich muss mich mit Kollegen treffen, und ich werde allmählich sauer.

R: Das verstehe ich, Mr. Bryant. Es tut mir schrecklich Leid. So etwas kommt normalerweise nicht vor.

JB: Das will ich schwer hoffen! Ich werde wohl morgen mit dem Manager sprechen müssen.

R: Gewiss. Darf ich Ihnen inzwischen auf Kosten des Hauses eine Flasche Sekt aufs Zimmer schicken? Bitte nehmen Sie unsere Entschuldigung an, Mr. Bryant.

JB: Nun, okay. Das ist nett von Ihnen. Es tut mir Leid, dass ich mich so aufgeregt habe – ich habe einen langen Flug hinter mir. Sieht so aus, als würde mein Aufenthalt hier nicht gerade optimal beginnen.

R: Kein Problem, Mr. Bryant. Wir bemühen uns, alles zu Ihrer Zufriedenheit in Ordnung zu bringen.

Exercises

1 Please listen to the following sentences and then repeat them.

1. Could you send someone to replace it, please?
2. Nothing seems to work here! This is going to cause me a delay!
3. I think I'll have to speak to the manager tomorrow.

2 Please listen to the following sentences and choose the correct definition.

1. The light bulb seems to have gone.
   To have gone. *Does this mean:* The light bulb is missing? *or:* The light bulb is broken?
   To have gone *means:* To be broken.
2. We'll get everything in order for you.
   To get in order. *Does this mean:* To tidy up *or:* To make sure everything is all right?
   To get in order *means:* To make sure everything is all right.
3. I send the janitor up to take a look.
   Janitor. *Does this mean:* manager *or:* caretaker?
   Janitor *means:* caretaker.

3 Please listen to the dialogue again, paying particular attention to the hotel room. Then answer the following questions.

1. *What is John's room number?*
   John's room number is 112.

2. *Who is the receptionist sending to replace the light bulb?*
   The receptionist is sending the janitor to replace the light bulb.

3. *Why is John in such a hurry?*
   Because he wants to take a shower and get ready before meeting his colleagues.

ℹ A "janitor" in the States is what the English call a "caretaker". He is in charge of the building and its technical appliances.

Vocabulary

light bulb Glühbirne
to replace *s.th.* *etwas* ersetzen
How can I help you? Was kann ich für Sie tun?
janitor (AE) Hausmeister
I haven't got much time. Ich habe nicht viel Zeit.
Nothing seems to work here! Hier scheint ja nichts zu funktionieren!
delay Verzögerung; Verspätung
This is no good! Das geht wirklich nicht!; So etwas darf einfach nicht vorkommen!
to fix reparieren
to be jet-lagged unter Jetlag leiden
I'm terribly sorry! Das tut mir schrecklich Leid!
This doesn't normally happen. Das kommt normalerweise nicht vor.
I certainly hope not! Das will ich schwer hoffen!
with the compliments of the house auf Kosten des Hauses
to accept the apology die Entschuldigung annehmen
That's nice of you. Das ist nett von Ihnen.
to get *s.th.* in order *etwas* in Ordnung bringen

7 First encounters

▲ Here we listen to greetings and introductions, making small talk and ordering a meal in a restaurant.

John Bryant is in the hotel foyer and is met by his business partner, Tony McNamara, and Tony's personal assistant, Lee Bernstein. They go to a nearby restaurant and talk about arrangements for the following day.

TM: = Tony McNamara; JB: = John Bryant; LB: = Lee Bernstein; W: = Waiter

TM: Hi there, John! It's great to meet you! Can I introduce you to Lee, my personal assistant?
JB: Nice to meet you both.

Das erste Treffen

▲ Hier hören wir, wie sich die Geschäftsfreunde begrüßen, sich vorstellen, ein bisschen Small Talk machen und in einem Lokal etwas zu Essen bestellen

John Bryant ist im Foyer seines Hotels und trifft dort seinen Geschäftspartner Tony McNamara und dessen Assistentin Lee Bernstein. Sie fahren zu einem nahe gelegenen Restaurant und besprechen den Ablauf des folgenden Tages.

TM: Hallo. John! Schön, dass wir uns endlich kennen lernen! Darf ich Sie Lee vorstellen, meiner Assistentin?
JB: Freut mich auch, Sie beide kennen zu lernen.

LB: Likewise. It's good to have you here. I hope you'll like Chicago.
TM: I hear you had a lousy flight.

JB: Well, there was a delay of two hours and I had problems at Customs because I tried to bring you some English cheese!

TM: Oh, too bad. We are very tough on food imports; I had the same trouble when I went to Europe last year!

TM: Well, how about going to eat right away – I'm so hungry I could eat a horse! How about you, John?
JB: I'm famished, to tell you the truth. I didn't eat anything on the plane.
TM: I don't blame you. Airline food is awful, isn't it? Now, there's a neat little restaurant downtown which I know you're going to love. What do you think? Do you like Italian food?
JB: Oh yes! Sounds good to me!
LB: You'll like it. I always go there. The pasta dishes are heaven!
TM: Well, let's go. The car's outside.

Tony, Lee and John are at the restaurant. The maitre d'… shows them to their table and hands them the menus. They order their meals and talk about the next day.
TM: It's good we booked a table – it gets kinda crowded here. Say, John, how about an aperitif, eh?
JB: Good idea.
W: Good evening. Can I get you anything to drink while you're looking at the menu?

TM: You sure can! I'll have a dry martini. What about you, John?
JB: I'd like a whisky on the rocks, please.
LB: I'll just have a glass of dry white wine.
(They study the menu.)
JB: Can you recommend anything?
TM: Well, I always have the minestrone followed by the penne arrabbiate – that's if you like it hot!

LB: Ganz meinerseits. Schön, dass Sie hier sind. Hoffentlich gefällt es Ihnen in Chicago.
TM: Wie ich hörte, hatten Sie keinen besonders guten Flug?
JB: Tja, wir hatten zwei Stunden Verspätung, und dann bekam ich noch Probleme mit dem Zoll, weil ich Ihnen etwas englischen Käse mitbringen wollte!
TM: Wie ärgerlich! Wir sind hier sehr strikt, was die Einfuhr von Lebensmitteln angeht. Ich hatte genau dasselbe Problem, als ich letztes Jahr in Europa war!
TM: Was halten Sie davon, wenn wir jetzt gleich Essen gehen? Ich habe einen Bärenhunger. Und Sie, John?
JB: Ehrlich gesagt, ich bin völlig ausgehungert. Ich habe im Flieger nichts gegessen.
TM: Das kann ich gut verstehen. Das Essen im Flugzeug ist wirklich grauenhaft. Ich kenne da ein nettes kleines Restaurant in der Stadtmitte, das Ihnen garantiert gefällt. Was meinen Sie? Essen Sie gerne Italienisch?
JB: Aber ja! Das klingt gut.
LB: Es wird Ihnen gefallen. Ich gehe immer dorthin. Die Nudelgerichte sind himmlisch!
TM: Also gehen wir. Das Auto steht gleich vor der Tür.
Tony, Lee und John sind im Restaurant. Der Oberkellner führt sie zu einem Tisch und bringt ihnen die Speisekarte. Sie bestellen ihre Gerichte und sprechen über den nächsten Tag.
TM: Wie gut, dass wir reserviert haben – es wird hier immer schnell voll. John, was halten Sie von einem Aperitif?
JB: Gute Idee.
W: Guten Abend. Darf ich Ihnen schon etwas zu trinken bringen, während Sie das Essen aussuchen?
TM: Ja, bitte. Ich nehme einen trockenen Martini. Und Sie, John?
JB: Einen Whisky bitte. Mit Eis.
LB: Für mich nur ein Glas trockenen Weißwein.
(Sie studieren die Speisekarte.)
JB: Können Sie etwas Bestimmtes empfehlen?
TM: Also ich nehme immer die Minestrone und danach die Penne arrabbiate – falls Sie gerne scharf essen!

LB: And I always have the spaghetti with pesto and a side salad.

JB: I think I'll go for the spaghetti, too. And maybe a minestrone to start with.

TM: Waiter? We'd like to order now.

...

(Tony, Lee and John order their meals. They are fond of Italian food. After dinner they discuss the timing for the next day.)

JB: That was simply fantastic! I certainly needed that!

LB: It *is* good here, don't you think?

TM: I love this place. I'm glad you like it, too. Coffee?

JB: Oh, yes, good idea.

LB: Waiter? Three coffees, please.

TM: Okay. Let's talk business for a moment. I guess you'd like to sleep in a bit tomorrow after your long flight, so I thought we could meet a little later, say around eleven. Is that okay?

JB: Yes, fine. I just have to pick up the car I hired from the airport.

LB: Well, that's no problem. Either Neil or I can take you there tomorrow morning and then you can follow in your car.

JB: I also have a problem in that one of my suitcases didn't arrive. Unfortunately, it has all my papers for tomorrow's meeting. On the other hand, I've got most of the details in my head, anyway. So it won't mean that we can't start, even if my luggage doesn't turn up.

TM: Lee? Can you see to that? Phone the airport and check it out!

LB: Don't worry - I'll call first thing in the morning. Oh – look at the time! I didn't realise it was so late!

TM: John? You must be tired. I'll ask for the check.

JB: Well, to tell you the truth, I could do with some sleep, but it was a lovely evening. Thanks.

LB: Und ich esse immer die Spaghetti mit Pesto und einen kleinen Salat.

JB: Ich glaube, ich probiere auch die Spaghetti. Und vielleicht als Vorspeise eine Minestrone.

TM: Herr Ober? Wir würden jetzt gern bestellen.

...

(Tony, Lee und John geben dem Ober ihre Bestellung auf. Sie genießen das italienische Essen. Anschließend besprechen sie kurz die Planung für den nächsten Tag.)

JB: Das war einfach fantastisch! Genau das habe ich jetzt gebraucht.

LB: Die Küche hier ist wirklich gut, nicht wahr?

TM: Ich komme sehr gern hierher. Ich freue mich, dass es Ihnen auch gefällt. Noch einen Kaffee?

JB: Ja, gute Idee.

LB: Herr Ober? Drei Kaffee, bitte.

TM: Okay, reden wir einen Moment übers Geschäft. Ich könnte mir vorstellen, dass Sie nach dem langen Flug morgen früh ein bisschen länger schlafen möchten. Deshalb dachte ich, wir treffen uns vielleicht etwas später, sagen wir so gegen elf. Ist Ihnen das recht?

JB: Ja, prima. Ich muss nur irgendwann meinen Mietwagen am Flughafen abholen.

LB: Kein Problem. Neil oder ich können Sie morgen Vormittag hinbringen, und dann können Sie mit Ihrem Auto hinter uns her zurück in die Stadt fahren.

JB: Ich habe da allerdings noch ein Problem: Einer meiner Koffer ist nicht angekommen. Ausgerechnet der mit meinen ganzen Unterlagen für das morgige Meeting. Allerdings habe ich das meiste ohnehin im Kopf. Wir können also anfangen, auch wenn mein Gepäck noch nicht wieder aufgetaucht ist.

TM: Würden Sie sich darum kümmern, Lee? Rufen Sie am Flughafen an und sehen Sie zu, dass Sie das abgängige Stück auftreiben.

LB: Keine Sorge – ich rufe gleich morgen früh dort an. Oh – so spät ist es schon? Die Zeit ist ja unheimlich schnell vergangen!

TM: John, Sie sind sicher müde. Ich lasse die Rechnung kommen.

JB: Ja, ehrlich gesagt könnte ich jetzt etwas Schlaf vertragen. Aber es war ein wirklich netter Abend. Vielen Dank.

Exercises

1 Please listen to the following sentences and then repeat them.

1. Can I introduce you to Lee, my personal assistant?
2. We are very tough on food imports.
3. I'm so hungry I could eat a horse.

2 Please listen to the following expressions and choose the correct definition.

1. I'm famished, to tell you the truth.
   To tell you the truth. *Does this mean:* I must tell you the truth *or:* to be honest with you?
   To tell you the truth *means:* to be honest with you.

2. I don't blame you.
   I don't blame you. *Does this mean:* I don't think you committed a crime *or:* I can understand you.
   I don't blame you *means:* I can understand you.

3. I'll ask for the check.
   I'll ask for the check. *Does this mean:* Somebody is going to give us some money *or:* We need to get the bill?
   I'll ask for the check *means:* We need the bill.

3 Please listen to the dialogue again, paying particular attention to meeting new business partners and ordering a meal in a restaurant. Then answer the following questions.

1. *What is Tony's personal assistant called?*
   Tony's personal assistant is called Lee.

2. *What kind of restaurant do Tony, John and Lee go to?*
   Tony, John and Lee go to an Italian restaurant.

3. *What does John drink as an aperitif?*
   John drinks a whisky on the rocks as an aperitif.

Vocabulary

personal assistant	persönliche(r) Assistent(in)
a nearby restaurant	ein Restaurant in der Nähe
waiter	Kellner
likewise	ebenso
lousy	lausig
tough	hart; strikt
famished	ausgehungert
I don't blame you.	Das kann ich gut verstehen.
Sounds good!	Klingt gut!
maitre d'…	Oberkellner
to book	reservieren
kinda (= kind of)	ein bisschen; irgendwie
How about an aperitif?	Wir wäre es mit einem Aperitif?
menu	Speisekarte
You sure can!	Aber sicher!; Ja, bitte!
to recommend *s.th.*	*etwas* empfehlen
I think I'll go for the spaghetti.	Ich glaube, ich probiere die Spaghetti.
We'd like to order now.	Können wir jetzt bitte bestellen?
I certainly needed that!	Genau das habe ich jetzt gebraucht!
Let's talk business.	Reden wir übers Geschäft.
Say around eleven.	Sagen wir so gegen elf.
Yes, fine.	Ja, prima.
to check *s.th.* out	*etwas* herausfinden
check (AE)	Rechnung (im Restaurant)
bill	Rechnung
to tell you the truth …	um ehrlich zu sein …; ehrlich gesagt …
I could do with some sleep.	Ich könnte etwas Schlaf vertragen.

8 A conference at *EZ Pack*

▲ We follow John Bryant as he arrives at *EZ Pack's* headquarters, gets his security pass and is taken to the conference room.

John Bryant arrives at EZ Pack. He and Lee Bernstein are greeted by Anne Watson, the secretary. They then go to the conference room, where they are joined by Tony McNamara and Neil Cosby.

JB: = John Bryant; LB: = Lee Bernstein; AW: = Anne Watson; TM: = Tony McNamara; NC = Neil Cosby

JB: Well, Lee. Thanks for taking me to the airport to pick up the car. Driving here isn't as bad as I thought!

LB: A pleasure. People get the idea that we drive like in the movies – you know, the car chases? But actually we're careful drivers.

JB: It's a shame that I haven't got my suitcase back yet.

LB: Well, I got in touch with the airport this morning and they said that they'd send it to the office by midday.

JB: Excellent.

AW: Good morning, sir. Good morning, Lee.

LB: Anne, this is Mr Bryant. We have a conference at eleven.

AW: I have your security card ready, Mr Bryant. Here you are. You need this to get in and out of the building. You can clip it on your lapel. Please give it back to us when you leave.

JB: Oh, thank you.

LB: Let's go up to the conference room.

JB: Where's the lift?

LB: Just follow me.

Lee Bernstein and John Bryant go up to the conference room, where Tony Mc Namara is waiting for them.

TM: Hey, John. Did you have a good sleep?

Eine Konferenz bei *EZ Pack*

▲ Wir begleiten John Bryant zur Zentrale von *EZ Pack*, wo er einen Besucherausweis bekommt und in den Konferenzraum geführt wird.

John Bryant kommt bei EZ Pack an. Die Sekretärin Anne Watson begrüßt ihn und Lee Bernstein. Sie gehen zusammen in den Konferenzraum, wo sie Tony McNamara und Neil treffen.

JB: Noch einmal vielen Dank, Lee, dass Sie mich zum Flughafen gebracht haben, um den Mietwagen abzuholen. Das Autofahren hier geht besser, als ich gedacht hatte!

LB: Gern geschehen. Viele Leute meinen tatsächlich, wir fahren hier so wie im Film – Sie wissen schon, die wilden Verfolgungsjagden. In Wahrheit sind wir sehr vorsichtige Autofahrer.

JB: Zu dumm, dass ich meinen Koffer noch immer nicht wiederhabe.

LB: Ja, ich habe heute früh am Flughafen angerufen, und die haben mir versprochen, ihn bis gegen Mittag hierher ins Büro zu schicken.

JB: Herzlichen Dank.

AW: Guten Morgen, Sir. Guten Morgen, Lee.

LB: Anne, das ist Mr. Bryant. Wir haben um elf eine Besprechung.

AW: Ich habe Ihren Besucherausweis, Mr. Bryant. Hier bitte. Sie brauchen ihn, um hier ins Haus zu kommen und auch zum Verlassen des Gebäudes. Sie können ihn sich ans Revers klipsen. Bitte geben Sie ihn ab, wenn Sie abreisen.

JB: Danke sehr.

LB: Gehen wir hinauf in den Konferenzraum.

JB: Wo ist der Aufzug?

LB: Folgen Sie mir.

Lee Bernstein und John Bryant gehen hinauf zum Konferenzraum, wo Tony McNamara schon auf sie wartet.

TM: Hallo, John. Gut geschlafen?

JB: Not too good, actually. It took me a long time to get to sleep, and then the alarm call woke me. I'm still a bit tired.

TM: Well, we'll soon wake you up! Lee, could you get us some coffee, please?

LB: Sure.

NC: Hi, John. Did you like the restaurant last night?

JB: Morning, Neil. Yes, it was fantastic. Do you know it?

NC: Sure do. I go there quite a lot with my wife. She's crazy about Italian food.

TM: Okay, John. Have a seat. I hear your papers haven't arrived yet.

JB: Unfortunately not. But I have all the information on my laptop and most of it in my head.

TM: That's what I like to hear! A man with something in his head!

LB: Here's the coffee.

TM: Good. Thanks, Lee. Well, let's get going, then.

JB: Ehrlich gesagt, nicht besonders. Erst konnte ich lange nicht einschlafen, und dann kam schon der Weckruf. Ich bin immer noch etwas müde.

TM: Wir werden Sie schon wach kriegen! Lee, würden Sie uns bitte Kaffee besorgen?

LB: Natürlich.

NC: Hallo, John. Hat Ihnen das Lokal gestern Abend gefallen?

JB: Guten Morgen, Neil. Ja, es war fantastisch. Kennen Sie es?

NC: Aber sicher. Ich gehe oft mit meiner Frau hin. Sie ist ganz verrückt nach italienischer Küche.

TM: Okay, John. Bitte nehmen Sie doch Platz. Ich habe gehört, Ihre Unterlagen sind noch nicht da?

JB: Leider nein. Aber ich habe alle wichtigen Informationen auf meinem Laptop und das Meiste sowieso im Kopf.

TM: Das hört man gern! Ein Mann, der was im Kopf hat!

LB: Hier kommt der Kaffee.

TM: Prima. Danke, Lee. Fangen wir also an.

Exercises

1 Please listen to the following sentences and repeat them.

1. Thanks for taking me to the airport.
2. It's a shame I haven't got my suitcase back yet.
3. I have your security card ready.

2 Please listen to the following sentences and form new sentences using "*Let's …*".

1. *We can go up to the conference room.*
   Let's go up to the conference room.
2. *We can have some coffee.*
   Let's have some coffee.
3. *We can get going now.*
   Let's get going now.

3 Please listen to the dialogue again, paying particular attention to taking part in a conference. Then answer the following questions.

1. *What does John need to get in and out of the building?*
   John needs a security card to get in and out of the building.
2. *How do John and Lee go up to the conference room?*
   John and Lee go by the lift up to the conference room.
3. *Where are John's papers?*
   John's papers are in the missing suitcase, but he has all the information on his laptop and most of it in his head.

Vocabulary

headquarters (Pl.)	Zentrale; Hauptverwaltung
security pass; -card	Besucherausweis
to greet *s.o.*	*j-n* begrüßen
to join	dazu kommen; dazu stoßen
A pleasure!	Gern geschehen!
People get the idea that …	Die Leute meinen immer …
car chase	Verfolgungsjagd (mit dem Auto)
actually	tatsächlich
careful	vorsichtig
It's a shame!	Es ist zu dumm!
to clip *s.th.* on *one's* lapel	sich *etwas* ans Revers heften/befestigen
It took me a long time to get to sleep.	Ich konnte lange nicht einschlafen.
to be crazy about *s.th.*	verrückt sein nach *etwas*
to take a seat	Platz nehmen
That's what I like to hear!	Das höre ich aber gern!
Let's get going.	Fangen wir an.

9 The meeting

▲ We listen to how John Bryant presents the product *Earth Pax* and talks about its benefits.

John, Tony, Lee and Neil are discussing their business.

TM: = Tony McNamara; JB: = John Bryant; LB = Lee Bernstein; NC: = Neil Cosby; SC: = Sarah Coen

TM: Okay, John. Let's get down to business. Lee? Could you take the minutes, please? You got in touch with us to make a deal concerning your product – which I must say is very interesting – *Earth Pax*. Now as you know, we are a market leader in the field of packaging, but you have some new method of producing packaging which I would like to talk about.

JB: Yes. At *Galaxy Pax UK* we have been working on biodegradable packaging for some time now, and have developed a product which we are proud of. Together with you, we would like to bring it to the US market.

Die Besprechung

▲ Wir hören, wie John Bryant das Produkt *Earth Pax* präsentiert und dessen Stärken hervorhebt.

John Bryant, Tony McNamara, Lee Bernstein und Neil Cosby besprechen das Projekt.

TM: Okay, John. Kommen wir zur Sache. Lee? Könnten Sie bitte Protokoll führen? Sie haben sich mit unserer Firma in Verbindung gesetzt, weil Sie bezüglich Ihres Produktes *Earth Pax* – das mir übrigens sehr interessant erscheint – ein Geschäft abschließen wollen. Wie Sie wissen, sind wir Marktführer auf dem Gebiet Verpackungen. Und Sie haben ein neues Herstellungsverfahren für Verpackungen entwickelt, über das ich gerne mit Ihnen sprechen würde.

JB: So ist es. Wir von *Galaxy Pax UK* beschäftigen uns seit geraumer Zeit mit biologisch abbaubaren Verpackungen und haben jetzt ein Produkt entwickelt, auf das wir sehr stolz sind. Und genau dieses würden wir nun gerne in Zusammenarbeit mit Ihnen auf den amerikanischen Markt bringen.

TM: So you want to go global?
JB: We'd like to, yes. We're convinced that this is a breakthrough in ecologically friendly packaging because it breaks down into its basic components within a few months.

TM: Sie streben also weltweiten Absatz an?
JB: Das wäre schön, ja. Wir sind überzeugt, dass dieses Produkt einen Durchbruch auf dem Gebiet umweltfreundlicher Verpackung darstellt, weil es sich innerhalb weniger Monate wieder in seine Grundbestandteile zersetzt.

TM: How does that happen?
JB: Sunlight, water, air. They all help to break down the material.
NC: But isn't there the problem that products will have a shorter shelf-life? That things will fall apart after a few months in the shops?
JB: We've thought about that. There *are* certain storage directives. People have to be careful how and where they place the products. It's just a matter of organisation, but the obvious ecological advantages, in my opinion, make these precautions worthwhile.

TM: Und wie funktioniert das?
JB: Sonnenlicht, Wasser, Luft. Sie alle tragen dazu bei, das Material aufzuspalten.
NC: Aber entsteht dann nicht das Problem verkürzter Lagerfähigkeit? Zerfallen die Produkte nicht, wenn sie ein paar Monate lang in den Geschäften liegen?
JB: Dieses Problem haben wir auch bedacht. Natürlich *gibt es* gewisse Richtlinien für die Lagerung. Man muss auf die richtige Platzierung achten. Aber das ist nur eine Frage der Organisation. In meinen Augen machen die offensichtlichen ökologischen Vorzüge diese Vorsichtsmaßnahmen mehr als wett.

TM: Hmm. Well, that *would* mean educating our customers, but we could sell them the ecological aspect, I guess.

TM: Hm. Das *würde* bedeuten, dass wir unsere Kunden entsprechend schulen müssten, aber ich denke, wir können ihnen den ökologischen Aspekt verkaufen.

JB: Exactly. The consumer of today is becoming more and more aware of the environment, so I don't think there should be a great problem. We'd have to organise a good advertising campaign.
LB: The ecological angle would certainly be a unique selling point.
TM: Got you. I like it. We just have to work out a few more details.

JB: Genau. Der Verbraucher von heute wird zunehmend umweltbewusster, deshalb sollte dies eigentlich kein allzu großes Problem darstellen. Wir müssten uns nur eine gute Werbekampagne einfallen lassen.
LB: Der ökologische Aspekt wäre garantiert ein überzeugendes Verkaufsargument.
TM: Das stimmt. Mir gefällt die Idee. Natürlich müssen wir noch einige Einzelheiten ausarbeiten.

JB: As you know, I haven't got my papers with me, but maybe I could print out something from my laptop.

JB: Leider habe ich ja meine Unterlagen nicht hier, wie Sie wissen, aber vielleicht könnte ich Ihnen etwas von meinem Laptop ausdrucken?

LB: That's no problem at all. Shall we print it right now?
TM: It would be a good idea to have the information in front of us.
NC: Can this packaging be used for *any* products? Or are there any things which are not suitable?

LB: Gar kein Problem. Wollen wir das gleich machen?
TM: Es wäre nicht schlecht, wenn wir die Details vor Augen hätten.
NC: Eignet sich diese Verpackung denn für *alle* Produkte? Oder gibt es Dinge, für die sie nicht eingesetzt werden sollte?

JB: Our tests have shown that we can use *Earth Pax* with any …
(Sarah is coming in.)
SC: Sorry, Mr McNamara, but there's a gentleman from *A-box* on the line – he says it's urgent.
TM: Didn't you say I was in a meeting? Can't he call back later?

SC: I'm sorry. I did tell him, but he insists it's urgent.
TM: Would you excuse me for a moment?

JB: No problem.
(Sarah and grumbling McNamara are leaving the room.)
LB: It's like this all the time. You get used to it!

NC: Too right!

JB: Unsere Testreihen haben gezeigt, dass *Earth Pax* praktisch für alle …
(Sarah kommt herein.)
SC: Verzeihen Sie, Mr. McNamara, aber da ist ein Herr von *A-Box* am Telefon, und er sagt, es sei dringend.
TM: Haben Sie ihm nicht gesagt, dass ich in einer Besprechung bin? Kann er nicht später wieder anrufen?
SC: Tut mir Leid. Ich habe es ihm gesagt, aber er meinte, es sei wirklich dringend.
TM: Bitte entschuldigen Sie mich einen Augenblick.
JB: Kein Problem.
(Sarah und ein murrender McNamara verlassen den Raum.)
LB: So ist das hier immer. Aber man gewöhnt sich daran.
NC: Das ist leider nur zu wahr!

Exercises

1 Please listen to the following sentences and then repeat them.

1. We're convinced that this is a breakthrough.
2. We could sell them the ecological aspect.
3. It would be a good idea to have the information in front of us.

2 Please listen to the following questions and then form new sentences using "*Yes, I think we should …*".

1. *Shall we get down to business now?*
Yes, I think we should get down to business now.
2. *Shall we go global?*
Yes, I think we should go global.
3. *Shall we print it out right now?*
Yes, I think we should print it out right now.

3 Please listen to the dialogue again, paying particular attention to presenting a new product. Then answer the following questions.

1. *What sort of packaging has Galaxy Pax UK been working on?*
Galaxy Pax UK has been working on biodegradable packaging.
2. *What is the name of the new packaging?*
The name of the new packaging is *Earth Pax.*
3. *What would be a unique selling point?*
The ecological angle would be a unique selling point.

If you want to pass on information to somebody at a meeting but do not want to interrupt the conference, you can use the expression *"Sorry, but …"* plus a sort of explanation as in the examples:
– *Sorry, but there's a gentleman on the phone.*
– *Sorry, but can you sign this, please?*
– *Sorry, but there's an important fax for you here.*
– *Sorry, but this e-mail has just arrived.*

Vocabulary

agenda	Tagesordnung
to take the minutes	Protokoll führen
market leader	Marktführer
in the field of	auf dem Gebiet
packaging	Verpackung(en)
for some time now	seit einiger Zeit
to develop *s.th.*	*etwas* entwickeln
to be proud of *s.th.*	stolz sein auf *etwas*
to bring *s.th.* to the market	*etwas* auf den Markt bringen
to go global	weltweit einführen
to break down	*hier:* aufspalten; zerfallen
shelf	Regal
shelf-life	*hier:* Lagerfähigkeit
to fall apart	auseinanderfallen
storage	Lagerung
directives	Vorgaben; Bestimmungen; Richtlinien
a matter of	eine Frage von
obvious	offensichtlich
ecological advantages	ökologische Vorzüge
to make *s.th.* worthwhile	der Mühe wert sein; *hier: etwas* wettmachen
precaution	Vorsichtsmaßnahme
aware	bewusst
environment	Umwelt
angle	Blickwinkel; Aspekt
unique selling point (USP)	einzigartiges Verkaufsargument; Alleinstellungsmerkmal
urgent	dringend
Would you excuse me for a moment?	Bitte entschuldigen Sie mich einen Augenblick.
You get used to it!	Man gewöhnt sich daran.

10 Concluding business

▲ We hear John Bryant saying goodbye to his business partners and making arrangements for the future.

John Bryant has concluded his business trip and is satisfied with the outcome of the meetings. He now decides to travel around the country for a few days before returning home and says goodbye to his new business partners.

TM: = Tony McNamara; JB: = John Bryant; LB: = Lee Bernstein; R: = Receptionist

TM: Well, John. That was a really productive meeting we had. It's going to be great working with you. Very exciting.
JB: I feel the same. I'm glad that we could come to an agreement, and it looks like I'll be over to Chicago quite a lot in future.

TM: But I hope you'll let me come to England, too!
JB: I'd like that.
TM: So we'll be in touch when you get back. Where are you heading for now?
JB: I'm not sure. I've got a bit of leave and just want to drive around and see where I end up!
TM: Well, John, this is America – you can drive and drive and get nowhere! Lee? Have you got any information brochures on the area?

LB: I think there are some in my office. I'll have a look. But I know the area quite well. I could give you a few tips.

JB: That'd be really good. Thanks, Lee.
TM: Lee, you've got vacation coming up. You could show John around, couldn't you?

LB: Er ... sure. I'd like that. If it's all right with you, John.

JB: That would be great. I don't know my way around here, and it would be nice to have some company.

Abschluss der Verhandlungen

▲ Wir hören, wie John Bryant sich von seinen Geschäftspartnern verabschiedet und das weitere Vorgehen bespricht.

John Bryant hat den geschäftlichen Teil seiner Reise abgeschlossen und ist mit dem Ergebnis der Besprechungen zufrieden. Jetzt will er sich noch ein paar Tage die Umgebung ansehen, bevor er wieder nach Hause fliegt. Er verabschiedet sich von seinen neuen Geschäftspartnern.

TM: Also, John. Das war ein wirklich produktives Treffen. Wir freuen uns auf die Zusammenarbeit. Das Ganze wird sehr spannend.
JB: Mir geht es genauso. Ich bin froh, dass wir eine Einigung erzielen konnten. So, wie es aussieht, werde ich in Zukunft wohl öfter in Chicago sein.
TM: Aber ich hoffe, ich kann auch einmal nach England kommen!
JB: Das würde mich freuen.
TM: Wir hören voneinander, wenn Sie wieder daheim sind. Was haben Sie jetzt noch vor?
JB: Ich bin mir noch nicht sicher. Ich habe noch etwas Urlaub und möchte einfach ein bisschen herumfahren; mal sehen, wo ich lande.
TM: Naja, John, wir sind in Amerika – Sie können fahren und fahren und nie irgendwo ankommen! Lee, haben Sie nicht ein paar Prospekte von der Umgebung hier?
LB: Ich glaube, es liegen welche in meinem Büro. Ich sehe mal nach. Aber ich kenne mich hier auch recht gut aus. Ich könnte Ihnen ein paar Tipps geben.
JB: Das wäre wunderbar. Danke, Lee.
TM: Lee, Sie haben doch auch noch Urlaub. Wollen Sie nicht John ein wenig die Gegend zeigen?
LB: Äh ... warum nicht. Doch, das würde ich gern machen. Natürlich nur, wenn es Ihnen recht ist, John.
JB: Das wäre fantastisch. Ich kenne mich hier ja überhaupt nicht aus, und es würde mich freuen, Gesellschaft zu haben.

TM: Well, it sure looks like we're consolidating our business connections!
JB: I suppose we are. Are you sure that's all right, Lee?
LB: Sure. I need a break. And it's been a successful week. I guess we deserve it.

TM: Okay. That's settled. John, enjoy the rest of your stay. You're in good hands.

LB: Tony!
JB: Thanks for everything, Tony. I'll be in touch as soon as I get back.
TM: You do that. Take care now!
LB: We could meet this evening at your hotel and talk about the trip if you like?

JB: Yes, I'm checking out tomorrow. Shall we say this evening at seven in the hotel bar – would that be okay?
LB: Sure. See you later, then, John.
Lee comes to the hotel while John is checking out the next day. They met the evening before and planned their trip.

R: I hope you enjoyed your stay with us, Mr Bryant.
JB: Well, it started off badly but got better!

R: I am sorry about the problems you had. That doesn't usually happen; I do hope you'll stay with us again.
JB: I'll probably be in Chicago again, and I'll stay here again, I'm sure.

R: Thank you. How would you like to pay?

JB: By credit card. Here it is.
R: Thank you. Just one moment please.
...
Could you sign here please?
JB: Right.
R: And here's your receipt. Have a nice trip.

JB: Thanks. Lee, are you ready?
LB: Sure. I'm looking forward to it. Let's go.

TM: Tja, es scheint, wir vertiefen unsere Geschäftsbeziehungen in jeder Hinsicht!
JB: Sieht so aus. Sind Sie sicher, dass Sie das wirklich wollen, Lee?
LB: Klar. Ich kann ein bisschen Erholung brauchen. Und es war eine erfolgreiche Woche. Ich denke, wir haben es uns verdient.
TM: Okay. Dann ist ja alles klar. John, genießen Sie Ihre Zeit hier noch. Sie sind ja in guten Händen.
LB: Tony!
JB: Vielen Dank für alles, Tony. Ich melde mich, sobald ich wieder daheim bin.
TM: Ja bitte. Passen Sie auf sich auf!
LB: Wenn Sie wollen, können wir uns heute Abend in Ihrem Hotel treffen und alles Weitere besprechen.
JB: Ja. Ich checke morgen aus dem Hotel aus. Sagen wir heute Abend um sieben in der Hotelbar? Wäre Ihnen das recht?
LB: Klar. Bis dann, John.
Lee kommt zum Hotel, als John gerade seine Rechnung bezahlt. Sie haben sich am vorhergehenden Abend getroffen und ihre Reise besprochen.
R: Ich hoffe, Sie hatten einen angenehmen Aufenthalt in unserem Haus, Mr. Bryant.
JB: Naja, der Anfang war nicht so berühmt, aber dann wurde es besser.
R: Ich bedaure sehr, dass Sie solchen Ärger hatten. Das ist sicher nicht die Regel. Ich hoffe, Sie kommen trotzdem wieder.
JB: Wahrscheinlich bin ich schon bald wieder in Chicago, und dann werde ich auch sicher wieder hier absteigen.
R: Danke. Das würde uns freuen. Wie möchten Sie bezahlen?
JB: Mit Kreditkarte. Hier bitte.
R: Danke. Einen Augenblick bitte.
...
Würden Sie bitte hier unterschreiben.
JB: Ja.
R: Und hier Ihr Beleg. Ich wünsche Ihnen eine gute Reise.
JB: Danke. Lee, sind Sie so weit?
LB: Sicher. Ich freue mich schon. Gehen wir.

Exercises

1 Please listen to the following sentences and then repeat them.

1. I'm glad that we could come to an agreement.
2. It looks like we're consolidating our business connections.
3. So we'll be in touch when you get back. Where are you heading for now?

2 Please listen to the following expressions and choose the correct definition.

1. Where are you heading for now?
   Does this mean: Where do you intend to go?
   Or: In which direction are you looking?
   Where are you heading for now?
   means: Where do you intend to go?

2. You`ve got vacation coming up.
   Does this mean: You will soon be able to go on holiday *or:* You want to go on holiday but you can`t?
   You`ve got vacation coming up *means:* You will soon be able to go on holiday.

3 Please listen to the dialogue again, paying particular attention to concluding a business trip. Then answer the following questions.

1. *Are John and Tony satisfied with the outcome of their meetings?*
   Yes, John and Tony are satisfied with the outcome of their meetings.

2. *Who is going to show John around Chicago?*
   Lee is going to show John around Chicago.

3. *Where and when will Lee and John meet in the evening?*
   Lee and John will meet this evening at seven in the bar of John's hotel.

Vocabulary

to conclude *s.th.*	*etwas* zu Ende bringen; abschließen
to be satisfied with *s.th.*	zufrieden sein mit *etwas*
I feel the same.	So geht es mir auch.
to be in touch	in Verbindung bleiben; *hier:* voneinander hören
a bit of leave	etwas Urlaub
to end up	landen; enden
to have some company	Gesellschaft haben
to consolidate	festigen; *hier:* vertiefen
I need a break.	Ich brauche Erholung.
to deserve *s.th.*	*etwas* verdienen; verdient haben
That's settled.	Das ist abgemacht.; Das steht fest.; Das ist klar.
Take care!	Passen Sie auf sich auf!
That doesn't usually happen.	Das ist nicht die Regel.
to pay by credit card	mit Kreditkarte bezahlen
receipt	Quittung; Beleg

Liste der ID-Nummern für CD 2: Geschäftsreisen

Inhalt der CD	ID-Nummer:		
Vorspann	**1**	**Dialogue 6**	**22**
Dialogue 1	**2**	Exercise 1	23
Exercise 1	3	Exercise 2	24
Exercise 2	4	Exercise 3	25
Exercise 3	5	**Dialogue 7**	**26**
Dialogue 2	**6**	Exercise 1	27
Exercise 1	7	Exercise 2	28
Exercise 2	8	Exercise 3	29
Exercise 3	9	**Dialogue 8**	**30**
Dialogue 3	**10**	Exercise 1	31
Exercise 1	11	Exercise 2	32
Exercise 2	12	Exercise 3	33
Exercise 3	13	**Dialogue 9**	**34**
Dialogue 4	**14**	Exercise 1	35
Exercise 1	15	Exercise 2	36
Exercise 2	16	Exercise 3	37
Exercise 3	17	**Dialogue 10**	**38**
Dialogue 5	**18**	Exercise1	39
Exercise 1	19	Exercise 2	40
Exercise 2	20	Exercise 3	41
Exercise 3	21	End	42

Meetings / Inhalt

1 Arranging a meeting

▲ In this dialogue, we hear about arranging a meeting and finding suitable dates …

Mary Robbins is the Managing Director of Frontpoint Communications. She has asked her PA, Sally Webb, to arrange a meeting with Paul, Clare, Ben and Mark … all members of the sales team. Frontpoint has its headquarters in Manchester and another large office in New York. Mary would prefer the meeting to take place in Manchester, so Sally needs to find out when everyone is available … She phones Keith Roberts, her counterpart in New York.

K: = Keith Roberts; S: = Sally Webb

K: Frontpoint Communcations. Keith Roberts speaking.
S: Hello, Keith, it's Sally here.
K: Hi there, Sally, good to speak to you! How are you doing?
S: I'm fine, thanks. How about you?
K: Fine, thanks. What can I do for you?
S: Mary's asked me to set up the sales meeting. I need to check when you have time so that we can fix a date. Sometime in November would be best.

K: Okay, I'll just get the sales team members' diaries up on the screen … here we are … Should we start with Paul first? He's always the most difficult one to pin down … let's see … it looks like he can only do November tenth and eleventh and November twenty-ninth. Where's the meeting going to be held?

S: Mary wants to hold it in Manchester this time.
K: We'd better discount the twenty-ninth – it's too close to Thanksgiving! Paul would never forgive me!
S: So, we'll start with the tenth of November. What does Clare's diary look like?

Eine Sitzung organisieren

▲ In diesem Dialog hören wir, wie man eine Besprechung organisiert und passende Termine findet …

Mary Robbins ist Geschäftsführerin von Frontpoint Communications. Sie hat ihre Chefsekretärin, Sally Webb, gebeten, eine Besprechung mit Paul, Clare, Ben und Mark zu organisieren, die alle Mitglieder des Verkaufsteams sind. Frontpoint hat seinen Sitz in Manchester und ein weiteres großes Büro in New York. Mary ist es lieber, das Treffen in Manchester durchzuführen. Sally muss also herausfinden, wer wann Zeit hat … Sie ruft Keith Roberts an, ihren Kollegen in New York.

K: Frontpoint Communications, Keith Roberts am Apparat.
S: Hallo, Keith, hier Sally.
K: Hallo, Sally, schön, dich zu hören! Wie geht es dir?
S: Sehr gut, danke. Und dir?
K: Gut, danke. Was kann ich für dich tun?
S: Mary hat mich gebeten, die Verkaufsbesprechung zu organisieren. Von dir muss ich wissen, wann du Zeit hast, damit wir einen Termin festsetzen können. Irgendwann im November wäre am günstigsten.
K: Alles klar, ich rufe als Erstes die Terminkalender der Mitglieder des Verkaufsteams auf dem Bildschirm auf … So, da haben wir sie … Sollen wir mit Paul anfangen? Er ist immer am schwierigsten festzunageln … So … es sieht so aus, als ob er nur am zehnten, am elften und am neunundzwanzigsten November kann. Wo findet die Besprechung statt?
S: Mary meint, sie sollte diesmal in Manchester stattfinden.
K: Den neunundzwanzigsten sollten wir streichen. Der liegt zu nahe an Thanksgiving. Das würde Paul mir nie verzeihen!
S: Also fangen wir mit dem zehnten November an. Wie sieht es bei Clare aus?

K: She has a meeting on the tenth, but perhaps I could persuade her to rearrange it. What's it looking like at your end?
S: Hmm. Mary's free then, but I'm not sure Ben will be able to make it. Mark's free though … Perhaps Ben can change his dates. I'll check with him. In the meantime, can you pencil in the tenth for Clare and Paul?
K: Sure will. Will they be doing presentations again?
S: I'm not sure. Mary hasn't put an agenda together yet. I think she's going to be calling them this week to discuss it.

K: Well, let me know and I'll get things organized at this end.
S: Great. And I'll email you the agenda as soon as it's confirmed.
K: That's fine. I'll speak to you soon.
S: Great, and thanks for your help, Keith.

K: Sie hat am zehnten schon eine Besprechung, aber ich könnte sie vielleicht überreden, sie zu verschieben. Wie sieht es bei euch aus?
S: Hm. Mary ist frei, aber ich bin nicht sicher, dass Ben dann kann. Mark ist auch frei … Vielleicht kann Ben seine Termine ja umstellen. Ich werde ihn fragen. Kannst du inzwischen den zehnten bei Clare und Paul vormerken?
K: Klar. Werden sie wieder Präsentationen machen?
S: Da bin ich nicht sicher. Die Tagesordnung hat Mary noch nicht zusammengestellt. Ich denke, sie wird noch diese Woche anrufen, um das zu besprechen.
K: Gut. Gib mir Bescheid und ich organisiere alles, was ich kann.
S: Wunderbar. Ich werde dir die Tagesordnung mailen, sobald sie steht.
K: Fein, dann hören wir bald wieder voneinander.
S: Gut, und danke für deine Hilfe, Keith.

Exercises

1 Listen to the following sentences and repeat them please.

1. Mary's asked me to set up the sales meeting.
2. What's it looking like at your end?
3. In the meantime, can you pencil in the tenth?
4. I'll get things organized at this end.

2 Please listen to the following expressions and choose the correct definition.

1. I need to check when you have time so that we can fix a date.
   To fix a date. *Does this mean:* to leave a message *or:* to arrange an appointment?
   To fix a date *means:* to arrange an appointment.

2. He's always the most difficult one to pin down.
   To pin somebody down. *Does this mean:* to arrange a meeting with somebody *or:* to exchange ideas with somebody?
   To pin somebody down *means:* to arrange a meeting with somebody.

3. I'm not sure Ben will be able to make it.
   To make it. *Does this mean:* to be there *or:* to confirm something?
   To make it *means:* to be there.

3 Please listen to the dialogue again, paying particular attention to the dates when people are available. Then answer the following questions.

1. *Which dates can Paul do?*
   Paul can do November tenth, eleventh and twenty-ninth.

2. *Why had they better discount the twenty-ninth?*
   They'd better discount the twenty-ninth because it's too close to Thanksgiving.

3. *What does Clare have on November tenth?*
   Clare has a meeting on November tenth.

4. *Are Mark and Mary free on the tenth of November?*
   Yes, they are free on the tenth of November.

ℹ Electronic diary organizers make arranging a meeting more straightforward. You can check the availability of those who are meant to attend, send an invitation and attach an agenda. An electronic system will also track changes, allow you to send updates and amendments, and remind you of the date of the meeting.

Vocabulary

to arrange a meeting	eine Sitzung organisieren
suitable	passend; geeignet
Managing Director	Geschäftsführer(in)
PA (Personal Assistant)	Chefsekretär(in)
sales team	Verkaufsteam
headquarter	Hauptsitz
to prefer	lieber haben; vorziehen
to take place	stattfinden
counterpart	Gegenüber, Gegenstück; *hier:* Kollege, Kollegin
to set up	errichten; aufbauen
to fix a date	einen Termin festsetzen
diary	Kalender
screen	Bildschirm
to pin down	festnageln
We'd better discount the twenty-ninth.	*etwa:* Den neunundzwanzigsten sollten wir streichen.
Thanksgiving (Day), (AE)	Thanksgiving (amerikanischer Feiertag am vierten Donnerstag im November)
Paul would never forgive me!	Das würde Paul mir nie verzeihen!
to look like	aussehen
to persuade	überreden
to rearrange	verschieben; umstellen; ändern
to pencil in	vormerken
presentation	Präsentation; Vortrag
to put an agenda together	eine Tagesordnung zusammenstellen
to confirm	bestätigen
electronic diary organizer	elektronischer Terminkalender
straightforward	einfach; aufrichtig
to track	*hier:* verfolgen
amendment	Änderung

2 The agenda

▲ Now let's have a look at preparing the agenda for a meeting, deciding on the items to be discussed and setting the priorities …

Mary Robbins, the managing director of Frontpoint Communications, is discussing the agenda for the forthcoming sales meeting with her deputy, Paul Crane.

M: = Mary Robbins; P: = Paul Crane

M: … so you see Paul, we need to include this in the agenda.
P: Guess you're right, Mary. So what does that give us now?
M: So far we have … quarterly figures, targets and forecasts, new customers and recruitment of additional sales managers for Europe and the US.
P: We should add relocation to those, which will give us five items. Where do you intend starting?
M: Before we launch into our meeting, I would like to bring in a guest speaker to talk about market expansion. I've heard him speak at a dinner I went to and he's very inspirational.
P: Good idea. How long should he speak for?
M: I thought he could kick off the meeting with a thirty-minute talk, then we could break for fifteen minutes before continuing with the agenda.
P: Which item would you start off with?
M: Well, the relocation is going to be a slightly thorny issue, so I thought we should start with this quarter's figures and then cover forecasts and targets. All of those are positive and should create an upbeat note.

P: Until the issue of relocation comes up!
M: I don't think they'll see it as such a negative thing. We are doing so well and the future is looking good. Relocating is a natural step to take.

Die Tagesordnung

▲ Lassen Sie uns nun einen Blick darauf werfen, wie man eine Tagesordnung vorbereitet, wie man festsetzt, welche Punkte besprochen werden müssen und wie man Prioritäten setzt …

Mary Robbins, Geschäftsführerin von Frontpoint Communications, bespricht die Tagesordnung für das bevorstehende Verkaufsmeeting mit ihrem Stellvertreter, Paul Crane.

M: … also Paul, du siehst, wir müssen diesen Punkt auf der Tagesordnung haben.
P: Ja, Mary, wahrscheinlich hast du Recht. Also, was haben wir bis jetzt?
M: Bis jetzt haben wir … Quartalszahlen, Ziele und Prognosen, Neukunden und die Einstellung von zusätzlichen Verkaufsleitern für Europa und die USA.
P: Den Umzug sollten wir auch mitzählen. Dann haben wir fünf Punkte. Mit welchem willst du beginnen?
M: Bevor wir mit der Sitzung anfangen, würde ich gerne einen Gastredner vorstellen, der über Marktexpansion sprechen wird. Ich habe ihn schon bei einem Geschäftsessen reden hören. Er ist sehr inspirierend.
P: Gute Idee. Wie lange soll er reden?
M: Ich dachte, er könnte mit einer Präsentation von etwa dreißig Minuten den Anfang machen. Danach machen wir eine fünfzehnminütige Pause, bevor wir mit der Tagesordnung fortfahren.
P: Mit welchem Punkt würdest du anfangen?
M: Also, der Umzug wird ein ziemlich heikles Thema sein, deshalb dachte ich, wir sollten mit den Quartalszahlen beginnen, dann legen wir Ziele und Prognosen fest. Das sind alles positive Punkte, die eine optimistische Stimmung erzeugen sollten.
P: Bis wir zum Thema „Umzug" kommen!
M: Ich glaube nicht, dass sie ihn als ganz so negativ betrachten werden. Bei uns läuft alles recht gut und die Zukunft sieht auch gut aus. Der Umzug ist der nächste logische Schritt.

P: In that case, we might as well leave it until the end and cover new customers and the sales managers first.

M: No, I don't think that's the right order. If the team feel even a little negative about the relocation, suggesting new sales managers might make them think we're replacing them.

P: Hmm. How about leaving the new customers until the end? We need to give the team a sense of being valued.

M: Yes, I think that's the right order. So, the agenda will be … guest speaker, quarterly figures, targets and forecasts, new sales managers, relocation and new customers. Have I got everything?

P: Looks like it. Now on to another subject …

P: In dem Fall könnten wir ihn genauso gut als letzten Punkt behandeln und zuerst über Neukunden und neue Verkaufsleiter sprechen.

M: Nein. Ich glaube nicht, dass das die richtige Reihenfolge ist. Wenn das Team auch nur ein wenig negativ wegen des Umzugs gestimmt ist, könnte der Vorschlag, neue Verkaufsleiter einzustellen, ihnen das Gefühl geben, wir wollten sie ersetzen.

P: Hm. Wie wäre es, wenn wir das Thema Neukunden bis zum Schluss aufheben? Wir müssen dem Team das Gefühl geben, dass es geschätzt wird.

M: Ja, das ist die richtige Reihenfolge. So, die Tagesordnung ist also … Gastredner, Quartalszahlen, Ziele und Prognosen, neue Verkaufsleiter, Umzug und Neukunden. Habe ich alles?

P: Sieht so aus. Nun, ein weiteres Thema …

Exercises

1 Please listen to the following sentences and repeat them.

1. We need to include this in the agenda.
2. We should add relocation, too.
3. Which item would you start off with?

2 Please listen to the following sentences and answer the questions using *"No, I don't …"* or: *"No, I wouldn't …"*.

1. *Would you like to talk about market expansion?*
   No, I wouldn't like to talk about market expansion.
2. *Do you want to break for thirty minutes?*
   No, I don't want to break for thirty minutes.
3. *Would you see it as a negative thing?*
   No, I wouldn't see it as a negative thing.

3 Please listen to the following extract from the dialogue.

M: Well, the relocation is going to be a slightly thorny issue, so I thought we should start with this quarter's figures and then cover forecasts and targets. All of those are positive and should create an upbeat note.

P: Until the issue of relocation comes up!

M: Hmm, I don't think they'll see it as such a negative thing. We are doing so well and the future is looking good. Relocating is a natural step to take.

P: In that case, we might as well leave it until the end and cover new customers and the sales managers first.

M: No, I don't think that's the right order. If the team feel even a little negative about the relocation, suggesting new sales managers might make them think we're replacing them.

P: Hmm. How about leaving the new customers until the end? We need to give the team a sense of being valued.

M: Yes, I think that's the right order. So, the agenda will be … guest speaker, quarterly figures, targets and forecasts, new sales managers, relocation and new customers. Have I got everything?

P: Looks like it. Now on to another subject …

And now it is your turn. Please take the role of Mary. You'll hear one answer as a model. Other solutions are, of course, possible.

1. Until the issue of relocation comes up!
   And now tell Paul that they will not see it as a negative thing, that you are doing well and the future looks good.
   I don't think they'll see it as such a negative thing. We are doing so well and the future is looking good.

2. In that case, we might as well leave it until the end and cover new customers and the sales managers first.
   Please say that you do not think that is the right order and that suggesting new sales managers might make them think you are replacing them.
   No, I don't think that's the right order. Suggesting new sales managers might make them think we're replacing them.

3. Hmm. How about leaving the new customers until the end? We need to give the team a sense of being valued.
   Please tell Paul that you think that is the right order, and that the agenda will begin with guest speaker and finish with new customers.
   Yes, I think that's the right order. So, the agenda will begin with … guest speaker and finish with new customers.

> ℹ The agenda is essential groundwork for any meeting. It provides a focus to ensure the time will be used effectively; it identifies which objectives the meeting aims to achieve and gives the person who is chairing the meeting an ideal tool for bringing attention back to the purpose of the meeting.

Vocabulary

agenda	Tagesordnung
item	*hier:* Punkt
to set priorities	Prioritäten setzen
deputy	Stellvertreter(in)
to include in the agenda	auf die Tagesordnung setzen
Guess you're right. (AE)	Du hast wahrscheinlich Recht.
quarterly figures	Quartalszahlen
target	Ziel
forecast	Prognose
recruitment	Einstellung
additional	zusätzlich
relocation	Umzug
to launch into (a meeting)	(mit einer Sitzung) anfangen
guest speaker	Gastredner(in)
market expansion	Marktexpansion
inspirational	inspirierend
to kick off	den Anfang machen
to break	Pause machen
slightly	leicht; etwas
a thorny issue	ein heikles Thema
to create an upbeat note	eine optimistische Stimmung erzeugen
We might as well leave it until the end.	Wir könnten es auch als letzten Punkt behandeln.
order	Reihenfolge
to suggest	vorschlagen
to replace	ersetzen
sense of being valued	Gefühl der Wertschätzung
subject	Thema
groundwork	Vorarbeit
to provide	stellen; geben
to chair a meeting	eine Sitzung leiten
tool	Werkzeug
purpose	Zweck

3 The sales meeting

▲ Here we listen in as Mary Robbins of Frontpoint Communications has some exciting news to deliver to the sales team, which consists of Clare, Paul and Ben, at their annual meeting …

Frontpoint has had its best year yet. The industry has expanded rapidly from a shaky start two years ago. More new clients are being signed up, giving Frontpoint significant market share.

M:= Mary Robbins; C: = Clare Jones; P: = Paul Crane

M: … as you can see from the graph, we've had a marvellous quarter. The downturn we experienced back in early April has been reversed and we have achieved a growth rate of 35% in this sector.

C: Do you think we can maintain that rate?

M: I don't believe the market has reached saturation point, although it's difficult to predict. Our competitors are catching up fast, with Montano leading the pack.

P: I understand Montano has been courting Robinsons recently.

M: Yes, we mustn't become complacent. Any slip on our part and someone will fill the gap.

B: Mary, what would you say are the biggest risks for us over the coming year?

M: Hmm … I would say … losing our people to our competitors – their skills are constantly in demand. And secondly, failing to deliver either because we have over-stretched ourselves or are resting on our laurels.

C: I'd really like to know how we're going to handle the extra clients. What plans has the board of directors made?

M: I'll come to that in a minute. First let's look at the next set of figures. It shows the clients we have signed up in the past three

Die Verkaufsbesprechung

▲ Hier erfahren wir, wie Mary Robbins bei der Jahresversammlung von Frontpoint Communications eine aufregende Neuigkeit für das Verkaufsteam hat, das aus Clare, Paul und Ben besteht …

Dieses Jahr war für Frontpoint bis jetzt das beste. Die Industrie hat sich rasch von einem holprigen Anfang vor zwei Jahren erholt. Es wurden mehr Neukunden gewonnen, wodurch Frontpoint einen beträchtlichen Marktanteil hinzubekam.

M: … wie Sie dem Diagramm entnehmen können, haben wir ein hervorragendes Quartal gehabt. Der Abwärtstrend vom frühen April hat sich in diesem Sektor umgekehrt und wir haben eine Wachstumsrate von 35 % erzielt.

C: Meinen Sie, wir können diese Rate aufrechterhalten?

M: Meines Erachtens hat der Markt seinen Sättigungspunkt noch nicht erreicht, obwohl es schwierig ist, eine Vorhersage zu machen. Unsere Mitbewerber holen auf, angeführt von Montano.

P: Ich höre, dass Montano seit neuestem Robinsons den Hof macht.

M: Ja, wir dürfen nicht überheblich werden. Wenn wir einen Fehler machen, schließt ein anderer die Lücke.

B: Mary, was birgt Ihrer Meinung nach für uns im kommenden Jahr die größten Risiken?

M: Hm … ich würde sagen … unsere Mitarbeiter an die Konkurrenz zu verlieren – ihre Fähigkeiten sind sehr gefragt. Unsere Versprechungen nicht einzuhalten, sei es weil wir uns verausgabt haben oder weil wir uns auf unseren Lorbeeren ausruhen.

C: Ich möchte wirklich wissen, wie wir die neuen Kunden betreuen sollen. Welche Pläne hat der Vorstand?

M: Darauf komme ich gleich. Schauen wir uns zuerst die nächste Statistik an. Sie zeigt die Kunden, die wir in den letzten drei Monaten

months, our biggest scoop being Bradford plc. Um … this has meant that we have already had to beef up our operation considerably …

P: … leading to major changes in our structure …

M: Right. And it has also required a huge increase in our workforce. We are currently looking for another twenty sales managers.

B: Where are we going to fit all these people in? Our offices are bursting at the seams right now.

P: Ben, you have just jumped the gun and brought up the next item on the agenda. Mary, shall I explain at this point?

M: Go ahead Paul.

P: As Ben has correctly identified, the situation here in Manchester has become critical and we no longer have the necessary capacity. The board has been looking at a number of options, the most likely involving relocation to Leeds.

C: And what about New York?

P: For the time being, the office in New York is sufficient …

(The discussion starts to get lively as people realize the implications of relocation.)

gewonnen haben. Unser größter Fang ist Bradford plc. Hm … das bedeutet, dass wir unser Vorgehen schon beträchtlich verschärfen mussten …

P: … was zu gravierenden Veränderungen in unserer Struktur führte …

M: Richtig. Und es hat auch einen riesigen Bedarf an Personal geweckt. Zurzeit suchen wir noch zwanzig weitere Verkaufsleiter.

B: Wo werden wir all diese Leute unterbringen? Unser Gebäude platzt schon jetzt aus allen Nähten.

P: Ben, Sie sind voreilig und haben schon den nächsten Punkt auf der Tagesordnung angesprochen. Mary, soll ich diesen Punkt erläutern?

M: Bitte, Paul.

P: Wie Ben das Problem schon richtig erkannte, ist die Lage hier in Manchester kritisch geworden und wir haben keine Kapazitäten mehr. Der Vorstand hat einige Möglichkeiten untersucht, und am wahrscheinlichsten scheint ein Umzug nach Leeds.

C: Und wie ist es mit New York?

P: Im Moment haben wir in New York genügend Platz …

(Die Besprechung wird lebhaft, als die Teilnehmer die Bedeutung des Umzugs erkennen.)

Exercises

1 Please listen to the following expressions and choose the correct definition.

1. Do you think we can maintain that rate?
   To maintain something. *Does this mean:* to keep something up *or:* to increase something?
   To maintain something *means:* to keep something up.

2. Their skills are constantly in demand.
   In demand. *Does this mean:* achieved *or:* required?
   In demand *means:* required.

3. You have just jumped the gun and brought up the next item.
   To jump the gun. *Does this mean:* to act too quickly *or:* to include in the agenda?
   To jump the gun *means:* to act too quickly.

2 Please listen to the following sentences and answer the questions using "*Yes, we have …*".

1. *Have you had a marvellous quarter?*
   Yes, we have had a marvellous quarter.
2. *Have you achieved a growth rate of 35%?*
   Yes, we have achieved a growth rate of 35%.
3. *Have you signed up any new clients?*
   Yes, we have signed up some new clients.

3 Please listen to the dialogue again, paying particular attention to the news that Mary Robbins is delivering to the sales team at the meeting. Then answer the questions.

1. *Who has been courting Robinsons recently?*
   Montano has been courting Robinsons recently.

2. *How many new sales managers is Frontpoint looking for?*
   Frontpoint is looking for twenty new sales managers.

3. *Where is Frontpoint most likely to relocate?*
   Frontpoint is most likely to relocate to Leeds.

Vocabulary

exciting	spannend; aufregend
annual meeting	Jahresversammlung
to expand	wachsen; erweitern
shaky start	holpriger Anfang
to sign up	Geschäft abschließen
market share	Marktanteil
graph	Diagramm
downturn	Abwärtstrend
to experience	erfahren; durchmachen
to reverse	umkehren; zurückstellen
to achieve	erzielen
growth rate	Wachstumsrate
to maintain	aufrechterhalten
saturation point	Sättigungspunkt
to predict	vorhersagen
competitor	Konkurrent(in); Mitbewerber(in)
to catch up	aufholen
to lead the pack	anführen
to court	*etwa:* den Hof machen
complacent	überheblich; selbstzufrieden
slip	Fehler
to fill the gap	dem Abstand aufholen; die Lücke schließen
their skills are in demand	ihre Fähigkeiten sind gefragt
to be in demand	gefragt sein
to fail to deliver	*etwa:* Versprechungen nicht einhalten
to overstretch	überfordern; verausgaben
to rest on one's laurels	sich auf seinen Lorbeeren ausruhen
to handle	*hier:* betreuen
board of directors	Vorstand
set of figures	Statistik
scoop	*hier:* Fang
to beef up	*etwa:* verstärken
major	bedeutend
to require	benötigen
huge	riesig
increase	Zuwachs; Zunahme
workforce	Belegschaft
currently	zur Zeit
to fit in	*hier:* unterbringen
to burst at the seams	aus allen Nähten platzen
to jump the gun	voreilig sein; einen Frühstart machen
most likely	am wahrscheinlichsten
sufficient	genügend

4 The guest speaker

▲ Simon Leonard lectures on cultural diversity in business. Frontpoint Communications has hired him for their annual meeting. Let's hear what he has to say …

Once a year, Frontpoint Communications holds a general meeting for all its employees. As a company that is growing internationally, the need to manage across cultures is more important than ever. Clare, Paul and Ben have questions to ask …

Si: = Simon Leonard; C: = Clare Jones; B: = Ben Adams; P: = Paul Crane

Si: … we take our cues from the society we know; the one we grew up in. These cues are not universally understood, however, and we may easily misinterpret the reaction of our audience.

C: Could you give us an example of this?
Si: Certainly. Western speakers can fall into the trap of assuming a Japanese audience to be asleep. Whilst they may have their eyes closed, this is more likely to be a sign of concentration.
C: So it wouldn't mean they were bored?

Si: Not at all, and if you assumed this to be the case, you would be caught off guard when the questions start …
B: What do you think are the main pitfalls for inexperienced managers when working abroad?
Si: The biggest danger is a complete lack of awareness of how other cultures function. Failing to understand local etiquette is likely to result in more than embarrassment; it will probably carry a heavy business cost in terms of lost contracts.

B: Isn't there a danger we could become too inhibited for fear of offending people?

Der Gastredner

▲ Simon Leonard hält Vorträge über kulturelle Vielfalt im Geschäftsleben. Frontpoint Communications hat ihn für seine Jahresversammlung engagiert. Hier hören wir, was er zu sagen hat …

Einmal im Jahr findet eine Jahresversammlung für alle Arbeitnehmer von Frontpoint Communications statt. Da es ein Unternehmen ist, das weltweit wächst, ist das Bedürfnis nach kulturübergreifender Zusammenarbeit größer denn je. Clare, Paul und Ben haben viele Fragen …

Si: … wir richten uns nach der Gesellschaft, die wir kennen, in der wir aufgewachsen sind. Die Regeln dieser Gesellschaft werden jedoch nicht weltweit verstanden und wir können die Reaktionen unserer Zuhörer leicht missverstehen.
C: Können Sie uns ein Beispiel dafür geben?
Si: Gewiss. Redner aus dem Westen tappen in eine Falle, wenn sie glauben, japanische Zuhörer schlafen. Dass sie die Augen geschlossen haben, ist eher ein Zeichen der Konzentration.
C: Dann bedeutet es nicht, dass sie sich langweilen?
Si: Nicht im Geringsten, und wenn Sie glauben, dies sei der Fall, werden Sie überrascht sein, wenn es mit den Fragen losgeht …
B: Was, glauben Sie, sind die Hauptfallstricke für unerfahrene Manager, die im Ausland arbeiten?
Si: Die Hauptgefahr ist ein Mangel an Bewusstsein für die Bräuche anderer Kulturen. Hat man kein Verständnis für fremde Gewohnheiten, kann dies mehr als peinlich werden; es würde wahrscheinlich auch ein hohen Preis an verlorenen Geschäftsverträgen fordern.
B: Besteht nicht die Gefahr, dass wir vor lauter Angst, andere zu beleidigen, zu gehemmt werden?

Si: Having an awareness is not the same as being an expert. If we learn to interpret the cues, we can respond accordingly. Let's consider personal space. Not only does it vary from one culture to another, we also need to consider the difference between urban and rural communities.

P: What does that mean in practical terms for us?

Si: As an urban Brit, your personal space is probably between two to three feet. As a rural American, it's potentially much greater – perhaps six feet or more. As an urban Japanese, it's probably around one foot. So an urban Japanese meets a rural American and a "dance" ensues as each tries to get a comfortable distance from the other … These are the kind of cues that you quickly need to become aware of …

Si: Verständnis haben heißt nicht, dass man ein Experte sein muss. Wenn wir lernen, die Regeln zu verstehen, können wir entsprechend reagieren. Denken wir an den persönlichen Mindestabstand. Er variiert nicht nur zwischen den Kulturen, sondern auch zwischen städtischen und ländlichen Gemeinden.

P: Was bedeutet das praktisch für uns?

Si: Als städtischer Brite liegt Ihr persönlicher Mindestabstand vermutlich zwischen 60 und 80 cm. Als ländlicher Amerikaner ist er potenziell viel größer – vielleicht 2 m oder mehr. Als städtischer Japaner liegt er wahrscheinlich bei 30 cm. Trifft ein städtischer Japaner auf einen ländlichen Amerikaner, entsteht ein „Tanz", wobei beide versuchen, eine angenehme Distanz zueinander zu finden … Es sind diese Unterschiede, deren man sich schnell bewusst werden muss …

Exercises

1 Please listen to the following sentences and answer the questions using *"Yes, I could …"* or *"Yes, I would …"*.

1. *Couldn't you give us an example of this?*
   Yes, I could give you an example of this.
2. *Couldn't you learn to interpret the cues?*
   Yes, I could learn to interpret the cues.
3. *Wouldn't you need to consider personal space?*
   Yes, I would need to consider personal space.

2 Please listen to the following extract from the dialogue.

Si: Not at all, and if you assumed this to be the case, you would be caught off guard when the questions start …

B: What do you think are the main pitfalls for inexperienced managers when working abroad?

Si: The biggest danger is a complete lack of awareness of how other cultures function. Failing to understand local etiquette is likely to result in more than embarrassment; it will probably carry a heavy business cost in terms of lost contracts.

B: Isn't there a danger we could become too inhibited for fear of offending people?

And now it's your turn! Please take the role of Ben. You'll hear one answer as a model. Other solutions are, of course, possible.

1. Not at all, and if you assumed this to be the case, you would be caught off guard when the questions start …
   Please ask what the main pitfalls for inexperienced managers working abroad are.
   What do you think are the main pitfalls for inexperienced managers when working abroad?

2. The biggest danger is a complete lack of awareness of how other cultures function. Failing to understand local etiquette is likely to result in more than embarrassment; it will probably carry a heavy business cost in terms of lost contracts.

Please ask if there is a danger you could become too inhibited for fear of offending people.
Isn't there a danger we could become too inhibited for fear of offending people?

3 Please listen to the dialogue again, paying particular attention to cultural diversity. Then answer the following questions.

1. *Why may Japanese people have their eyes closed?*
   Japanese people may have their eyes closed because this is a sign of concentration.
2. *What could failing to understand local etiquette result in?*
   Failing to understand local etiquette could result in lost contracts.
3. *How great is the personal space of a rural American?*
   The personal space of a rural American is six feet or more.

ℹ Humour is one of those areas that can land people in trouble. It does not translate well across languages and frequently not across cultures. If you are giving a presentation or attending a meeting abroad and you are not sure of the local culture, the inclusion of jokes is probably best avoided!

Vocabulary

to lecture	Vorträge halten
diversity	Vielfalt
to hire	engagieren
need	Bedürfnis
to take cues from	sich richten nach
cue	*hier:* Regel
universally	weltweit
to misinterpret	falsch verstehen
audience	Zuhörerschaft
to fall into the trap	in die Falle gehen
to assume	annehmen
to be bored	gelangweilt sein; sich langweilen
to be caught off guard	überrascht werden; überrumpelt werden
pitfall	Fallstrick
inexperienced	unerfahren
abroad	*hier:* im Ausland
lack of	Mangel an
awareness	Verständnis; Bewusstsein
etiquette	Verhaltensregeln
embarrassment	Verlegenheit; Peinlichkeit
inhibited	gehemmt
accordingly	entsprechend
to offend	beleidigen
space	Raum; Platzbedarf
to vary	verschieden sein; variieren
urban	städtisch
rural	ländlich
to ensue	entstehen
to become aware of *s.th.*	sich *einer Sache* bewusst werden
to land in trouble	in Schwierigkeiten geraten
to translate	übertragen; übersetzen

5 The presentation

▲ Paul Crane is updating his colleagues on the latest developments in the US operation. Has he checked that the technical equipment is working? Let's listen to his presentation …

Frontpoint Communications aims to keep ahead of the game. One way it does this is to hold regular updates to see how the competition is faring. Here we join the management team at one of their meetings.

P: = Paul Crane; M: = Mary Robbins; B:= Ben Adams

P: I have to tell you guys this: I was doing a presentation in Cincinnati last week when the beamer failed to work. I had this wonderful presentation lined up in PowerPoint and ended up doing everything on a flip chart!
M: Which proves that sometimes the old methods are the most trustworthy!
P: Sure, but I'm out of touch with those now. Slide projectors, flip charts … they're somewhat passé!
B: Did you check that *this* projector's working?
P: Oh yes. I won't get burned like that again! Anyway, let's get started. I'm going to give you guys a run-down on what has been happening over in New York. Please interrupt me if you want anything clarified. I'll take questions at any time.
B: Before you start Paul, are these notes here for handing out?
P: Yep. I've prepared a pack which contains a summary of this presentation and more detail which you might find of interest later.
P: … I'll move on now to my next set of figures. As you can see from the chart, market share for ProNet has increased significantly over the last quarter. This can mainly be attributed to their take-over of GemSystems. The latter previously had a sizeable market share.

Die Präsentation

▲ Paul Crane macht seine Kollegen mit dem neuesten Stand der Entwicklungen des US-Projekts vertraut. Hat er aber auch überprüft, ob die technischen Geräte funktionieren? Hören wir uns doch seine Präsentation an …

Frontpoint Communications strebt eine Spitzenposition an. Eine Möglichkeit, dies zu erreichen, ist die regelmäßige Beobachtung der Konkurrenz. Hier sind wir bei einer Sitzung des Führungsteams.

P: Ich muss Ihnen Folgendes erzählen: Letzte Woche hatte ich eine Präsentation in Cincinnati. Der Beamer funktionierte aber nicht. Ich hatte eine wunderbare Präsentation mit PowerPoint vorbereitet und musste schließlich alles auf einem Flipchart machen!
M: Was beweist, dass die alten Methoden manchmal die zuverlässigsten sind!
P: Sicher, aber jetzt kenne ich mich damit nicht mehr aus. Diaprojektoren, Flipcharts … das ist alles irgendwie überholt!
B: Haben Sie *diesen* Projektor überprüft?
P: Aber sicher. Ich möchte mir nicht noch einmal so die Finger verbrennen! Also, fangen wir an. Ich werde Ihnen erzählen, was in New York los ist. Bitte unterbrechen Sie mich, wenn etwas unklar ist. Ich bin immer bereit, Fragen zu beantworten.
B: Bevor Sie anfangen, Paul, sollen diese Blätter hier verteilt werden?
P: Ja. Ich habe eine Zusammenfassung dieser Präsentation sowie weitere Einzelheiten vorbereitet, die vielleicht später interessant sind.
P: … Ich zeige Ihnen jetzt die nächsten Zahlen. Wie Sie der Tabelle entnehmen können, ist der Marktanteil für ProNet im letzten Quartal erheblich gewachsen. Dies ist hauptsächlich auf ihre Übernahme von GemSystems zurückzuführen. Die hatten schon vorher einen beträchtlichen Marktanteil.

B: They must have lost some of GemSystems' customers in the process. I heard the transition was not too smooth.

P: You're right there. The two organisations were not compatible. ProNet took an aggressive approach and frightened off a number of GemSystems' longstanding clients.

M: Did we manage to pick any of those up?

P: Sure. We gained Freemasons and Celeb, but ProNet is marketing hard to get them back. We will need to prove our worth to keep them.

...

M: Paul, I'd like to thank you for taking us through this. It has been a very comprehensive review.

B: Die müssen bei diesem Prozess einige Kunden von GemSystems verloren haben. Ich habe gehört, der Wechsel war nicht so reibungslos.

P: Da haben Sie Recht. Die beiden Unternehmen waren nicht kompatibel. ProNet ging aggressiv vor und schreckte damit etliche langjährige Kunden von GemSystems ab.

M: Haben wir einige davon auffangen können?

P: Sicher. Wir haben Freemasons und Celeb gewonnen, aber ProNet kämpft schwer darum, sie zurückzugewinnen. Wir werden unseren Wert beweisen müssen, wenn wir sie behalten wollen.

...

M: Paul, ich möchte Ihnen danken, dass Sie uns all das erläutert haben. Es war ein sehr ausführlicher Überblick.

Exercises

1 Please repeat the following sentences.

1. I was doing a presentation when the projector failed to work.
2. Sometimes the old methods are the most trustworthy.
3. It has been a comprehensive review.

2 Please listen to the following expressions and choose the correct definition.

1. I'm out of touch with those now.
   To be out of touch. *Does this mean:* to be caught off guard *or:* to be unfamiliar with something?
   To be out of touch *means:* to be unfamiliar with something.

2. I'm going to give you guys a run-down on what has been happening.
   A run-down. *Does this mean:* a report *or:* a forecast?
   A run-down *means:* a report.

3. Did we manage to pick any of those up?
   To pick up. *Does this mean:* to gain *or:* to lose?
   To pick up *means:* to gain.

3 Please listen to the following extract from the dialogue.

P: Sure, but I'm out of touch with those now. Slide projectors, flip charts ... they're somewhat passé!

B: Did you check that *this* projector's working?

P: Oh yes. I won't get burned like that again! Anyway, let's get started. I'm going to give you guys a run-down on what has been happening over in New York. Please interrupt me if you want anything clarified. I'll take questions at any time.

B: Before you start Paul, are these notes here for handing out?

And now it is your turn. Please take the role of Ben. You'll hear one answer as a model. Other solutions are, of course, also possible.

1. Sure, but I'm out of touch with those now. Slide projectors, flip charts ... they're somewhat passé!
   And now ask if Paul checked that this projector is working.
   Did you check that *this* projector's working?

2. Oh yes. I won't get burned like that again! Anyway, let's get started. I'm going to give you guys a run-down on what has been happening over in New York. Please interrupt me if you want anything clarified. I'll take questions at any time.

And now ask Paul if these are the notes for handing out.
Before you start Paul, are these notes here for handing out?

ℹ Alcohol is hardly ever present at a business meeting in the States and drinking it during the day is likely to be frowned upon. In the UK, the situation is a little more relaxed with a small amount of wine or beer sometimes made available. Even then it is best not to overindulge!

Vocabulary

to update – auf den neuesten Stand bringen
development – Entwicklung
equipment – Gerät; Ausrüstung
to work – *hier:* funktionieren
to aim – anstreben
to be ahead of the game – *etwa:* der/die Führende sein
to fare – *hier:* gehen
to have *s.th.* lined up – *etwas* vorbereitet haben
trustworthy – zuverlässig
slide – Dia
to get burned – sich die Finger verbrennen
to give *s.o.* a run-down – *j-n* informieren
to interrupt – unterbrechen
to clarify – klären
to hand out – austeilen
summary – Zusammenfassung
chart – *hier:* Tabelle
significantly – wesentlich
to attribute *s.th.* to *s.th.* – *etwas* auf *etwas* zurückführen
take-over – Übernahme
latter – letztgenannter
previously – vorher
transition – Wechsel
smooth – reibungslos
to take an approach – herangehen
to frighten off – abschrecken
longstanding – langjährig
to pick up – aufschnappen
to gain – gewinnen
to market – vermarkten; vertreiben
comprehensive – ausführlich
to frown – die Stirn runzeln
amount – Betrag; Summe; Höhe
to overindulge – *hier:* übermäßig frönen

6 Project meeting with the client

▲ Two of Frontpoint's consultants are discussing the proposal they have put together for a new client. There are several points to be covered and some changes to be made before agreement is reached …

Frontpoint Communications has tendered for a project to redesign Crampon Inc.'s marketing strategy. The client team – Jane Martin and Helen Allen – are asking some searching questions. Paul Crane and Ben Adams are being kept on their toes!

J: = Jane Martin; P: = Paul Crane;
H: = Helen Allen; B: = Ben Adams

J: We have several questions regarding the proposal you've put together. Should we go through them one at a time?
P: Yes, where would you like to start?
J: In the executive summary, you state that you expect to raise our direct marketing uptake to 15% within a twelve-month period. That's quite a claim: do you think you can deliver on this?

P: Direct marketing normally yields low results – 3% would be considered reasonable. This is an area we have had much success in and the best evidence for this comes from previous clients.
H: Can you give us an example?
P: I can. Eighteen months ago, we worked with GlobalPower who were struggling to increase their market share following deregulation. We applied our strategy and they saw their direct marketing response increase to 12%.

H: Hmm. That's interesting. What about your suggestion that you can increase our market share within six months?

Projektbesprechung mit dem Kunden

▲ Zwei Frontpoint-Berater besprechen mit einem Kunden einen Vorschlag, den sie für ihn ausgearbeitet haben. Einige Punkte müssen abgedeckt und einige Änderungen vorgenommen werden, ehe man zu einer Einigung kommt …

Frontpoint Communications hat ein Angebot für ein Projekt zur Neugestaltung der Marketingstrategie von Crampon Inc. eingereicht. Das Kundenteam – Jane Martin und Helen Allen – stellen bohrende Fragen. Paul Crane und Ben Adams werden auf Trab gehalten!

J: Wir haben einige Fragen zum Vorschlag, den Sie vorbereitet haben. Sollen wir die Punkte nacheinander durchgehen?
P: Ja. Wo möchten Sie anfangen?
J: In der Zusammenfassung, die Sie für den Vorstand ausgearbeitet haben, stellen Sie fest, dass Sie das Ergebnis unseres Direktmarketings innerhalb von zwölf Monaten auf 15 % erhöhen wollen. Das ist ein starkes Versprechen. Glauben Sie, dass Sie dieses Versprechen halten können?
P: Direktmarketing bringt normalerweise niedrige Resultate – 3 % werden schon als ein gutes Ergebnis betrachtet. Auf diesem Gebiet haben wir viel Erfolg gehabt. Der Beweis sind unsere bisherigen Kunden.
H: Können Sie uns ein Beispiel geben?
P: Ja. Vor achtzehn Monaten arbeiteten wir mit GlobalPower zusammen. Sie hatten Probleme, nach der Deregulierung ihren Marktanteil auszubauen. Wir haben unsere Strategie angewandt, und sie sahen, wie die Resonanz auf das Direktmarketing auf 12 % anstieg.
H: Hm. Das ist interessant. Wie ist es mit Ihrem Vorschlag, dass Sie unseren Marktanteil innerhalb von sechs Monaten erhöhen können?

B: Again, this is a tried and tested process. We used this strategy with another client, Evolve Industries, to raise their flagging profile.

H: And how are they doing now?

B: Evolve now has a market share of 27 % compared with 5 % four years ago.

H: Would any of your previous clients be willing to talk to us?

P: No problem at all. We can provide you with any contacts you want.

(They continue discussions for another thirty minutes.)

J: … so if we make this adjustment to the specification, how much is that likely to increase the fee?

P: We'll need to take another look at it to give you an accurate figure. But I could guess that it would not be more than $ 10,000.

H: Good, then we'll wait to hear from you.

(They shake hands and depart.)

B: Noch einmal: Das ist ein erprobtes und bewährtes Verfahren. Diese Strategie haben wir bei einem anderen Kunden angewandt, Evolve Industries, um sein schwaches Erscheinungsbild zu verstärken.

H: Und wie läuft es jetzt bei denen?

B: Jetzt hat Evolve einen Marktanteil von 27 % – verglichen mit 5 % vor vier Jahren.

H: Wären irgendwelche Ihrer ehemaligen Kunden bereit, mit uns zu reden?

P: Das ist überhaupt kein Problem. Wir können jeden Kontakt herstellen, den Sie wünschen.

(Sie reden noch dreißig Minuten.)

J: … Also: Wenn wir diese Korrektur im Entwurf machen, um wieviel wird das das Honorar erhöhen?

P: Wir müssten das noch einmal anschauen, um Ihnen eine genaue Summe nennen zu können. Aber ich schätze, es würden nicht mehr als $ 10.000 werden.

H: Gut. Dann warten wir, bis Sie wieder auf uns zukommen.

(Sie schütteln sich die Hände und gehen.)

Exercises

1 Please listen to the following expressions and choose the correct definition.

1. They were struggling to increase their market share.
   To struggle. *Does this mean:* to jump the gun *or:* to have problems?
   To struggle *means:* to have problems.

2. We used this strategy to raise their flagging profile.
   Flagging. *Does this mean:* falling *or:* varying?
   Flagging *means:* falling.

3. How much is that likely to increase the fee?
   A fee. *Does this mean:* an amount of money *or:* a board of directors?
   A fee *means:* an amount of money.

2 Please, listen to the following sentences and form questions using *"Do you think you …?"*

1. *They can deliver on this claim.*
   Do you think you can deliver on this claim?

2. *We have had much success in this area.*
   Do you think you have had much success in this area?

3. *They will increase our market share within six months.*
   Do you think you will increase our market share within six months?

3 Please listen to the dialogue again, paying particular attention to percentages. Then answer the following questions.

1. *GlobalPower saw their direct marketing response increase to how much?*
   GlobalPower saw their direct marketing response increase to 12 %.
2. *Evolve now has a market share of how much?*
   Evolve now has a market share of 27 %.
3. *Four years ago, Evolve had a market share of how much?*
   Four years ago, Evolve had a market share of 5 %.

Vocabulary

consultant	Berater
proposal	Vorschlag
to cover	*hier:* behandeln; abdecken
to reach (an) agreement	zu einer Einigung kommen
to tender	ein Angebot einreichen
to redesign	neu gestalten
searching	durchdringend; bohrend
to be kept on *one's* toes	auf Trab gehalten werden
regarding	bezüglich
executive	leitende(r) Angestellte(r); Manager(in)
to state	feststellen; konstatieren
uptake	Aufnahme
claim	Versprechen; Behauptung
to yield	ergeben
reasonable	gut; reell
evidence	Beweis
previous	ehemalig
to struggle	*hier:* Probleme haben
to apply	anwenden
tried (and tested)	erprobt; bewährt
flagging	nachlassend; erlahmend
adjustment	Korrektur
fee	Gebühr; Honorar
accurate	genau
to guess	schätzen

7 Overcoming disagreement

▲ Not every meeting runs smoothly. Here we listen in as Clare and Ben have a difference of opinion. It's important to hear everyone's views and to seek agreement …

Two of Frontpoint's employees, Ben Adams and Clare Jones, are having a disagreement prior to the monthly meeting with their team. Clare is annoyed at Ben's attitude over a deadline they have both been working towards.

C: = Clare Jones; B: = Ben Adams

C: Ben, this is not what we agreed. Last week we said that we would publish the document today.
B: Clare, that might be *your* record of events. I don't recall reaching any agreement on deadlines.
C: Of course we agreed it, it's here in the minutes. Look, "framework document", action: BA and CJ. 31 July.
B: Let me see that! It's a bit vague isn't it? It doesn't actually say "complete"!
C: I think you're splitting hairs. What else would it imply?
B: And I think you're getting worked up over nothing!
C: I take offence at that comment. We have a meeting with the team in two hours and they will be expecting us to deliver. What do *you* propose we do?
B: OK, OK. It shouldn't take too long to put together an outline …
C: … but it must be sufficiently clear for the team to feel confident …
B: … if you'd just let me finish! What I was trying to say was that we could put together a draft outline of our proposals. It doesn't have to be in a final version. In fact it's better in draft form as it offers an opportunity for debate.

Eine Meinungsverschiedenheit ausräumen

▲ Nicht alle Besprechungen laufen reibungslos ab. Hier hören wir, wie Clare und Ben eine Meinungsverschiedenheit haben. Es ist wichtig, alle Meinungen zu hören und eine Einigung zu suchen …

Zwei Mitarbeiter von Frontpoint, Ben Adams und Clare Jones, haben kurz vor einem Treffen mit dem Team eine Meinungsverschiedenheit. Clare ist verärgert über Bens Einstellung zu einem Termin, auf den sie beide hingearbeitet haben.

C: Ben, so haben wir es nicht abgemacht. Letzte Woche haben wir vereinbart, das Dokument heute zu veröffentlichen.
B: Clare, so haben *Sie* es vielleicht verstanden. Ich kann mich nicht erinnern, dass wir eine Einigung über Termine erzielt haben.
C: Natürlich haben wir das abgemacht. Es steht hier im Protokoll. Sehen Sie: „Rahmendokument", Handlung: BA und CJ, 31. Juli.
B: Zeigen Sie her! Das ist ein bisschen vage, nicht wahr? Es steht da nicht deutlich „fertig"!
C: Sie treiben Haarspalterei! Was soll das denn sonst bedeuten?
B: Und Sie regen sich umsonst auf!
C: Diese Bemerkung nehme ich übel. In zwei Stunden findet ein Treffen mit dem Team statt und es wird erwartet, dass wir etwas vorweisen. Was schlagen *Sie* vor, sollen wir tun?
B: OK, OK. Es sollte nicht zu lange dauern, einen Entwurf zusammenzustellen …
C: … aber er muss klar genug sein, damit das Team zuversichtlich ist …
B: … wenn Sie mich mal ausreden lassen würden! Ich wollte sagen, dass wir einen Entwurf unserer Vorschläge zusammenstellen könnten. Es muss nicht die endgültige Version sein. In der Tat ist ein Entwurf besser, weil das eine Gelegenheit zur Diskussion bietet.

C: OK, let's get on with it. I don't want to postpone the meeting.
(Two hours later)
B: ... look Clare, I'll meet you halfway on this point, otherwise we'll never reach agreement.
C: Good; and how about this item?
B: I have grave concerns about this one. I don't think the proposal has been properly thought out. I think it will end up costing much more than our existing set-up ...
C: You have a point there. I'm beginning to wonder whether we are rushing this too much. Should we re-schedule the team meeting to allow ourselves more time?
B: Yes. I think they'd be disappointed with a half-baked proposal.
C: Do you realize we actually agreed on something?
B: That makes a change!

C: OK, lassen Sie uns anfangen. Ich möchte das Treffen nicht verschieben.
(Nach zwei Stunden)
B: ... also Clare, in diesem Punkt komme ich Ihnen auf halbem Weg entgegen, sonst werden wir uns nie einigen.
C: Gut, und bei diesem Punkt?
B: Über den mache ich mir ernsthafte Sorgen. Ich finde, der Vorschlag ist nicht gut durchdacht. Es kostet uns im Endeffekt viel mehr als unser jetziger Plan ...
C: Da haben Sie wahrscheinlich Recht. Ich fange an zu glauben, dass wir dies zu schnell durchziehen. Sollen wir das Teammeeting doch verschieben, um Zeit zu gewinnen?
B: Ja. Über einen unausgegorenen Vorschlag wären sie enttäuscht.
C: Da haben wir uns doch noch geeinigt!
B: Das ist mal was Neues!

Exercises

1 Please repeat the following sentences.

1. I take offence at that comment.
2. It shouldn't take too long to put together an outline.
3. Should we re-schedule the team meeting to allow more time?

2 Please listen to the following extract from the dialogue.

C: Ben, this is not what we agreed. Last week we said that we would publish the document today.
B: Clare, that might be *your* record of events. I don't recall reaching any agreement on deadlines.
C: Of course we agreed it, it's here in the minutes. Look, "framework document", action: BA and CJ. 31 July.
B: Let me see that! It's a bit vague isn't it? It doesn't actually say "complete"!
C: I think you're splitting hairs. What else would it imply?
B: And I think you're getting worked up over nothing!

Now it is your turn. Please take the role of Ben.

1. Ben, this is not what we agreed. Last week we said that we would publish the document today.
   Tell Clare that your record of events does not include reaching an agreement on deadlines.
   Clare, that might be your record of events. I don't recall reaching any agreement on deadlines.

2. Of course we agreed it, it's here in the minutes. Look, "framework document", action: BA and CJ. 31 July.
   Ask to see the document, which seems a bit vague and does not actually say "complete".
   Let me see that! It's a bit vague isn't it? It doesn't actually say "complete"!

3. I think you're splitting hairs. What else would it imply?
   Now say that you think Clare is getting worked up over nothing.
   And I think you're getting worked up over nothing!

3 Please listen to the dialogue again, paying particular attention to seeking agreement. Then answer the following questions.

1. *What does Ben suggest ?*
   Ben suggests they put together a draft outline of their proposals.
2. *What could Ben and Clare do about the meeting?*
   Ben and Clare could postpone the meeting.
3. *What do Ben and Clare finally agree on?*
   Ben and Clare finally agree that the team will be disappointed with a half-baked proposal.

Vocabulary

smoothly reibungslos
difference of opinion Meinungsverschiedenheit
disagreement Uneinigkeit
prior to (be)vor
annoyed genervt; verärgert
attitude Einstellung
deadline (Abgabe-)Termin
to publish veröffentlichen
record of events *etwa:* Erinnerung
to recall erinnern
minutes Protokoll
framework *etwa:* Gerüst; Rahmen
vague vage
to split hairs Haarspalterei treiben
to imply andeuten
to get worked up sich aufregen
to take offence at *s.th.* *etwas* übelnehmen
comment Kommentar; Bemerkung
outline Grundriss
sufficiently genug; genügend
draft Entwurf
debate Debatte; Diskussion
to postpone verschieben
to meet *s.o.* halfway *j-m* auf halbem Weg entgegenkommen
set-up Projekt, Plan
to rush *s.th.* *etwas* schnell erledigen, durchpeitschen
half-baked unausgegoren

8 Chairing a meeting

▲ Mary Robbins is chairing the management meeting. This means she has to make sure the agenda is followed, to keep the discussion moving, and to manage those attending. Let's hear how she does it …

Frontpoint's management team are all busy people. The agenda is long and time is short.

M: = Mary Robbins; B: = Ben Adams; C: = Clare Jones; P: = Paul Crane

M: Ben, we haven't heard your view on this: what do you think?
B: I think it's an excellent proposal and one that we should go with …
C: … but we haven't considered all the options yet …
M: Let's listen to what Ben has to say first and then we'll hear your reservations, Clare.

B: I was going to say … I feel the proposal is based on sound principles and I haven't got any concerns about it.
M: Clare, do you have anything else to add?
C: Well, the reason I am concerned is that I don't feel this company has enough experience. We are taking them a bit on face value and I'm not sure that's wise.

M: Any more comments from anyone at this stage?
P: If Clare has concerns, I think they should be explored …
B: That's just going to delay the start even more …
C: Well, that's better than going full steam ahead and getting it wrong.
M: Shall we call another meeting to discuss this proposal? There are obviously a number of issues here which have been highlighted and we don't have time to cover them here. Clare, can you arrange it?

C: Yes, I'll set that up.

Ein Meeting leiten

▲ Mary Robbins leitet das Managementsitzung. Sie hat dafür zu sorgen, dass die Tagesordnung eingehalten wird, dass die Diskussion in Gang bleibt und dass alle Teilnehmer geführt werden. Hier hören wir, wie sie das anstellt …

Alle Mitglieder des Managementteams von Frontpoint sind sehr beschäftigt. Die Tagesordnung ist lang und die Zeit ist kurz.

M: Ben, wir haben Ihre Meinung hierzu noch nicht gehört: Was denken Sie?
B: Ich denke, der Vorschlag ist hervorragend und wir sollten ihn akzeptieren …
C: … aber wir haben noch nicht alle Möglichkeiten erwogen …
M: Lassen Sie uns hören, was Ben zu sagen hat, dann kommen wir auf Ihre Bedenken, Clare.
B: Ich wollte sagen … Ich finde, der Vorschlag ist gut begründet und ich habe keine Bedenken.
M: Clare, möchten Sie noch etwas dazu sagen?
C: Also, der Grund für meine Bedenken ist, dass ich nicht sicher bin, ob diese Firma genügend Erfahrung hat. Wir glauben ihnen unbesehen, und ich bin mir nicht sicher, ob das vernünftig ist.
M: Hat noch jemand etwas hierzu zu sagen?

P: Wenn Clare Bedenken hat, finde ich, sollten wir darüber diskutieren.
B: Das wird den Anfang noch mehr hinauszögern.
C: Es ist aber besser, als mit voller Kraft loszulegen und eventuell Fehler zu machen.
M: Wollen wir noch eine Sitzung einberufen, um diesen Vorschlag zu besprechen? Es gibt offensichtlich einige Punkte, die wir herausgestellt haben. Wir haben jetzt keine Zeit, sie zu behandeln. Clare, können Sie das organisieren?
C: Ja, das mache ich.

M: Thank you. Now, as time is limited, shall we move on to the next item? Paul, would you like to take us through this one?
P: OK, this is an idea that my team came up with …
(Sixty minutes later:)
M: … I'm going to suggest that we adjourn here. We've already overrun by thirty minutes and the agenda is not finished. I have another meeting in fifteen minutes and I'm sure you all need to be getting on with other things. Shall we arrange to meet again tomorrow?
(The team agrees and the meeting finishes.)

M: Vielen Dank. Da die Zeit kurz ist, kommen wir zum nächsten Punkt. Paul, würden Sie bitte übernehmen?
P: OK, dies ist eine Idee, die mein Team ausgebrütet hat …
(Sechzig Minuten später:)
M: Ich schlage vor, wir machen hier Schluss. Wir haben schon dreißig Minuten überzogen und die Tagesordnung ist noch nicht erledigt. Ich habe in fünfzehn Minuten noch eine Sitzung und ich bin sicher, Sie alle haben auch noch anderes zu tun. Wollen wir uns morgen wieder treffen?
(Das Team stimmt zu und die Sitzung ist zu Ende.)

Exercises

1 Please listen to the following expressions and choose the correct definition.

1. It's better than going full steam ahead and getting it wrong.
   To go full steam ahead. *Does this mean:* to use all one's energy *or:* to meet somebody halfway?
   To go full steam ahead *means:* to use all one's energy.

2. We don't have time to cover all the issues.
   Issues. *Does this mean:* fees to be paid *or:* questions to be discussed?
   Issues *means:* questions to be discussed.

3. I'm going to suggest that we adjourn here.
   To adjourn. *Does this mean:* to reach an agreement *or:* to have a break?
   To adjourn *means:* to have a break.

2 Please listen to the following sentences and answer the questions using *"No, I haven't …"*.

1. *Have you considered all the options yet?*
   No, I haven't considered all the options yet.
2. *Have you got anything else to add?*
   No, I haven't got anything else to add.
3. *Have you finished the agenda?*
   No, I haven't finished the agenda.

3 Please listen to the following extract from the dialogue.

C: … but we haven't considered all the options yet …
M: Let's listen to what Ben has to say first and then we'll hear your reservations, Clare.
B: I was going to say … I feel the proposal is based on sound principles and I haven't got any concerns about it.
M: Clare, do you have anything else to add?
C: Well, the reason I am concerned is that I don't feel this company has enough experience. We are taking them a bit on face value and I'm not sure that's wise.
M: Any more comments from anyone at this stage?

Now it is your turn. Please take the role of Mary. You'll hear one answer as a model. Other solutions are, of course, possible.

1. … but we haven't considered all the options yet …
   And now suggest listening to what Ben has to say and hearing Clare's reservations.

Let's listen to what Ben has to say first and then we'll hear your reservations, Clare.

2. I was going to say … I feel the proposal is based on sound principles and I haven't got any concerns about it.
   And now ask if Clare has anything to add.
   Clare, do you have anything else to add?

3. Well, the reason I am concerned is that I don't feel this company has enough experience. We are taking them a bit on face value and I'm not sure that's wise.
   And now ask if anyone else has any more comments at this stage.
   Any more comments from anyone at this stage?

Vocabulary

to chair (a meeting)	den Vorsitz (bei einer Sitzung) führen
to consider	betrachten
option	Möglichkeit
reservation	Einschränkung; Vorbehalt
to be based on *s.th.*	beruhen, basieren auf
sound	vernünftig; gründlich
principle	Prinzip; Grundsatz
to have concerns about *s.th.*	wegen *etwas* Bedenken haben
to add	etwas hinzufügen
to take *s.th.* on face value	*etwas* für bare Münze nehmen; unbesehen glauben
stage	Phase
to explore	*hier:* diskutieren
to delay	verzögern
to go full steam ahead	mit Volldampf loslegen
obviously	offensichtlich
issue	Frage
to **highlight**	hervorheben, herausstellen
to cover	behandeln
limited	kurz; beschränkt
to adjourn	(Sitzung) beenden, schließen
to overrun	überziehen
to come up with *s.th.*	sich *etwas* ausdenken

9 Deciding on action points

▲ At the end of a meeting, there are always tasks to be assigned, deadlines to be agreed and follow-ups to be arranged. Here we listen in as Paul Crane makes sure everyone leaves with something to do …

As in any business, meetings form a major part of daily life. However, they are not simply opportunities to spend an hour in discussion. Every meeting is followed up with minutes containing action points.

P: = Paul Crane; B: = Ben Adams;
C: = Clare Jones; M: = Mary Robbins

P: Ben, when can you have that ready by?
B: Friday should be OK.
P: Good, that's agreed then. Item six, action BA. Now item seven. Clare will you be able to take this one on?
C: Hmm, probably, although I do have another project due for completion by early next week.
P: What support do you need to get that finished?
C: I could do with some administrative support …
P: Agreed! Let me know afterwards how much assistance you need and I'll make sure it's there for you.
C: Thank you.
M: I'll take care of item eight. I'm seeing this client later today and should have a better idea of what they want after that meeting.

P: Great! That just leaves item nine now. I think this one should be down to me. Let's look at follow-up now. Ben, you said you could be ready by Friday. Clare, would you be ready by then?
C: No, that is not enough time. I could commit myself to next Wednesday though.
P: Mary, how about you?
M: At a push I could probably have something together by Friday but would prefer a bit more time.

Aufgaben verteilen

▲ Am Ende einer Sitzung gibt es immer Aufgaben zu übertragen, Abgabetermine zu vereinbaren und Folgemaßnahmen, die eingeleitet werden müssen. Hier hören wir, wie Paul Crane sicherstellt, dass jeder etwas zu tun hat …

In allen Geschäftsbereichen machen Sitzungen einen Teil des Alltags aus. Sie sind jedoch nicht bloß Gelegenheiten, eine Stunde mit Diskutieren zu verbringen. Jeder Sitzung folgt ein Protokoll, das weitere Handlungsschritte enthält.

P: Ben, bis wann haben Sie das fertig?
B: Freitag sollte möglich sein.
P: Gut, abgemacht. Punkt sechs, wird von BA (Ben Adams) erledigt. Also jetzt Punkt sieben. Clare, werden Sie das übernehmen können?
C: Hmm, wahrscheinlich schon, obwohl ich ein anderes Projekt habe, das Anfang nächster Woche fertig sein muss.
P: Welche Unterstützung brauchen Sie, um es zu beenden?
C: Ich könnte Unterstützung bei der Organisation gebrauchen …
P: Abgemacht! Geben Sie mir nachher Bescheid, wieviel Hilfe Sie brauchen und ich werde dafür sorgen, dass Sie sie bekommen.
C: Vielen Dank.
M: Ich erledige Punkt acht. Ich bin heute mit diesem Kunden verabredet und müsste nach dem Treffen eine genauere Vorstellung davon haben, was er will.
P: Fein! Dann ist nur noch Punkt neun offen. Ich denke, den werde ich übernehmen. Schauen wir mal, was veranlasst werden muss. Ben, Sie haben gesagt, Sie könnten bis Freitag fertig sein. Clare, würden Sie das auch schaffen?
C: Nein, das ist zu wenig Zeit. Ich könnte mich jedoch auf nächsten Mittwoch festlegen.
P: Mary, wie ist es mit Ihnen?
M: Im Notfall könnte ich bis Freitag schon etwas zusammenstellen, aber mir wäre etwas mehr Zeit lieber.

P: Can I suggest we reconvene next Wednesday to follow up? Does that give everyone enough time?

(Everyone gives their agreement.)

P: Good, that's settled then. Next Wednesday it is.

P: Dann schlage ich vor, wir treffen uns für die weitere Planung nächsten Mittwoch wieder. Ist das Zeit genug für alle?

(Jeder stimmt zu.)

P: Gut, das ist also abgemacht. Bis nächsten Mittwoch.

Exercises

1 Please repeat the following sentences.

1. When can you have that ready by?
2. What support do you need to get that finished?
3. I could commit myself to next Wednesday though.

2 And now listen to the following sentences and respond using *"Yes, I'll …"*.

1. *Will you be able to take this one on?*
   Yes, I'll be able to take this one on.
2. *Will you need some administrative support?*
   Yes, I'll need some administrative support.
3. *Will you see this client later today?*
   Yes, I'll see this client later today.

3 Please listen to the dialogue again, paying particular attention to tasks to be assigned. Then answer the following questions.

1. *When will Ben have item six ready by?*
   Ben will have item six ready by Friday.
2. *Will Ben be ready with follow-up by Friday?*
   Yes, Ben will be ready with follow-up by Friday.
3. *When will the team reconvene?*
   The team will reconvene next Wednesday.

Vocabulary

task	Aufgabe
to assign	stellen; geben
to follow-up	*etwa:* weiterverfolgen
action point	*etwa:* Handlung, Maßnahme
to take *s.th.* on	*etwas* übernehmen
Agreed!	Abgemacht!
to be due for completion by …	bis … fertig sein müssen
completion	Fertigstellung
to decide (on)	*hier:* bestimmen, entscheiden
support	Unterstützung
afterwards	nachher
at a push	im Notfall
assistance	Hilfe
to take care of *s.th.*	*etwas* erledigen
to commit *oneself* to *s.th.*	sich auf *etwas* festlegen
to reconvene	wieder zusammenkommen
That's settled then.	Das ist also abgemacht.

10 Meeting the mentor

▲ Paul Crane is meeting his mentor, Sharon Walton, to discuss the challenges of management …

Frontpoint set up a mentoring scheme last year. Each month, every manager has a one-hour meeting with his or her mentor to discuss personal development and to reflect on what has been happening.

Sh: = Sharon Walton; P: = Paul Crane

Sh: How are you doing? Good to see you again.
P: Great thanks. I really look forward to these sessions; it's a break from the daily routine!

Sh: I'm glad you find them beneficial. Which points would you like to discuss today?

P: I was talking to you last time about the difficulties I had getting an answer from my boss.
Sh: Yes, as I remember, you thought he was reluctant to discuss your prospects.

P: That's right. I've been giving it some thought, but I haven't found an opportunity to tackle it with him yet.
Sh: And how do you feel about that?
P: I feel it's just dragging on and I really want a decision now. If not, I'm gonna have to look for another job.

Sh: What's the worst thing that can happen if you ask him directly?
P: We could end up with a fractured relationship – and I still have to work with him.

Sh: What steps could you take to avoid that?

P: Not sure. I need your guidance on this.

Sh: Try and think yourself into his situation. What do you feel?
P: I guess I feel a little threatened. My authority is being tested.

Treffen mit dem Mentor

▲ Paul Crane trifft sich mit seinem Mentor, Sharon Walton, um die Herausforderungen des Managements zu besprechen …

Frontpoint hat letztes Jahr ein Mentorenprogramm eingeführt. Jeden Monat hat jeder Manager eine einstündige Sitzung mit seinem oder ihrem Mentor, um die persönliche Entwicklung zu besprechen und um über Geschehenes nachzudenken.

Sh: Wie geht es Ihnen? Schön, Sie wiederzusehen.
P: Gut, danke. Ich freue mich wirklich auf diese Treffen; sie sind eine Abwechslung in der täglichen Routine.
Sh: Es freut mich, dass Sie sie nützlich finden. Welche Punkte möchten Sie heute besprechen?
P: Das letzte Mal habe ich Ihnen von den Schwierigkeiten erzählt, eine Antwort von meinem Vorgesetzten zu bekommen.
Sh: Ja, wie ich mich erinnere, waren Sie der Meinung, dass er nicht bereit war, über Ihre Karriereaussichten zu diskutieren.
P: Das ist richtig. Ich habe weiter nachgedacht, aber ich habe noch keine Gelegenheit gefunden, mit ihm darüber zu reden.
Sh: Und wie fühlen Sie sich dabei?
P: Ich denke, das zieht sich einfach in die Länge, und ich will jetzt wirklich eine Entscheidung. Wenn nicht, werde ich mir eine neue Stelle suchen müssen.
Sh: Was ist das Schlimmste, das passieren könnte, wenn Sie ihn direkt fragen?
P: Es könnte zu einem gestörten Verhältnis führen – und ich werde dennoch weiter mit ihm arbeiten müssen.
Sh: Welche Maßnahmen könnten Sie ergreifen, um das zu vermeiden?
P: Ich bin mir nicht sicher. Dabei brauche ich Ihre Hilfe.
Sh: Versuchen Sie, sich in seine Lage zu versetzen. Was empfinden Sie?
P: Ich denke, ich fühle mich irgendwie bedroht. Meine Autorität wird auf die Probe gestellt.

Sh: Why do you think that is?
P: I've got this young manager here who is pushing hard for his career. Why can't he be more patient?
Sh: Is that your assumption or has he given you a reason to think that?
P: *(Pauses to think.)* I guess it's more my assumption.
Sh: What approach would you feel more comfortable with?
P: Um … I suppose an approach that preserves my authority. I'm not sure what exactly.

Sh: Do you think it might work if you appeal to his experience?
P: As a kind of mentor you mean?
Sh: Yes, just that. People generally feel flattered if we ask for their opinion. If he is feeling insecure, this may be one way to get around that.

P: Hmmm, it's worth trying.
(We leave them to continue their discussion.)

Sh: Woran, glauben Sie, liegt das?
P: Da ist dieser junge Manager, der weiterkommen will. Warum kann er nicht geduldiger sein?
Sh: Ist das Ihre Vermutung oder hat er Ihnen einen Grund für diese Annahme gegeben?
P: *(Macht eine Denkpause.)* Ich denke, das ist eher meine Annahme.
Sh: Bei welcher Vorgehensweise würden Sie sich wohler fühlen?
P: Hm … ich glaube, mit einer Vorgehensweise, die meine Autorität schützt. Ich bin mir nicht sicher, wie das aussehen könnte.
Sh: Meinen Sie, es könnte klappen, wenn Sie an seine Erfahrungen appellieren?
P: Meinen Sie, so wie bei einem Mentor?
Sh: Ja, genau das. Die Leute fühlen sich normalerweise geschmeichelt, wenn wir sie nach ihrer Meinung fragen. Wenn er sich nicht sicher fühlt, kann das ein Weg sein, dies zu umgehen.
P: Hmmm, es lohnt sich, das zu versuchen.
(Wir lassen sie ihre Besprechung weiterführen.)

Exercises

1 Please repeat the following sentences.

1. I feel it's just dragging on and I really want a decision now.
2. What steps could you take to avoid that?
3. My authority is being tested.

2 Please listen to the following expressions and choose the correct definition.

1. I'm glad you find them beneficial.
   Beneficial. Does *this mean:* accurate
   or: useful?
   Beneficial *means:* useful.

2. I guess I feel a little threatened.
   Threatened. *Does this mean:* at a push
   or: at risk?
   Threatened *means:* at risk.

3. If he is feeling insecure, this may be one way to get around that.
   Insecure. *Does this mean:* unsure
   or: complacent?
   Insecure *means:* unsure.

3 Please listen to the following extract from the dialogue.

Sh: How are you doing? Good to see you again.
P: Great thanks. I really look forward to these sessions; it's a break from the daily routine!
Sh: I'm glad you find them beneficial. Which points would you like to discuss today?
P: I was talking to you last time about the difficulties I had getting an answer from my boss.

Sh: Yes, as I remember, you thought he was reluctant to discuss your prospects.
P: That's right. I've been giving it some thought, but I haven't found an opportunity to tackle it with him yet.
Sh: And how do you feel about that?

Now it is your turn. Please take the role of Sharon. You'll hear one answer as a model. Other solutions are, of course, also possible.

1. Great thanks. I really look forward to these sessions; it's a break from the daily routine!
   And now tell Paul you are glad he finds them beneficial and ask him which points he would like to discuss today.
   I'm glad you find them beneficial. Which points would you like to discuss today?

2. I was talking to you last time about the difficulties I had getting an answer from my boss.
   Now say you remember that Paul thought his boss was reluctant to discuss his prospects.
   Yes, as I remember, you thought he was reluctant to discuss your prospects.

3. That's right. I've been giving it some thought, but I haven't found an opportunity to tackle it with him yet.
   Now ask Paul how he feels about that.
   And how do you feel about that?

> Is mentoring a new fad? Mentoring is becoming big business, both in the US and the UK. It creates personal time for a manager to discuss his or her development with someone who can act as a sounding board. It is used to nurture the skills of those starting out in business, individuals entering management roles for the first time, through to senior managers approaching retirement.

Vocabulary

challenge	Herausforderung
to mentor	betreuen; beraten; unterstützen
scheme	System; Programm; Projekt
session	Besprechung; Sitzung
beneficial	nützlich; vorteilhaft
reluctant	unwillig
prospect	Aussicht
to tackle	angehen
It's just dragging on.	Es zieht sich einfach in die Länge.
to take steps	Maßnahmen ergreifen
guidance	*hier:* Hilfe
threatened	bedroht
to push hard	*etwa:* durchsetzen
patient	geduldig
assumption	Annahme; Vermutung
approach	Methode; Vorgehensweise
to preserve	schützen
to appeal to *s.th.*	an *etwas* appellieren
flattered	geschmeichelt
insecure	unsicher
fad	Trend
to act as a sounding board	als Testperson fungieren
to nurture	pflegen
to approach retirement	bald pensioniert werden, bald in Rente gehen

Liste der ID-Nummern für CD 3: Meetings

Inhalt der CD	ID-Nummer:
Vorspann	1
Dialogue 1	2
Exercises	3–5
Dialogue 2	6
Exercises	7–9
Dialogue 3	10
Exercises	11–13
Dialogue 4	14
Exercises	15–17
Dialogue 5	18
Exercises	19–21
Dialogue 6	22
Exercises	23–25
Dialogue 7	26
Exercises	27–29
Dialogue 8	30
Exercises	31–33
Dialogue 9	34
Exercises	35–37
Dialogue 10	38
Exercises	39–41

Verhandlungen / Inhalt

1 Introducing a new product

▲ In this dialogue you will learn how to present a new product and how to deal with questions and queries.

Flair is a medium-sized clothing company based in Watford, just outside London. Flair is the British subsidiary of the blue-chip enterprise, Future Fabrics, Inc. whose headquarters are in New York. Today, the President of the New York firm, Guy Russell, has come to Flair to present a new product to the management team.

MR: = Mark Reynolds (Managing Director *Flair*); GR: = Guy Russell (President *Future Fabrics, Inc.*); SB: = Stephanie Beecham (Mark's personal assistant); JS: = Julia Spencer (Marketing Manager); SE: = Sam Elliot (Sales Manager)

MR: Good morning everyone and thanks for coming together at such short notice. I'd like to personally introduce you to our "big boss" from the States, Guy Russell, as most of you only know him from our video conferences.

GR: Yeah. The wonders of modern technology.

MR: Guy has come over for a few weeks to help us to launch a new product. Far be it from me to give the game away. Over to you, Guy. Er ... Stephanie, would you take the minutes of the meeting, please.

SB: Of course ... er, Mr Russell, please make yourself at home. Would you like something to drink? Tea, coffee or perhaps a cold drink?

GR: Thanks very much, Stephanie. Please call me Guy, by the way. You British are so polite! I'll just have some water, thanks. OK. Let's get down to business. As you all know, I'm the President of *Future Fabrics* and I am sure you'll agree that we have come a long way since we started out five years ago with around 40 million dollars turnover per annum, 800 employees and 20 branches worldwide

Ein neues Produkt vorstellen

▲ In diesem Dialog hören wir, wie man ein neues Produkt vorstellt und wie man mit Fragen und Einwänden umgeht.

Flair ist ein mittelgroßes Bekleidungsunternehmen mit Sitz in Watford, einem Vorort von London. Flair ist die britische Tochterfirma des Blue-Chip-Unternehmens Future Fabrics, dessen Hauptsitz in New York ist. Heute ist der Präsident von Future Fabrics, Guy Russell, im Hause, um dem Managementteam ein neues Produkt vorzustellen.

MR: Guten Morgen und danke, dass Sie so kurzfristig zusammengekommen sind. Ich möchte Ihnen unseren „Big Boss" aus den Staaten, Guy Russell, persönlich vorstellen, da Sie ihn zum größten Teil nur von unseren Videokonferenzen kennen!

GR: Jawohl. Die Wunder der Technik.

MR: Guy ist für ein paar Wochen nach England gekommen, um uns bei der Einführung eines neuen Produktes zu helfen. Ich will jedoch nicht gleich alles verraten. Guy, bitte schön! Stephanie, würden Sie bitte Protokoll führen?

SB: Natürlich. Hm, Mr. Russell, bitte fühlen Sie sich wie zu Hause. Möchten Sie etwas trinken? Tee, Kaffee oder lieber etwas Kaltes?

GR: Vielen Dank, Stephanie. Bitte nennen Sie mich doch Guy. Ihr Engländer seid so höflich! Nur Wasser für mich, bitte. Okay. Kommen wir zur Sache. Wie Sie bereits wissen, bin ich der Präsident von *Future Fabrics,* und ich bin mir sicher, Sie stimmen mir zu, dass wir es seit unserer Geschäftsgründung vor fünf Jahren mit rund 40 Millionen Dollar Umsatz pro Jahr, 800 Mitarbeitern und weltweit 20 Nieder-

and with one subsidiary in Europe, here in Watford.

JS: Are you planning further expansion into Europe?

GR: Sure. That's our number one priority. Things are really happening in Europe, which is why I have come here today to introduce this new product. This is our new baby! A scientific breakthrough in fabric design. Here are some samples. Could you pass them round the table, Julia?

SE: It feels really nice. Is it silk?

GR: Strictly speaking it *is* silk, but not as we all know it.

SE: Oh, I'm not sure we're onto a winner with silk. We have seen a slump in goods made of silk. It's fragile and it creases too easily.

GR: You've jumped the gun a bit there, Sam. As I said, it is a different type of silk. Just crumple that sample in your hand. Actions speak louder than words.

SE: Impressive. Not a crease or even a fingermark.

GR: This fabric is a real innovation. We've called it *Silkease* and its selling point is that it is 100 % natural silk but more resistant. It doesn't crease or mark easily and you don't have to dry clean it.

SE: What sort of price are we looking at?

GR: I don't want to get bogged down in figures at this preliminary stage. Let's save figures and strategies for our sales meeting tomorrow.

lassungen weit gebracht haben. Eine Tochterfirma haben wir in Europa, hier in Watford.

JS: Ist eine weitere Expansion in Europa vorgesehen?

GR: Sicher. Das ist unsere höchste Priorität. Gerade in Europa tut sich zur Zeit sehr viel, und deswegen bin ich heute hier, um Ihnen dieses neue Produkt vorzustellen. Dies ist unser neues Baby! Ein wissenschaftlicher Durchbruch im Stoffdesign. Hier sind einige Stoffmuster. Julia, würden Sie sie bitte weiterreichen?

SE: Fühlt sich ja gut an. Ist das Seide?

GR: Genaugenommen schon, aber nicht Seide, wie wir sie kennen.

SE: Ah, was Seide angeht, bin ich eher skeptisch. Die Nachfrage nach Kleidung aus Seide hat sehr nachgelassen. Der Stoff ist einfach zu fein und knittert zu leicht.

GR: Nicht so voreilig, Sam. Wie ich bereits erwähnt habe, handelt es sich hier um eine neue Form von Seide. Zerknittern Sie die Stoffprobe in der Hand. Das Ergebnis spricht für sich.

SE: Eindrucksvoll. Keine Falte, nicht mal ein Abdruck.

GR: Dieser Stoff ist eine wahre Innovation. Wir haben ihn *Silkease* genannt. Seine Verkaufsstärke ist die Tatsache, dass er 100 % Seide ist, jedoch widerstandsfähiger. Er knittert kaum, ist fleckunempfindlich und muss nicht chemisch gereinigt werden.

SE: Und über welche Preiskategorie sprechen wir?

GR: Ich möchte mich in diesem Anfangsstadium eigentlich noch nicht in Zahlen vertiefen. Heben wir uns Preise und Strategien für unsere Verkaufsversammlung morgen auf.

Exercises

1 Please repeat the following sentences.

1. Thanks for coming together at such short notice.
2. We have come a long way since we started out.
3. Are you planning further expansion into Europe?

2 Listen to the dialogue again, paying particular attention to the qualities of *Future Fabrics*' new product. Then answer the following questions.

1. *What kind of product does Guy Russell present?*
   Guy Russell presents a new kind of silk.
2. *What is different about it?*
   It is different because it doesn't crumple or crease.
3. *What's the name of the new product?*
   The name of the new product is *Silkease*.

3 Please listen to the following expressions and choose the correct definition:

1. Let's get down to business.
   To get down to business. *Does this mean:* to get on with the business of the day
   or: to put off business until later?
   To get down to business *means:* to get on with the business of the day.

2. We have seen a slump in goods made of silk.
   A slump. *Does this mean:* a rise in sales
   or: a fall in sales?
   A slump *means:* a fall in sales.

3. I don't want to get bogged down ...
   To get bogged down. *Does this mean:* to be slowed down by too much information
   or: to run through something?
   To get bogged down *means:* to be slowed down by too much information.

Vocabulary

query	Rückfrage; Zweifel
medium-sized	mittelgroß
MD = Managing Director	Generaldirektor
PA = Personal Assistent	Persönliche(r) Assistent(in)
at short notice	kurzfristig
far be it from me	es liegt mir fern
to give the game away	etwas verraten
Make yourself at home!	Fühlen Sie sich wie zu Hause!
Let's get down to business.	Lassen Sie uns zur Sache kommen.
to have come a long way	weit gekommen sein; es weit gebracht haben
turnover	Umsatz
subsidiary	Tochterfirma
expansion	Verbreitung; Expansion
number one priority	Dringlichkeitsstufe eins; höchste Priorität
breakthrough	Durchbruch
sample	Probestück; Muster
to be onto a winner	Erfolg versprechend sein
slump	Rückgang; Absinken
to crease	(zer)knittern
sensitive	empfindlich
to jump the gun	voreilig sein
to crumple	(zer)knüllen
Actions speak louder than words.	Das Ergebnis spricht für sich selbst.
impressive	beeindruckend
crease	Falte
fingermark	(Finger)Abdruck
selling point	Verkaufsargument
to mark	Flecken machen; schmutzig machen
to get bogged down	steckenbleiben; sich festfahren; sich verzetteln
figures	Zahlen

2 The sales and marketing briefing

▲ In this dialogue you will learn how to participate in a sales and marketing briefing and how to set deadlines and priorities.

Here Guy Russell, the President of Future Fabrics in New York, chairs the sales and marketing briefing for the launch of the new product Silkease into the UK market. Mark Reynolds, the MD of Flair UK, and his sales team, Sam Elliot, Julia Spencer and Tom McHugh, have lots to say.

GR: = Guy Russell; SE: = Sam Elliot; JS: = Julia Spencer; MR: = Mark Reynolds; TH: = Tom McHugh (Press and Promotions);

GR: Good morning everyone. Now that you've all had the chance to familiarize yourselves with *Silkease*, I'm sure that the question on everyone's lips is how to market the product in Britain.

SE: Exactly. We must offer the right marketing mix to our customers. First and foremost I'd like to see some sales statistics.

GR: Sure thing, Sam. I think I can whet your appetite when I tell you that this product has boosted our profit margin by 40 % in just three months. Let me show you a couple of sales charts here ...

JS: Staggering. This could be just the lift we need. The rag trade in the UK is on a real downward spiral.

SE: You can say that again. Lots of big names have gone to the wall in the past year alone.

MR: What price do you charge per yard of fabric in America, Guy?

GR: We sell the fabric to our wholesalers at 20 dollars a yard with a discount of 10 % per 100 yards of material.

TH: Phew! That's pretty steep ... about 15 quid. I think we need to pitch our prices lower here.

Die Verkaufs- und Marketingbesprechung

▲ Hier verfolgen Sie eine Verkaufs- und Marketingbesprechung und erfahren, wie man Termine und Prioritäten festlegt.

Guy Russell, Chef von Future Fabrics in New York, führt den Vorsitz der Verkaufsbesprechung zur Einführung des neuen Produkts Silkease auf dem britischen Markt. Mark Reynolds, Chef der Tochterfirma Flair UK, und sein Verkaufsteam Sam Elliot, Julia Spencer und Tom McHugh haben viel dazu zu sagen.

GR: Guten Morgen, allerseits. Nun, da Sie alle Gelegenheit hatten, sich mit *Silkease* vertraut zu machen, möchten Sie bestimmt wissen, wie wir das Produkt in Großbritannien vermarkten wollen.

SE: Genau. Wir müssen die richtigen Marketingstrategien im Hinblick auf unsere Kunden finden. Zu allererst würde ich gerne einige Verkaufsstatistiken sehen.

GR: Aber natürlich, Sam. Ich glaube, ich kann Ihnen den Mund wässerig machen, wenn ich Ihnen sage, dass dieses Produkt unseren Gewinn in nur drei Monaten um 40 % gesteigert hat. Darf ich Ihnen hier ein paar Verkaufstabellen zeigen ...

JS: Umwerfend. Das könnte genau der Auftrieb sein, den wir brauchen. Die Bekleidungsindustrie in England befindet sich im Moment wirklich in einem starken Abwärtstrend.

SE: Das können Sie laut sagen. Allein im letzten Jahr sind etliche namhafte Unternehmen Bankrott gegangen.

MR: Was verlangen Sie pro Yard Stoff in Amerika, Guy?

GR: Wir verkaufen den Stoff für 20 Dollar per Yard an den Großhandel – mit 10 % Rabatt pro 100 Yard.

TH: Puh! Das ist ganz schon viel ... ungefähr 15 Pfund. Ich denke, dass unsere Preise hier niedriger sein müssen.

GR: More than likely. Back home in the US, price is not as important as quality.

TH: The economic climate in Britain is not as favourable and there is fierce competition among fashion retailers on the High Street. People tend to shop around more.

JS: Yes, but I do think that quality is becoming much more important to our customers according to our latest market research.

MR: What we are looking at then is to market the *image* of the product – its design, quality and the "feelgood factor" of *Silkease.*

JS: Mmm ... I think you've hit the nail on the head there, Mark. The clothing market for young people is pretty much saturated. Our consumer should be someone with lots of disposable income to spend on luxury, high quality goods.

TH: And our selling points fit the bill exactly – a natural and luxurious material which feels good and looks good and is a UK exclusive!

MR: Right then. Let's go back to the drawing board and set some strategies and deadlines. Tom we'll need a snazzy slogan and some up-market sales literature. Julia, promotional flyers a.s.a.p., please!

GR: Das kann gut sein. Bei uns in den Staaten spielt der Preis nicht so eine große Rolle wie die Qualität.

TH: Die Wirtschaftslage in Großbritannien ist nicht so günstig, und es gibt einen scharfen Wettbewerb im Bekleidungseinzelhandel in den Innenstädten. Die Leute wollen heute erst Preise vergleichen.

JS: Gewiss, aber laut unserer neuesten Marktforschung wird die Qualität auch für unsere Kunden immer wichtiger.

MR: Unser Ziel ist es dann also, das *Image* des Produktes zu vermarkten – sein Design, die Qualität und einfach den Wohlfühlfaktor von *Silkease.*

JS: Mmm ... Ich glaube, Sie haben den Nagel auf den Kopf getroffen, Mark. Der Bekleidungsmarkt für junge Leute ist ziemlich gesättigt. Unser Endverbraucher sollte jemand sein, der ein hohes verfügbares Einkommen hat, um Luxusartikel, eben Qualitätsprodukte zu kaufen.

TH: Und unsere Verkaufsargumente passen da genau rein: natürlicher und luxuriöser Stoff, der sich gut anfühlt und der gut aussieht, exklusiv auf dem britischen Markt!

MR: Genau. Also zurück an die Arbeit. Wir müssen Strategien und Termine festlegen. Tom, wir brauchen einen pfiffigen Slogan und anspruchsvolle Verkaufsunterlagen. Julia, Werbeprospekte, so schnell wie möglich, bitte.

Exercises

1 Please repeat the following sentences.

1. I think the question on everyone's lips is how to market the product.
2. We must offer the right marketing mix to our customers.
3. This product has boosted our profit margin by 40 %.

2 Please listen to the following expressions and choose the correct definition.

1. We must offer the right marketing mix to our customers.
   To offer the right marketing mix. *Does this mean:* to try different marketing strategies *or:* to combine marketing strategies effectively?
   To offer the right marketing mix *means:* to combine marketing strategies effectively.
2. This product has boosted our profit margin by 40 %.

To boost our profit margin. *Does this mean:* to increase profits *or:* to make profits decrease?
To boost our profit margin *means:* to increase profits.

3. People tend to shop around more.
To shop around. *Does this mean:* people like to go shopping in lots of different places *or:* people carefully compare product prices when they go shopping?
To shop around *means:* people carefully compare product prices when they go shopping.

3 Please listen to the dialogue again, paying particular attention to the marketing strategies for *Silkease*. Then answer the following questions.

1. *Are the sales figures for Silkease in America very good?*
Yes, *Silkease* has boosted the company's profit margin by 40 %.
2. *Is the rag trade in the UK doing well?*
No, it isn't. Many companies have gone to the wall.
3. *What is the price per yard of the fabric in America?*
The price is 20 dollars per yard for wholesalers.

ℹ There is often some confusion when foreign business people come to the UK regarding the issue of nationality. It is better to refer to "UK businesses" rather than "English businesses". This way you avoid stepping on people's toes by excluding businesses from the rest of the UK. When addressing business people in the UK, it is advisable to use the same diplomacy because people can be sensitive about nationality. Avoid talking about "English" or "England" and use "British" or "Britain" instead.

Vocabulary

to familiarize oneself with *s.th.*	sich mit *einer Sache* vertraut machen
question on everyone's lips	die Frage des Tages
first and foremost	an allererster Stelle
Sure thing! (AE)	Ganz bestimmt!
to whet *s.o.'s* appetite	*j-m* etwas schmackhaft machen; *j-m* den Mund wässrig machen
to boost (business)	(die Wirtschaft) ankurbeln
profit margin	Gewinnspanne
sales chart	Verkaufstabelle
staggering	umwerfend
lift	Aufschwung
rag trade (BE *coll.*)	Bekleidungsindustrie
to be on a downward spiral	einem Abwärtstrend folgen
to go to the wall	Bankrott gehen
to charge (price)	(einen Preis) verlangen
wholesaler	Großhändler
steep (price)	teuer
quid (BE)	Pfund
pitch (prices)	festsetzen
back home (AE)	*hier:* bei uns in den Staaten
economic climate	Wirtschaftslage
fierce	stark; heftig
retailer	Einzelhändler
to shop around	Preise vergleichen
feelgood factor	Wohlfühlfaktor
to hit the nail on the head	den Nagel auf den Kopf treffen
to be saturated (market)	gesättigt sein
consumer	Verbraucher
disposable income	verfügbares Einkommen
to fit the bill	passen
Let's go back to the drawing board!	Zurück an die Arbeit!
snazzy	pfiffig
up-market	anspruchsvoll
promotional flyers	Werbeprospekte
a.s.a.p. (as soon as possible)	so bald wie möglich

3 Launching a new product

▲ Here you learn how to present a new product to the buyers and how to receive feedback and negotiate over the new business.

Mark Reynolds and his sales team, Sam Elliot, Julia Spencer and Tom McHugh, are presenting Silkease to their main UK buyers. Guy Russell is also present.

MR: = Mark Reynolds; TH: = Tom McHugh; B: = Buyer; GR: = Guy Russell

MR: Testing,1, 2, 3 … Okay. Good morning and welcome to *Flair UK* for the national launch of our revolutionary new product, *Silkease.* I'm sure you're all brimming with questions and so let me pass you and this microphone over to my colleague, *Flair's* Product Promotions Manager, Tom McHugh. Tom …

TH: Thank you, Mark, and a warm Scottish welcome to you all. *Silkease.* Wearing silk has never been easier! That's our slogan but really, the quality of the product speaks for itself.

B: Do you think there is still a market for high quality textiles? The bulk of our customers buy the latest fashion fads and don't want to spend much money.

TH: You're right but we are not aiming at customers who buy off-the-peg fashion. *Silkease* is at the cutting edge of textile technology and so lends itself to the top notch of the consumer market. Furthermore, we are the sole suppliers of *Silkease* to the UK and in the rest of Europe.

B: Oh … so you don't manufacture *Silkease* in Britain?

TH: No, we don't manufacture any of our textiles in the UK. As most of you are aware, it is simply not cost-effective. In line with most suppliers nowadays, we import our textiles from the Far East, or, in this case, from the States.

B: Won't that push the price up? What with freight costs and taxes and the high value of the dollar …

Die Einführung eines neuen Produktes

▲ Hier erfahren Sie, wie man Käufern ein neues Produkt präsentiert, wie man Feedback erhält und über das neue Geschäft verhandelt.

Mark Reynolds und sein Verkaufsteam Sam Elliot, Julia Spencer und Tom McHugh präsentieren ihren britischen Hauptkunden das neue Produkt Silkease. Guy Russell ist ebenfalls anwesend.

MR: Test: 1, 2, 3 … Okay. Guten Morgen und willkommen bei *Flair UK* zum Start unseres revolutionären neuen Produktes *Silkease* auf dem britischen Markt. Ich bin mir sicher, dass Sie viele Fragen haben, und deshalb möchte ich Sie und dieses Mikrophon an meinen Kollegen Tom McHugh weitergeben, den Werbeleiter von *Flair.* Tom …

TH: Danke, Mark, und ein herzliches schottisches Willkommen an alle. Seide zu tragen ist easy mit *Silkease*! Das ist unser Slogan, aber eigentlich spricht das Produkt ja für sich.

B: Glauben Sie, dass es tatsächlich noch einen Markt für Qualitätstextilien gibt? Der Großteil unserer Kundschaft möchte den letzten Schrei kaufen und wenig Geld dafür ausgeben.

TH: Sie haben Recht, aber die Kunden, die Mode von der Stange kaufen, sind nicht unsere Zielgruppe. *Silkease* ist ein Spitzenprodukt der Textiltechnologie und gehört deshalb in das oberste Segment auf dem Verbrauchermarkt. Ich möchte noch hinzufügen, dass wir der einzige Lieferant von *Silkease* in Großbritannien und Europa sind.

B: Ah … *Silkease* wird also nicht in Großbritannien hergestellt?

TH: Nein, wir produzieren überhaupt keine Stoffe in Großbritannien. Wie Sie alle wissen, rechnet sich das einfach nicht. Wie die meisten Lieferanten heutzutage importieren wir unsere Stoffe aus Fernost oder – in diesem Fall – aus den Vereinigten Staaten.

B: Wird das nicht den Preis in die Höhe treiben? Was ist mit Frachtkosten und Steuern und dem hohen Dollarkurs …

TH: *Flair UK* is a subsidiary of *Future Fabrics* in the US and so we have special agreements which keep the costs to a minimum. I'm sure that you'll find our prices very competitive.

B: Fair enough, but won't customers in Britain flinch when they see that the product is not made over here?

GR: Let's face facts here. We're in a global marketplace now and Europe is on the verge of becoming a free trading market with the Euro. People look for the right quality and price ratio. That's the bottom line in selling these days!

B: Will you just be supplying us with the raw product?

TH: As we are still at the early stages of launching this product, we are mainly focused on selling the material but we have designed a range of clothing for niche markets.

GR: For example, a selection of exclusive tailor-made suits for discerning business people, eye-catching scarves for that last minute gift …

MR: Talking of last minute, we'll take a short tea break now. Thanks for your attention.

TH: *Flair UK* ist eine Tochtergesellschaft von *Future Fabrics, Inc.* in den USA, und daher haben wir spezielle Vereinbarungen, um die Kosten gering zu halten. Ich bin sicher, Sie werden unsere Preise konkurrenzfähig finden.

B: Schon gut, aber werden unsere britischen Kunden nicht zurückschrecken, wenn Sie feststellen, dass das Produkt nicht hier hergestellt wird?

GR: Wir müssen den Tatsachen ins Auge sehen. Wir haben heute einen globalen Markt, und mit dem Euro ist Europa im Begriff, ein freier Handelsmarkt zu werden. Der Verbraucher sucht das richtige Preis-Leistungs-Verhältnis. Das ist heute die Grundlage für den erfolgreichen Verkauf!

B: Haben Sie vor, uns nur das Rohprodukt zu liefern?

TH: Wir stecken noch im Anfangsstadium der Produkteinführung, und deshalb verkaufen wir erstmal schwerpunktmäßig das Material, aber wir haben schon eine Kollektion für Nischenmärkte entworfen.

GR: Zum Beispiel eine Auswahl maßgefertigter Anzüge für modebewusste Geschäftsleute und wunderschöne Tücher für das Geschenk in letzter Minute …

MR: Da wir gerade von „letzter Minute" sprechen – machen wir jetzt eine kurze Teepause. Danke für Ihre Aufmerksamkeit.

Exercises

1 Please repeat the following sentences.

1. The quality of the product speaks for itself.
2. *Silkease* is at the cutting edge of textile technology.
3. I'm sure that you'll find our prices very competitive.

2 Please listen to the dialogue again, paying particular attention to the facts of the *Silkease* launch. Then answer the following questions.

1. *What market niche is Flair UK aiming for?*
   Flair UK is aiming for the top notch of the consumer market.
2. *Why doesn't Flair manufacture any textiles in the UK?*
   It is not cost effective to manufacture textiles in the UK.
3. *Will British customers accept the fact that the products are not made in Britain?*
   This is a global marketplace now and people look for the right quality and price ratio.

3 Please listen to the following extract from the dialogue and pay close attention to what Tom Mc Hugh says.

B: Do you think there is still a market for high quality textiles? The bulk of our customers

buy the latest fashion fads and don't want to spend much money.

TH: You're right, but we are not aiming at customers who buy off-the-peg fashion. *Silkease* is at the cutting edge of textile technology and so lends itself to the top notch of the consumer market. Furthermore, we are the sole suppliers of *Silkease* to the UK and in the rest of Europe.

B: Oh … so you don't manufacture *Silkease* in Britain?

TH: No, we don't manufacture any of our textiles in the UK. As most of you are aware, it is simply not cost effective. In line with most suppliers nowadays, we import our textiles from the Far East, or, in this case, from the States.

B: Won't that push the price up? What with freight costs and taxes and the high value of the dollar.

TH: *Flair UK* is a subsidiary of *Future Fabrics* in the US and so we have special agreements which keep the costs to a minimum. I'm sure that you'll find our prices very competitive.

Now it's your turn. Please take the role of Tom McHugh. You'll hear one answer as a model. Other solutions are, of course, also possible.

1. The bulk of our customers buy the latest fashion fads and don't want to spend much money.
   And now it's your turn. Agree with the buyer but tell her that mass fashion is not the market you are aiming for.
   You are right, but we're not aiming at customers who buy off-the-peg fashion.
2. Oh … so you don't manufacture *Silkease* in Britain?
   And now it's your turn again. Tell the buyer that you don't manufacture textiles in the UK because it is too expensive.
   No, we don't manufacture any of our textiles in the UK because it is not cost-effective.
3. Won't that push the price up? What with freight costs and taxes.
   Reassure your buyer that the costs will be very low and that you will be able to offer a good price.
   We have special agreements which keep costs to a minimum. I'm sure you'll find our prices very competitive.

Vocabulary

launch	Markteinführung
to be brimming with questions	viele Fragen haben
bulk (of our customers)	Großteil (unserer Kunden)
fads	Modetrends
to aim at *s.o.*	(ab)zielen auf *j-n*
off-the-peg (BE)	(Kleidung) – von der Stange
off-the-rack (AE)	(Kleidung) – von der Stange
to be at the cutting edge of	an der Spitze sein
to lend itself to *s.th.*	sich für *etwas* eignen
top notch	Spitze
supplier	Lieferant
in line with *s.th.*	im Einklang mit *etwas*
to push the price up	den Preis in die Höhe treiben
to keep costs to a minimum	Kosten gering halten
competitive	konkurrenzfähig
fair enough	schon gut; na schön
to flinch	zurückzucken
to face facts	Tatsache ist …; den Tatsachen ins Auge sehen
to be on the verge of *s.th.*	im Begriff sein, zu …
ratio	Verhältnis; Relation
bottom line	Grundlinie
raw product	Rohprodukt
to be focused on *s.th.*	sich auf *etwas* konzentrieren
niche market	Marktlücke; Nischenmarkt
tailor-made	maßgeschneidert
discerning	anspruchsvoll
eye-catching	ins Auge springend; auffallend

4 Organising a conference

▲ The following dialogue will show you how to book conference facilities at a trade fair and how to make sure that the necessary technical equipment is organised.

It's the morning after the product launch. Mark Reynolds and Guy Russell are discussing invitations and mailshots. Stephanie Beecham books a stand for Flair UK at the National Exhibition Centre (NEC) in Birmingham.

SB: = Stephanie Beecham; MR: = Mark Reynolds; GR: = Guy Russell; S: = Susan (Conference Co-ordinator, NEC)

SB: Morning, Mark. You're in early! How did the product launch go yesterday?

MR: Well, you know how cagey buyers can be, but I feel we've made a good first impression with *Silkease.*

SB: Fantastic! So it's the green light for the Birmingham Fabric and Fashion Fair then?

MR: You've got it in one. We need to act quickly to keep the ball rolling and to keep ahead of the competition.

GR: Hi, guys! Sorry to butt in, but here are our invitations for our key accounts in the UK plus a list of contacts in Europe. Can I leave it with you, Stephanie?

SB: Of course, Guy.

MR: Oh, by the way, Stephanie, here's the itinerary for the conference. Could you go ahead and make the necessary arrangements, please?

SB: Right away.

S: Good morning, *NEC Birmingham*, Susan speaking. How can I help you?

SB: Good morning, Susan. Stephanie Beecham, *Flair UK*, here. I'd like to book a stand at the Fabric and Fashion Fair next month.

S: Of course. Can you give me your specifications, please?

SB: Yes, I'd like a medium-sized stand in a central position near the main entrance of the hall.

Eine Konferenz organisieren

▲ Hier erfahren wir, wie man Konferenzräume auf einer Handelsmesse bucht und wie man sicherstellt, dass die erforderliche technische Ausstattung bereitsteht .

Am Morgen nach der Produkteinführung besprechen Mark Reynolds und Guy Russell die Einladungen und Mailings. Stephanie Beecham bucht einen Messestand für Flair UK auf der NEC, Birmingham.

SB: Morgen, Mark. Sie sind ja früh dran. Wie ist es gestern gelaufen?

MR: Nun, Sie wissen, wie zurückhaltend Käufer sein können, aber ich denke schon, dass wir mit *Silkease* einen guten ersten Eindruck gemacht haben.

SB: Fantastisch! Das heißt also grünes Licht für die Stoff- und Modemesse in Birmingham?

MR: Ganz genau. Wir müssen schnell handeln, um das Ganze am Laufen zu halten und im Wettbewerb in Führung zu bleiben.

GR: Hallo, Leute! Entschuldigung, wenn ich mich einmische, aber hier sind die Einladungen für unsere Hauptkunden in Großbritannien und eine Liste unserer Kontakte in Europa. Können Sie das erledigen, Stephanie?

SB: Natürlich, Guy.

MR: Stephanie, hier ist übrigens der Ablaufplan für die Konferenz. Könnten Sie bitte gleich die nötigen Schritte in Angriff nehmen?

SB: Sofort, Mark.

S: Guten Morgen, *NEC Birmingham*, Susan am Apparat. Wie kann ich Ihnen helfen?

SB: Guten Morgen, Susan. Stephanie Beecham hier, *Flair UK*. Ich möchte einen Stand für die Stoff- und Modemesse im nächsten Monat buchen.

S: Gerne. Würden Sie mir bitte Ihre genauen Wünsche durchgeben?

SB: Ja. Ich möchte einen mittelgroßen Stand in zentraler Lage in der Nähe vom Haupteingang.

S: There is a surcharge of £ 200 for stands in prime positions in the main trading aisle.
SB: That's a bit pricey. How about if we order your special business package?

S: It's an excellent offer and means that we will provide you with all the multimedia facilities you need, plus technical support throughout the conference.

SB: Hm ...would we still have to pay the £ 200 surcharge if we take the package?

S: No, that is included as well as a private negotiations room which is preferable as many people would rather do business deals behind closed doors.

SB: That's settled then. We'll take the business package for the full three days of the conference. Can I reserve six single rooms at the *Park Hotel* as well?
S: Is that for the three nights inclusive?
SB: No, sorry, just two nights. We're checking out on Saturday.
S: Right then. Your conference and hotel bookings are made. I'll send you confirmation of your booking today along with the conference programme and complimentary invitations to our buffet on Friday night. And your address is?

S: Es gibt einen Zuschlag von £ 200 für Messestände im Hauptgang.
SB: Das ist ein bisschen viel. Wie sieht es aus, wenn wir Ihr spezielles Businessarrangement nehmen?
S: Das ist wirklich ein hervorragendes Angebot und bedeutet, dass wir Ihnen alle Multimediaeinrichtungen zur Verfügung stellen, die Sie benötigen, sowie technischen Support während der ganzen Messe.
SB: Hm ... wenn wir dieses Angebot annehmen, müssen wir dann immer noch den Zuschlag zahlen?
S: Nein. Der ist in dem Arrangement inbegriffen, ebenso wie ein privater Besprechungsraum. Der ist zu empfehlen, weil viele Leute ihre Geschäfte lieber unter vier Augen abschließen.
SB: Abgemacht. Wir nehmen das Arrangement für die drei Tage der Konferenz. Kann ich bei Ihnen auch sechs Einzelzimmer im *Park Hotel* reservieren?
S: Für drei Nächte?
SB: Nein, nur für zwei Nächte. Wir reisen am Samstag ab.
S: In Ordnung. Die Buchungen für die Konferenz und das Hotel werden erledigt. Ich schicke Ihnen die Buchungsbestätigung zusammen mit dem Konferenzprogramm und der Einladung zu unserem Buffet am Freitag Abend. Ihre genaue Anschrift ist ...

Exercises

1 Please repeat the following sentences.

1. Here are our invitations for our key accounts in the UK.
2. How did the product launch go yesterday?
3. I'd like a medium-sized stand in a central position.

2 Please listen to the following extract from the dialogue and pay close attention to what Stephanie Beecham says.

S: Can you give me your specifications, please?
SB: Yes, I'd like a medium-sized stand in a central position near the main entrance of the hall.
S: There is a surcharge of £200 for stands in prime positions in the main trading aisle.
SB: That's a bit pricey. How about if we order your special business package?
S: It's an excellent offer and means that we will provide you with all the multimedia facilities you need, plus technical support throughout the conference without additional charges.
SB: That's settled then.

Now it's your turn. Please take the role of Stephanie Beecham. You'll hear one answer as a model. Other solutions are, of course, also possible.

1. Can you give me your specifications?
   And now it's your turn. Tell Susan what kind of stand you want and where you'd like it to be.
   I'd like a medium-sized stand in a central position near the main entrance.
2. The surcharge for a stand in a prime position is £200.
   It's your turn again now. Tell Susan that you think it's too expensive. Ask about the special business package.
   That's a bit pricey. How about if we order your special business package?
3. It's an excellent offer and means that we will provide you with all the multimedia facilities you need, plus technical support throughout the conference without additional charges.
   Now it's your turn. Tell Susan that this offer is ok with you.
   That's settled then.

3 Please listen to the dialogue again and pay particular attention to organising and booking a conference. Then answer the following questions.

1. *Where will the Fabric and Fashion Fair be held?*
   The Fabric and Fashion Fair will be held at the *NEC* in Birmingham.
2. *What is the surcharge for a stand in a prime position?*
   There is a surcharge of £200 for a stand in a prime position.
3. *What does the business package include?*
   The business package includes multimedia facilities and technical support throughout the conference without additional charges.

ℹ You have already observed that in the UK and in the USA business colleagues use first name terms to address one another. First names are also often used over the phone when making bookings or asking for general information. This is intended to make customer service more personal and informal. However, remember that if you are representing your company with the intention of doing business rather than just giving information, you should always give your full name, your company name and title or position.

Vocabulary

facilities	Einrichtungen
trade fair	Handelsmesse
mailshot	Mailing
to be cagey	vorsichtig sein; „zugeknöpft" sein
to give the green light	grünes Licht geben
You've got it in one!	Sie haben es auf den Punkt gebracht!
to keep the ball rolling	die Sache in Gang halten
to keep ahead of the competition	der Konkurrenz voraus sein/bleiben
to butt in *s.th.*	sich in *etwas* einmischen
key account	*hier:* Hauptkunde
Can I leave it with you?	Kann ich Ihnen das überlassen?
itinerary	Ablaufplan
to make arrangements	*etwas* organisieren
specifications; spec(s)	(genaue) Angaben
medium-sized	mittelgroß
surcharge	Zuschlag; Aufpreis
prime position	wichtigster Standort
pricey *(coll.)*	teuer
technical support	technische Unterstützung
deal	Geschäft
to be preferable	vorzuziehen/besser sein
behind closed doors	unter vier Augen; hinter geschlossenen Türen; privat
confirmation	Bestätigung
complimentary	gratis; frei
That's settled then!	Abgemacht!

5 Making a business proposal

▲ Here Sam Elliot shows us how to make contact with a potential customer and how to define what the business package includes.

It's the first day of the Fabric and Fashion Fair in Birmingham and there is a lot of interest around the Flair UK stand. Tom McHugh and Julia Spencer are handing out leaflets. Meanwhile, Sam Elliot goes over to talk to a potential customer at the Silkease display.

JS: = Julia Spencer; SE: = Sam Elliot; MB: = Martin Berger; GR: = Guy Russell

JS: Would you like a leaflet, madam, … thanks.

SE: Good afternoon. Can I help you at all?

MB: Yes, I'm interested in this new product … *Silkease*, isn't it? Could you give me a rundown of the terms and conditions of your special trade offer?

SE: Certainly, er … Mr Berger. Pleased to meet you. We have several different promotions running during the fair. Perhaps you could tell me more about what line of business you're in and I'll see what I can do for you.

MB: Of course. I run a small sports and adventure boutique called *Pronatura Travel.*

SE: Actually, *Flair UK* doesn't do sportswear yet, although there is a range of golfwear being tried out in the States.

MB: I'm not interested in branded sports goods. My line of business is in casual but stylish clothes for the traveller and some outdoor wear. I'd be interested in purchasing the material … at the right price.

SE: Well, you won't find anything like *Silkease* elsewhere at the fair or on the market.

MB: Is it really silk though or does it have some synthetic components?

SE: Nothing manmade about *Silkease.* It's 100% natural silk, but it has the unique ad-

Ein Angebot machen

▲ Hier hören wir Sam Elliot, wie er den ersten Kontakt mit einem potenziellen Kunden herstellt und das Angebot erläutert.

Es ist der erste Tag der Stoff- und Modemesse, und der Flair-Stand ist von Interessenten umlagert. Tom McHugh und Julia Spencer verteilen Prospekte. Währenddessen geht Sam Elliot zu einem potenziellen Kunden, der beim Silkease-Display steht, um ein Gespräch anzufangen.

JS: Guten Tag, die Dame. Eine kleine Information über *Flair UK* … bitte schön.

SE: Guten Tag. Kann ich Ihnen behilflich sein?

MB: Ja. Ich interessiere mich für Ihr neues Produkt … *Silkease*, nicht wahr? Könnten Sie mir bitte eine kurze Zusammenfassung Ihrer Messeangebote geben?

SE: Sicherlich, Hm … Herr Berger. Freut mich. Wir haben verschiedene Angebote während der Messe. Vielleicht können Sie mir ein bisschen mehr über Ihren Geschäftszweig sagen, und dann sehen wir, was ich für Sie tun kann.

MB: Gerne. Ich habe eine kleine Boutique für Sport- und Outdoorbekleidung – *Pronatura Travel.*

SE: Nun, eigentlich produzieren wir noch keine Sportkleidung bei *Flair UK*, obwohl ein Sortiment von Golfkleidung zur Zeit in den Staaten getestet wird.

MB: Ich interessiere mich auch nicht für Sportartikel. Ich vertreibe sportliche, aber modische Bekleidung für Reisende und etwas Outdoorbekleidung. Ich könnte mir vorstellen, dieses Material zu kaufen … zum richtigen Preis.

SE: Nun, Sie werden nichts finden, was *Silkease* vergleichbar ist, nicht hier auf der Messe und auch sonst nirgendwo auf dem Markt.

MB: Ist es wirklich reine Seide, oder enthält das Material synthetische Bestandteile?

SE: Nichts Künstliches in *Silkease.* Es ist 100 % reine Seide, nur mit dem großen Vorteil,

vantage that it doesn't crease or mark. All down to our patented manufacturing process in America, but that's a trade secret.

MB: I see. And how has the fabric sold over there? *(Guy steps over.)*

GR: Great shakes – an absolute bestseller for us! Just feel that quality.

MB: It certainly feels very smooth and lightweight. What sort of price am I looking at per metre?

SE: We're charging a special trader's price of £ 15 per metre for up to ten metres of fabric. Orders over and above this at £ 12 a metre with a price freeze on all orders placed before the end of the month. Minimum down payment, 20 % of the order price.

MB: Hmm … £ 15 a metre. Rather more than I wanted to pay. I'll sleep on it and get back to you. Thanks for your time.

SE: You're welcome. Hope to see you again, soon.

dass es nicht knittert oder schmutzempfindlich ist. Das liegt an unserem patentierten Herstellungsverfahren in Amerika, aber das ist ein Geschäftsgeheimnis.

MB: Interessant. Und wie verkauft sich der Stoff drüben? *(Guy schließt sich dem Gespräch an.)*

GR: Sagenhaft – ein absoluter Bestseller für uns! Fühlen Sie nur diese Qualität.

MB: Es fühlt sich wirklich sehr glatt und leicht an. Und mit welchem Preis per Meter muss ich rechnen?

SE: Wir haben einen Sonderpreis für Messebesucher von £ 15 pro Meter, wenn Sie bis zehn Meter des Stoffes kaufen. Bestellungen darüber hinaus kosten nur £ 12 pro Meter. Dieser Preis gilt für alle Bestellungen bis Ende des Monats. Mindestanzahlung sind 20 % des Auftragsvolumens.

MB: Hm … £ 15 pro Meter. Deutlich mehr als ich ausgeben wollte. Ich muss das überschlafen und komme dann wieder. Danke, dass Sie sich die Zeit genommen haben.

SE: Nichts zu danken. Dann hoffentlich bis bald.

Exercises

1 Please repeat the following sentences.

1. Could you give me a rundown of the terms and conditions of your special trade offer?
2. Perhaps you could tell me more about what line of business you're in.
3. I'd be interested in purchasing the material at the right price.

2 Please listen to the following expressions and choose the correct definition:

1. I'm not interested in branded sports goods as such.
   Branded goods. *Does this mean:* certain types of goods and products *or:* the name given to goods and products which makes them recognizable?
   Branded goods *means:* the name given to goods and products which makes them recognizable.
2. There's a price freeze on all orders placed before the end of the month.
   Price freeze. *Does this mean:* the price of the goods is fixed *or:* the price of the goods is going to change?
   Price freeze *means:* the price of the goods is fixed.
3. Minimum down payment, 20 % of the order price.
   Down payment. *Does this mean:* to pay a deposit *or:* to get a price reduction?
   Down payment *means:* to pay a deposit.

3 Please listen to the following sentences and answer the questions using *"Yes, I'm interested in …"* or *"No, I'm not interested in …"*.

1. Are you interested in this new product, *Silkease*?

Yes, I'm interested in this new product, *Silkease.*

2. Are you interested in branded sportswear?
   No, I'm not interested in branded sportswear.
3. Are you interested in purchasing the material?
   Yes, I'm interested in purchasing the material.

ℹ The UK and the USA are often clubbed together in the global world of business because both countries have English as a first language. However the business styles of the UK and USA are quite different. In Britain people tend to be more factual and reserved when doing business and will give exactly the information that has been asked for. They will rarely push a client into buying a product. Americans are generally a lot less reserved and interact in a more open and informal way. It is important to be aware of these cultural differences when entering into negotiations.

Vocabulary

leaflet	Prospekt; Hand-/Reklamezettel
rundown	Bericht; kurze Zusammenfassung
terms and conditions	Geschäftsbedingungen
trade offer	Handelsangebot
promotions	Werbeangebote
line of business	Geschäftszweig; Branche
fair	Messe
to run (a business)	ein Geschäft führen
branded goods	Markenartikel
casual	salopp; sportlich (Kleidung)
to purchase	kaufen
stylish	modisch
man-made fibres	Kunst-/Chemiefasern
to place an order	einen Auftrag erteilen; eine Bestellung aufgeben
Great shakes! (AE)	Großartig!; Ausgezeichnet!
smooth	glatt; weich
to charge	(Preis) verlangen
trader	Händler
lightweight	leicht
over and above	darüber hinaus
price freeze	Preisgarantie
down payment (deposit)	Anzahlung
I'll sleep on it.	Ich werde es überschlafen.

6 Primary negotiations and setting up a business deal

▲ Here you learn how to enter into primary negotiations and how to set up a business deal.

It's the second day of the trade fair. There has been a lot of interest at the Flair UK stand and quite a few orders. The sales team know that today is vital for clinching business deals. Sam Elliot is excited when he sees Mr Berger again.

SE: = Sam Elliot; MB: = Martin Berger

SE: Good morning, Mr Berger. Nice to see you again. Goodness, it's like Piccadilly Circus out here today. Would you like to step into my office?

MB: Yes, please. I've come to talk to you about *Silkease* … in private, if possible.

SE: Naturally. … Right. How can I help you?

MB: I've been thinking about *Silkease* and I would like to place an order but I'm on a bit of a tight budget. You see, I've only just started out in this business … Is the price you quoted ex-warehouse?

SE: Yes, it is. We have set up a special contract with *Transexpress Carriers.* I'm sure I can offer you a highly competitive rate.

MB: As a first time buyer with your company, I'd like to start with an order of 200 metres and then we can take things from there. Could you give me a price estimate, please?

SE: Of course. …That's 200 times £ 12 which is £ 2,400 plus 17 % tax gives us £ 2,808 for the material. Then the haulier's flat rate for transport and insurance is £ 140 so the grand total is £ 2,948 which I'll round down to £ 2,900 all in.

MB: I'll go with that. Do you accept credit cards?

SE: As a norm we do, but not at fairs because of our special rates. However, we do accept che-

Vorverhandlungen führen und einen Geschäftsabschluss tätigen

▲ Hier erfahren Sie, wie man grundlegende Verkaufsverhandlungen führt und wie man einen Geschäftsabschluss tätigt.

Es ist der zweite Messetag. Viele Interessenten haben den Flair-Stand besucht und es hat ziemlich viele Bestellungen gegeben. Dem Verkaufsteam ist klar, dass dieser Tag entscheidend für den Abschluss von Geschäftsverhandlungen ist. Sam Elliot ist freudig erregt, als er Herrn Berger wiedersieht.

SE: Guten Morgen, Herr Berger. Es freut mich, Sie wiederzusehen. Mein Gott, heute geht es hier zu wie auf dem Piccadilly Circus. Darf ich Sie in mein Büro bitten?

MB: Ja, gerne. Ich möchte mich mit Ihnen über *Silkease* unterhalten … wenn möglich unter vier Augen.

SE: Natürlich. … So, wie kann ich Ihnen helfen?

MB: Ich habe über *Silkease* nachgedacht und möchte gerne eine Bestellung aufgeben, aber ich muss ziemlich scharf kalkulieren. Wissen Sie, ich bin neu in dieser Branche. Gilt der Preis, den Sie mir genannt haben, ab Werk?

SE: Ja, so ist es. Wir haben einen Sondervertrag mit der Spedition *Transexpress Carriers* abgeschlossen. Deshalb bin ich mir sicher, dass ich Ihnen einen guten Preis machen kann.

MB: Da ich zum ersten Mal bei Ihnen bestelle, möchte ich mit 200 Metern anfangen – und dann sehen wir weiter. Können Sie mir bitte einen Kostenvoranschlag machen?

SE: Sicher … Also 200 mal £ 12 ergibt £ 2400 plus 17 % Steuer, da kommen wir auf £ 2808 für den Stoff. Dazu die pauschalen Transport- und Versicherungskosten, macht £ 140. Das ergibt einen Gesamtbetrag von £ 2948, den ich auf £ 2900 abrunde, alles inklusive.

MB: Abgemacht! Nehmen Sie Kreditkarten?

SE: Normalerweise schon, aber nicht auf Messen, da wir hier Sonderpreise anbieten.

ques, cash ... naturally, or alternatively we can offer a confirmed irrevocable letter of credit.

MB: I'm sorry. Could you explain that as I'm not familiar with the term?

SE: Yes, er … you need to hold a UK bank account and basically your bank only releases the money to us when it receives confirmation that we have exported the goods to you.

MB: I see. I like that idea and it also means that I won't have to tie down my cash flow straight away. Could you recommend a good bank?

SE: Certainly. If you make your way to that stand over there on the right. Can you see it? It's called *Regent Bank.*

MB: Yes, I can see the blue logo. If you'll excuse me for a moment …

SE: No problem. I'll see you later, Mr Berger.

Wir nehmen jedoch Schecks, Bargeld … natürlich, oder wir können Ihnen ein bestätigtes unwiderrufliches Akkreditiv anbieten.

MB: Entschuldigung. Könnten Sie mir „bestätigtes unwiderrufliches Akkreditiv" erklären? Das ist mir kein Begriff.

SE: Klar. Sie brauchen ein britisches Girokonto. Ihre Bank überweist uns das Geld erst, wenn sie eine Bestätigung bekommt, dass die Ware an Sie abgeschickt worden ist.

MB: Hm – mir gefällt diese Idee, und es bedeutet, dass ich meine flüssigen Mittel nicht gleich festlegen muss. Können Sie mir eine gute Bank empfehlen?

SE: Gewiss. Gehen Sie rüber zu dem Stand dort rechts, sehen Sie ihn? Das ist die *Regent Bank.*

MB: Ja, ich kann das blaue Logo sehen. Bitte entschuldigen Sie mich einen Moment.

SE: Natürlich. Bis nachher dann, Herr Berger.

Exercises

1 Please repeat the following sentences.

1. Would you like to step into my office?
2. I'm sure I can offer you a highly competitive rate.
3. Could you give me a price estimate, please?

2 Please listen to the following sentences and choose the correct answer a), b) or c).

1.
a) *Mr Berger wants more information about Silkease.*
b) *Mr Berger wants to place an order.*
c) *Mr Berger hasn't got enough money to buy Silkease.*
The correct answer is **b)**: Mr Berger wants to place an order.

2.
a) *"Transexpress Carriers" is the German distributor of Flair UK.*
b) *Flair UK is a subsidiary of Transexpress Carriers.*
c) *Flair UK has a special contract with Transexpress Carriers.*
The correct answer is **c)**: Flair UK has a special contract with *Transexpress Carriers.*

3.
a) *The final price which Sam Elliot quotes to Mr Berger is £2,900.*
b) *The final price which Sam Elliot quotes to Mr Berger is £3,900.*
c) *The final price which Sam Elliot quotes to Mr Berger is £2,400.*
The correct answer is **a)**: The final price which Sam quotes to Mr Berger is £2,900.

3 Please listen to the following sentences and answer the questions using *"I'm afraid ..."* or *"I'm sure ..."*.

1. *Can you offer me a competitive rate?*
   I'm sure I can offer you a competitive rate.
2. *Do you accept credit cards?*
   I'm afraid we don't accept credit cards.
3. *Can you give me a price estimate?*
   I'm sure I can give you a price estimate.

Even though credit cards were not accepted at this trade fair, it is true to say that in the UK and in the USA credit cards are the most common form of payment in both private and business spheres. Most people will indeed have several credit cards.

Vocabulary

to set up a deal	ein Geschäft abschließen
primary negotiations	Vorverhandlungen
to clinch a deal	ein Geschäft sichern
in private	unter vier Augen
to be on a tight budget	knapp bei Kasse sein; scharf kalkulieren müssen
to start out in business	neu im Geschäft sein
to quote a price	einen Preis nennen
ex-warehouse	ab Werk
solely	ausschließlich
competitive rate	konkurrenzfähiger Preis
first time buyer	Erstkäufer
We can take things from there.	Dann sehen wir weiter.
price estimate	Kostenvoranschlag
tax	Steuer
haulier	Transportunternehmer; Spediteur
flat rate	Pauschalpreis
grand total	Gesamtsumme
to round down	abrunden
all in all	alles in allem
I'll go with that!	Abgemacht!
confirmed irrevocable letter of credit	bestätigtes unwiderrufliches Akkreditiv
to be familiar with *s.th.*	vertraut sein mit *etwas*; einen Begriff haben von *etwas*
to hold a current account	ein Girokonto haben
to release money	Geld freigeben
confirmation	Bestätigung
to tie down	fest anlegen
cash flow	Cashflow
to recommend	empfehlen

7 Asking for a bank loan

▲ Here you learn how to negotiate a business loan for your company and how to talk about interest rates and loan specifications.

Mr Berger is at the Regent Bank stand and he is talking to the Accounts Manager, Mrs Linda Fernandes.

MB: =Martin Berger; LF: = Linda Fernandes

LF: Good afternoon, I'm Linda Fernandes. How may I help you?
MB: Martin Berger. I'd like to open a bank account, please.
LF: Excuse me for asking but are you a UK resident?

Ein Darlehen beantragen

▲ Hier erfahren Sie, wie man ein Geschäftsdarlehen bei der Bank aushandelt und wie man über Zinsraten und Einzelheiten des Darlehens spricht.

Herr Berger ist am Stand der Regent Bank und unterhält sich mit der Kundenbetreuerin Mrs. Linda Fernandes.

LF: Guten Tag, ich bin Linda Fernandes. Wie kann ich Ihnen helfen?
MB: Martin Berger. Ich möchte ein Konto eröffnen.
LF: Entschuldigen Sie, wenn ich frage, aber haben Sie Ihren Wohnsitz in England?

MB: No, I live in Germany. Why, does that make a difference?
LF: Yes, it does. You have to be resident in the UK for three months before I can open an account for you.
MB: Well, that throws a spanner in the works because I'm finalizing a business deal and was told that I need to have an account here to obtain an irrevocable letter of credit.

LF: Not necessarily. Anyway there are lots of reasonable options open to international traders nowadays.
MB: But isn't there always a fee involved? Last time I sent a cheque to a company outside Germany, I had to pay a transfer fee of 25 euros. Which is ridiculous!
LF: Yes, I see your point but a cheque really is the slowest and most costly way to transfer money. I recommend International Money Orders.

MB: OK, but I also need to take out a loan.

LF: Can you tell me the name of your German bank?
MB: Yes, it's *Eurobank* in Freiburg.
LF: Then we can proceed. You see *Eurobank* is one of our European affiliates. How much would you like to borrow?

MB: A thousand pounds over a year. I want to keep interest rates to a minimum.
LF: Then a short term loan like this is your best option. I can offer you 11 % on an instant loan depending on your credit rating. If you'd just fill out the forms.

MB: Nein, ich lebe in Deutschland. Warum? Macht das einen Unterschied?
LF: Ja, leider. Sie müssen drei Monate in England wohnen, bevor ich für Sie ein Konto eröffnen kann.
MB: Nun, das wirft mir Knüppel zwischen die Beine, da ich gerade in der Abschlussphase einer Geschäftsverhandlung stecke. Mir wurde gesagt, dass ich hier ein Konto haben muss, um ein unwiderrufliches Akkreditiv zu bekommen.
LF: Nicht unbedingt. Es gibt heutzutage eine Menge vernünftiger Alternativen für den internationalen Handel.
MB: Aber ist damit nicht immer eine Gebühr verbunden? Das letzte Mal, als ich einen Scheck ins Ausland geschickt habe, musste ich 25 Euro bezahlen. Das ist lächerlich!
LF: Ja, ich bin ganz Ihrer Meinung, aber ein Scheck ist auch der langsamste und teuerste Weg Geld zu transferieren. Ich würde eine internationale Zahlungsanweisung empfehlen.
MB: Okay, aber außerdem brauche ich ein Darlehen.
LF: Wie heißt Ihre Bank in Deutschland?

MB: *Eurobank*, Freiburg.
LF: Dann können wir weitermachen. Wissen Sie, *Eurobank* ist eine unserer europäischen Tochtergesellschaften. Wie hoch soll der Kredit denn sein?
MB: Eintausend Pfund – für ein Jahr. Ich möchte den Zinssatz möglichst niedrig halten.
LF: Dann ist ein kurzfristiger Kredit genau das Richtige. Ich kann Ihnen ein Sofortdarlehen zu 11 % anbieten, abhängig von Ihrer Kreditwürdigkeit. Wenn Sie bitte diese Formulare ausfüllen würden.

Exercises

1 Please repeat the following sentences.

1. I'd like to take out a loan.
2. But isn't there always a fee involved?
3. I want to keep interest rates to a minimum.

2 Please listen to the following expressions and choose the correct definitions.

1. Excuse me for asking, but are you a UK resident?
   Are you a UK resident? *Does this mean:*
   Do you live in the UK? *or:* Are you British?

Are you a UK resident? *means:* Do you live in the UK?

2. Well, that throws a spanner in the works.
   To throw a spanner in the works. *Does this mean:* to make a process easier *or:* to make a process more difficult?
   To throw a spanner in the works *means:* to make a process more difficult.

3. I can offer you 11 % on an instant loan depending on your credit rating.
   Credit rating. *Does this mean:* the financial strength of your company *or:* the amount of money which you intend to borrow?
   Credit rating *means:* the financial strength of your company.

3 Please listen to the following extract from the dialogue and pay close attention to what Mr Berger says.

LF: I recommend International Money Orders.
MB: But I also need to take out a loan.
LF: Can you tell me the name of your German bank?
MB: Yes, it's *Eurobank* in Freiburg.
LF: Then we can proceed. You see *Eurobank* is one of our European affiliates. How much would you like to borrow?
MB: A thousand pounds over a year. I want to keep interest rates to a minimum.
LF: Then a short term loan like this is your best option. I can offer you 11 % on instant loan depending on your credit rating. If you'd just fill out the forms.

Now it's your turn. Please take the role of Mr Berger. You'll hear one answer as a model. Other solutions are, of course, also possible.

1. I recommend International Money Orders.
   Now it's your turn. Tell her that that is ok with you and that you also need to take out a loan.
   Ok, but I also need to take out a loan.

2. Can you tell me the name of your German bank?
   Now it's your turn. Tell her that your bank is the Eurobank in Freiburg.
   It's Eurobank in Freiburg.

3. How much would you like to borrow?
   Now it's your turn. Tell her that you'd like £1000 which you intend to pay back in a year so as to pay as little interest as possible.
   A thousand pounds over a year because I want to keep interest rates to a minimum.

ℹ In the UK and in the USA there is huge competition amongst banks and so it is worthwhile to shop around for the best deal before you make a decision about a loan. It is not just banks that offer loans but big supermarket chains and several independent organisations who just do business on-line.These types of business are called e-tailers.

Vocabulary

business loan	Geschäftskredit
resident	Einwohner
to throw a spanner in(to) the works (BE)	Sand ins Getriebe streuen
reasonable options	vernünftige Alternativen
I see your point.	Ich verstehe, was Sie meinen.
international traders	internationale Geschäftsleute
to transfer	transferieren
International Money Order	internationale Zahlungsanweisung
supplier	Lieferant
transaction	(Geschäfts)Abschluss
to take out a loan	ein Darlehen/Kredit aufnehmen
affiliate	Tochtergesellschaft
interest rates	Zinsen
short term	kurzzeitig
credit rating	Kreditwürdigkeit

8 Negotiating the business contract

▲ In this dialogue you learn how to finalise a business contract, negotiate prices, guarantees and after-sales services.

We are back at the Flair UK stand where Mr Berger has returned to settle the final terms of the business contract. He has business to discuss with Sam Elliot.

SE: = Sam Elliot; MB: = Martin Berger

SE: Mr Berger. Welcome back. How did you get on at the bank?
MB: The bank was very helpful and in fact I've been mulling your deal over in my mind.

SE: Oh ... how do you mean?
MB: You see, I'm still learning the ropes of this business and I'm very wary about signing anything before I've checked the small-print.
SE: I think that's very wise, but I can assure you that you can rely on the exceptional quality of our products as well as our customer service.

MB: Your track record is certainly admirable and I still want to place my order. In the meantime I'd like your assurance that I will get a pro forma invoice for my 20 % deposit and then I will pay the difference on receipt of the goods at my shop.

SE: Don't worry, Mr Berger. It's company policy to issue an invoice for any merchandise, regardless of the size of the order. Nowadays, with so many fly-by-night companies, you need to have everything in writing.

MB: Well, your professional attitude is certainly reassuring. Ordering a new product is always a gamble, especially with glamour stocks like sports clothing.
SE: Absolutely. Then again, nothing ventured, nothing gained!

Den Vertrag aushandeln

▲ Hier erfahren Sie, wie man einen Geschäftsvertrag abschließt und wie man über Preise, Garantien und Kundenservice verhandelt.

Wir befinden uns wieder am Stand von Flair UK. Herr Berger ist zurückgekommen, um die endgültigen Vertragsbedingungen abzusprechen. Er hat konkrete Fragen an Sam Elliot.

SE: Herr Berger! Schön, Sie wiederzusehen. Wie ist es Ihnen bei der Bank ergangen?
MB: Die Bank war sehr hilfsbereit. Inzwischen habe ich mir Ihr Angebot nochmals durch den Kopf gehen lassen.
SE: Wirklich? Inwiefern?
MB: Wissen Sie, ich bin ziemlich neu in diesem Geschäft und deshalb bin ich sehr vorsichtig, etwas zu unterschreiben, bevor ich nicht auch das Kleingedruckte geprüft habe.
SE: Ich finde, das ist klug, aber ich kann Ihnen versichern, dass Sie sich sowohl auf die herausragende Qualität unserer Produkte als auch auf unseren Kundendienst verlassen können.
MB: Ihr Ruf ist wirklich ausgezeichnet, und ich möchte meine Bestellung nach wie vor aufgeben. Vorher hätte ich jedoch gerne Ihre Zusicherung, dass ich für meine 20 % Anzahlung eine Proforma-Rechnung bekomme. Dann bezahle ich die Differenz nach Erhalt der Ware in meinem Laden.
SE: Keine Sorge, Herr Berger. Es ist ein Unternehmensgrundsatz, für alle unsere Waren eine Rechnung auszustellen, unabhängig vom Auftragsvolumen. Heutzutage braucht man immer eine schriftliche Bestätigung – bei so vielen windigen Unternehmen.
MB: Ihre Professionalität ist beruhigend. Ein neues Produkt zu bestellen ist immer ein Risiko, vor allem bei so heikler Ware wie Sportbekleidung.
SE: Ganz bestimmt, aber wer nicht wagt, der nicht gewinnt!

MB: Do I sign in duplicate?
SE: Yes, please. Here are the freight and insurance documents. Would you sign those as well.
MB: Before I do … are there any guarantees with *Silkease?*
SE: We offer a CIF contract which guarantees the goods while in transit and then you have 30 days to return any damaged garments, free of charge. *Silkease* itself carries a statutory guarantee of twelve months, subject to normal wear and tear.

MB: Soll ich beides unterschreiben?
SE: Ja, bitte. Hier sind die Fracht- und Versicherungspapiere. Würden Sie die bitte auch unterschreiben?
MB: Bevor ich das tue … wie sind die Garantieleistungen bei *Silkease*?
SE: Wir bieten einen Vertrag mit CIF-Klausel als Garantie für den Warentransport; und anschließend haben Sie eine dreißigtägige Frist, um die Ware kostenlos zurückzusenden, falls sie beschädigt ist. Das Produkt *Silkease* selbst hat eine gesetzliche Garantie von zwölf Monaten, ausgenommen normaler Verschleiß.

MB: And here are the papers for you to countersign and my £580 deposit.
SE: Thank you, Mr Berger. I'm sure that you'll be delighted with the product, and our after-sales service is second to none.

MB: Also hier sind die Papiere zum Gegenzeichnen und meine £580 Anzahlung.
SE: Danke, Herr Berger. Ich bin mir sicher, dass Sie mit dem Produkt zufrieden sein werden – und unser Kundenservice ist unübertroffen.

Exercises

1 Please repeat the following sentences.

1. I'd like your assurance that I will get a pro forma invoice.
2. It's company policy to issue an invoice for any merchandise.
3. Our after-sales service is second to none.

2 Please listen to the following sentences and choose the correct answer a), b) or c).

1.
a) *Mr Berger won't sign the contract without an assurance.*
b) *Mr Berger won't sign the contract without a proforma invoice.*
c) *Mr Berger won't sign the contract with a CIF.*

The correct answer is **b)**: Mr Berger won't sign the contract without a pro forma invoice.

2.
a) *A CIF contract guarantees the merchandise for 30 days.*
b) *A CIF contract guarantees the merchandise for twelve months.*
c) *A CIF contract guarantees the merchandise while in transit.*

The correct answer is **c)**: A CIF contract guarantees the merchandise while in transit.

3.
a) *Damaged garments can be returned free of charge.*
b) *Damaged garments can be returned subject to wear and tear.*
c) *Damaged garments can be returned with copyright.*

The correct answer is **a)**: Damaged garments can be returned free of charge.

3 Please listen to the following sentences and answer the questions using *"Yes, I …"*.

1. *Do you still want to place your order?*
   Yes, I still want to place my order.
2. *Have you signed the papers?*
   Yes, I have signed the papers.
3. *Will you pay the difference on receipt of the goods at your shop?*
   Yes, I will pay the difference on receipt of the goods at my shop.

Vocabulary

How did you get on?	Wie ist es gelaufen?
to mull *s.th.* over	sich *etwas* durch den Kopf gehen lassen
learning the ropes	sich einarbeiten; neu im Geschäft sein
wary	skeptisch; vorsichtig
smallprint	Kleingedrucktes
wise	vernünftig; weise
to rely on *s.th.*	sich auf *etwas* verlassen
track record	Ruf; Leumund
assurance	Zusicherung
pro forma invoice	Proforma-Rechnung
company policy	Unternehmens-grundsatz
regardless of	ohne Rücksicht auf; unabhängig von
fly-by-night company	windiges, anrüchiges Unternehmen
gamble	Risiko
glamour stock (BE); glamor inventory (AE)	heikle Waren
Nothing ventured, nothing gained.	Wer nicht wagt, der nicht gewinnt.
CIF (Cost, Insurance, Freight) Contract	CIF (Kosten-, Versi-cherungs- und Fracht-) Vertrag
free of charge (FOC)	kostenlos
subject to wear and tear	ausgenommen normaler Verschleiß
to countersign	gegenzeichnen
second to none	unübertroffen

9 Negotiating a follow-up deal

▲ Here we listen in as Martin Berger tries to bargain for a follow-up deal.

Sam Elliot and Guy Russell return to the sales office with samples from the golfwear range. Mr Berger is waiting to put his cards on the table …

GR: = Guy Russell; MB: = Martin Berger; SE: = Sam Elliot

GR: Hi, I'm Guy Russell of *Future Fabrics*, New York. Pleased to meet you. We met already, didn't we?
MB: Yes, back on the first day. Martin Berger, *Pronatura*, Freiburg. Nice to see you again. I'm interested in that golf clothing you talked about.
GR: Yeah. Sam told me and I've brought along some samples for you to see.

MB: You said your company is *Future Fabrics*? Are you an independent company or part of *Flair*?

GR: Well, you know us Americans. We kinda like to own companies, so *Flair* is our UK subsidiary and distributor in Europe.

MB: So the business terms are the same or do I have some leeway to do a little deal on those samples; as it's the last day of the fair and I'm a new customer …?
GR: You sure drive a hard bargain. I like that. What did you have in mind?

MB: So far, I've just ordered the material which means an inevitable lapse between the arrival of the fabric and the clothes being produced. What I want is to run a promotion of some ready-made clothing.

GR: Smart move. Initially you won't be looking at a big order, right?

Ein Folgegeschäft verhandeln

▲ Hier hören wir in das Gespräch hinein, wie Martin Berger ein Folgegeschäft aushandelt.

Sam Elliot und Guy Russell kehren mit Mustern von Golfkleidung zum Verkaufsbüro zurück. Herr Berger wartet gespannt darauf, seine Karten auf den Tisch zu legen …

GR: Hi, ich bin Guy Russell von *Future Fabrics*, New York. Freut mich. Wir haben uns schon kennen gelernt, oder?
MB: Ja, am ersten Tag. Martin Berger, *Pronatura*, Freiburg. Schön, Sie wiederzusehen. Ich interessiere mich für die Golfkleidung, über die Sie gesprochen haben.
GR: Ja, das hat mir Sam gesagt und ich habe Ihnen einige Ausstellungsstücke mitgebracht.
MB: Sie sagten, Ihre Firma heißt *Future Fabrics*? Sind Sie ein selbstständiges Unternehmen oder hängen Sie mit *Flair* zusammen?
GR: Tja. Sie kennen uns Amerikaner. Uns gefällt es irgendwie, Firmen zu besitzen, deshalb ist *Flair* unsere Tochtergesellschaft in Großbritannien und gleichzeitig unser Vertriebsunternehmen in Europa.
MB: Dann sind die Geschäftsbedingungen gleich – oder habe ich ein bisschen Spielraum zum Handeln? Es ist der letzte Messetag, und ich bin ein neuer Kunde …
GR: Sie sind ja ein harter Verhandlungspartner! Das gefällt mir. Was haben Sie sich vorgestellt?
MB: Nun ja, ich habe bis jetzt nur den Stoff bestellt. Das bedeutet eine unvermeidliche Zeitspanne vom Eintreffen des Stoffes bis zur Fertigstellung der Kleidungsstücke. Was ich möchte, ist eine Werbekampagne mit fertiger Konfektionskleidung.
GR: Ein geschickter Schachzug. Also Sie wollen nicht gleich eine große Bestellung aufgeben, richtig?

MB: Exactly. I'd like to buy a few items to see how they catch on with my customers.

GR: You won't put a foot wrong with these, Martin. Take a look for yourself.

MB: Hmm. Golf is certainly the up and coming sport in Germany. This could be my stepping stone into a very lucrative market. Could you give me a price for these off the top of your head?

GR: Let's see. There are 15 pieces. A little bit of mental arithmetic gives me a street value of £600. If you take the lot, I'll do you a special price of £400.

MB: And if I take the lot ... now ... for £350, cash in hand?

GR: Sam. What do you think? I guess this guy wants these clothes, badly?

MB: I think we should go for it. There are a lot of promising German golfers on the circuit. Think of all that free advertising!

GR: I guess you got yourself a deal there, Martin.

MB: Thanks for everything. It's been a pleasure doing business with you. Could I have your business cards for my records and your handy numbers?

SE: Handy? Ah! You mean mobile, ... cell phone. So much for this global English! Catch you later at the do.

MB: I'm looking forward to it. See you there.

MB: Genau. Ich möchte jetzt ein paar Artikel kaufen um zu sehen, wie sie bei meinen Kunden ankommen.

GR: Mit diesen Produkten machen Sie keinen Fehler, Martin. Sehen Sie selbst.

MB: Hm. Golf wird immer beliebter in Deutschland. Dieses Geschäft könnte mein Einstieg in einen sehr lukrativen Markt sein. Können Sie mir so auf Anhieb einen Preis hierfür nennen?

GR: Mal sehen. Es sind 15 Teile. So schnell im Kopf zusammengerechnet macht das einen Verkaufswert von £ 600. Wenn Sie alles kaufen, mache ich Ihnen einen Sonderpreis von £400.

MB: Und wenn ich alles nehme – gleich – für £350 bar auf die Hand?

GR: Sam, was meinen Sie? Ich habe das Gefühl, dass dieser Herr diese Kleidungsstücke unbedingt haben möchte.

MB: Ich glaube, wir sollten es tun. Es gibt ja etliche viel versprechende deutsche Golfspieler. Denken Sie an all die kostenlose Werbung!

GR: Ich glaube, Sie haben gerade ein gutes Geschäft gemacht, Martin.

MB: Vielen Dank für alles. Es ist mir eine Freude, mit Ihnen Geschäfte zu machen. Geben Sie mir noch Ihre Visitenkarte für meine Unterlagen und auch Ihre Handynummern?

SE: Handy? Ah! Sie meinen „mobile" ... „cell phone". Tja ... soviel zum Englischen als Weltsprache! Bis später dann auf einen Umtrunk.

MB: Ich freue mich darauf. Bis dann.

Exercises

1 Please repeat the following sentences.

1. Initially you won't be looking at a big order, right?
2. You sure drive a hard bargain.
3. Could you give me a price off the top of your head?

2 Listen to the dialogue again, paying particular attention to how Martin Berger negotiates for the golf clothing. Then answer the following questions.

1. *Why does Martin want to buy some ready-made clothing?*

Martin wants to see if his customers like the product.

2. *Why is Martin so interested in getting into the golf market?*
   Because the golf market is very lucrative.
3. *What price does Martin offer for the clothing?*
   Martin offers £350 for the clothing.

3 Please listen to the following expressions and choose the correct definitions.

1. Do I have some leeway to do a little deal on those samples?
   To have some leeway. *Does this mean:* to have some flexibility in the negotiation *or:* to have some discount on the samples?
   To have some leeway *means:* to have some flexibility in the negotiation.
2. You sure drive a hard bargain.
   To drive a hard bargain. *Does this mean:* to negotiate for something in a determined way *or:* to negotiate in a way that the other person can't understand?
   To drive a hard bargain *means:* to negotiate for something in a determined way.
3. Could you give me a price off the top of your head?
   To give a price off the top of one's head. *Does this mean:* to give someone an accurate price *or:* to give someone an approximate price?
   To give a price off the top of one's head *means:* to give someone an approximate price.

Vocabulary

follow-up deal	Folgegeschäft
to bargain for *s.th.*	*etwas* verhandeln
to put *one's* cards on the table	*seine* Karten auf den Tisch legen
sample	Probe; Muster
kinda (AE); *(coll. für)* kind of	ein bisschen; irgendwie
business terms	Geschäftsbedingungen
leeway	Handlungsspielraum
You drive a hard bargain!	Sie sind ein harter Verhandlungspartner!
lapse	Zeitspanne
to catch on	Anklang finden; sich durchsetzen
You won't put a foot wrong with these!	Damit können Sie nichts falsch machen!
to be up and coming	groß im Kommen sein
stepping stone	Einstieg; Sprungbrett
lucrative	lukrativ
off the top of *one's* head	spontan; aus dem Kopf
to take the lot	alles nehmen
cash in hand	bar auf die Hand
business card	Visitenkarte
record	Akten; Unterlagen
mobile (phone) (BE); cell phone (AE)	Handy
do (BE *coll.*)	Party

10 Post-conference socializing

▲ In this dialogue you will learn how to make small talk and how to mingle at the post-conference buffet and wine bar.

It's Friday evening and after all their hard work, the Flair team is exhausted but very pleased with their successful sales campaign. They are enjoying some food and a few drinks at the post-conference buffet.

GR: = Guy Russell; SE: = Sam Elliot; JS: =Julia Spencer; MB: = Martin Berger

GR: Hi there, guys. You two still talking shop? I reckon it's time for a change of scene.

SE: So, what's the alternative?

JS: I found a really nice wine bar about five minutes away. They do homemade food and have a great wine list.

SE: You've twisted my arm. Let's go for it then.

GR: Excuse me for interrupting, but would you like to join us for a drink in a nearby wine bar?

MB: I'd love to. Er … do they serve food there, only I'm starving?

JS: Yes … and it's homemade.

…

SE: I'll get this round. A bottle of Australian Chardonnay sound good to everyone?

MB: Oh … you don't have to get my drink. I'll pay when the waiter comes to the table.

JS: You have to pay for the drinks straight away at the bar in England and we all pay for a round. Your turn will come.

MB: But I insist on paying for my food.

JS: Yes, that's what we usually do. We take turns buying drinks but everyone gets their own food.

MB: I see. Could you recommend something which is typically English?

Ein Umtrunk nach der Messe

▲ Hier erfahren Sie, wie man Small Talk macht und sich mit seinen neuen Geschäftspartnern am Buffet und im Weinkeller zusammensetzt.

Es ist Freitagabend und nach all der harten Arbeit ist das Flair-Team erschöpft, jedoch sehr glücklich über seine erfolgreiche Verkaufskampagne. Sie genießen die Häppchen am Messeabschlussbuffet und trinken ein paar Gläser zusammen.

GR: Hallo, alle miteinander. Sie reden ja immer noch vom Geschäft. Ich glaube, wir brauchen einen Tapetenwechsel.

SE: Was schlagen Sie vor?

JS: Ich habe einen wirklich netten Weinkeller entdeckt, nur fünf Minuten von hier. Es gibt hausgemachte Gerichte und eine tolle Weinkarte.

SE: Sie haben mich überredet! Gehen wir hin.

GR: Entschuldigung, wenn ich unterbreche, aber hätten Sie nicht Lust, uns auf ein Glas Wein in einen Weinkeller hier um die Ecke zu begleiten?

MB: Sehr gerne. Hm … gibt es dort auch etwas zu essen? Ich bin am Verhungern!

JS: Jawohl … und es ist hausgemacht.

…

SE: Diese Runde geht auf mich. Wie wärs mit einer Flasche australischem Chardonnay?

MB: Oh, das muss nicht sein, Sam. Ich zahle meine Getränke selbst, wenn der Kellner kommt.

JS: In England muss man die Getränke gleich an der Bar bezahlen; wir alle zahlen eine Runde. Sie werden schon noch drankommen!

MB: Aber für mein Essen möchte ich schon selbst bezahlen.

JS: Ja, so machen wir das auch. Wir wechseln uns beim Bezahlen der Getränke ab, aber jeder zahlt sein Essen selbst.

MB: Verstehe. Können Sie mir etwas typisch Englisches empfehlen?

JS: I must say that it's hard to find typical English dishes. We tend to eat a wide range of food from curry to suchi! But you could try the Ploughman's. That's very English.

MB: What is it exactly?

JS: It's a mixed cheese board served with tomatoes, homemade brown bread and pickle.

MB: Mmm. That sounds tasty. I'll order that then.

...

GR: Badener Weissherbst? Who's bought this bottle?

MB: My round. It's one of the best wines from my home region of Baden. I hope you'll like it.

GR: Let's drink a toast then to Baden, to old friends and new friends.

ALL: To us. To us. Cheers!

JS: Wissen Sie, es ist schwierig etwas 'typisch Englisches' zu empfehlen. Heutzutage essen wir vielerlei unterschiedliche Gerichte – von Curry bis Sushi! Aber Sie könnten das Ploughman's versuchen. Das ist typisch Englisch.

MB: Was genau ist das?

JS: Es ist eine gemischte Käseplatte mit Tomaten, hausgemachtem dunklem Brot und sauren Gurken.

MB: Mmm. Klingt ja lecker. Ich bestelle das dann.

...

GR: Badener Weißherbst? Wer hat denn diese Flasche bestellt?

MB: Meine Runde! Dies ist einer der besten Weine meiner Heimatgegend Baden. Hoffentlich schmeckt er Ihnen.

GR: Dann trinken wir auf Baden, auf alte und auf neue Freunde.

Alle: Auf uns. Prost! Auf uns! Prost!

Exercises

1 Please repeat the following sentences.

1. I reckon it's time for a change of scene.
2. Would you like to join us for a drink in a nearby wine bar?
3. Let's drink a toast!

2 Please listen to the following example and pay special attention to making suggestions using "*I'll ...*".

1. *I want to pay for my food.*
   I'll pay for my food.

2. *I want to join you for a drink.*
   I'll join you for a drink.

3. *I want to get this round.*
   I'll get this round.

3 Listen to the dialogue again, paying particular attention to socializing with colleagues in the bar. Then answer the questions.

1. Who pays for the food?
   Everybody pays for their own food.

2. Where do you pay for your drinks?
   You pay for your drinks at the bar.

3. When you go out for a drink, who buys a round?
   Everybody buys a round.

ℹ In the UK it is common to be asked out for an informal drink after doing business and it helps foster good relations. Normally, the person who invites you will always buy the first round, but if you stay out for longer, you should always offer to pay for a round, too. The person who is buying the next round will ask you whether you would like the same again.

Vocabulary

socializing	Zusammenkommen
to mingle	sich unter die Leute mischen
to talk shop	fachsimpeln
to reckon (AE)	glauben; denken
homemade	hausgemacht
to join	beitreten; sich anschließen; *hier:* mitkommen
I'm starving!	Ich habe einen Bärenhunger!; Ich bin am Verhungern!
to eat out	(auswärts) Essen gehen
I'll get this round.	Dies ist meine Runde.
to insist on *s.th.*	auf *etwas* bestehen
to recommend *s.th.*	*etwas* empfehlen
a typical dish	ein (landes)typisches Gericht
tasty	lecker
Let's drink a toast to …	Trinken wir auf …
Cheers!	Zum Wohl!; Prost!
to foster	fördern

Liste der ID-Nummern für CD 4: Verhandlungen

Inhalt der CD	ID-Nummer:		
Vorspann	**1**	**Dialogue 6**	**22**
Dialogue 1	**2**	Exercise 1	23
Exercise 1	3	Exercise 2	24
Exercise 2	4	Exercise 3	25
Exercise 3	5	**Dialogue 7**	**26**
Dialogue 2	**6**	Exercise 1	27
Exercise 1	7	Exercise 2	28
Exercise 2	8	Exercise 3	29
Exercise 3	9	**Dialogue 8**	**30**
Dialogue 3	**10**	Exercise 1	31
Exercise 1	11	Exercise 2	32
Exercise 2	12	Exercise 3	33
Exercise 3	13	**Dialogue 9**	**34**
Dialogue 4	**14**	Exercise 1	35
Exercise 1	15	Exercise 2	36
Exercise 2	16	Exercise 3	37
Exercise 3	17	**Dialogue 10**	**38**
Dialogue 5	**18**	Exercise1	39
Exercise 1	19	Exercise 2	40
Exercise 2	20	Exercise 3	41
Exercise 3	21	End	42

Small Talk / Inhalt

1 On arrival

▲ In the following short conversations we hear how business colleagues are welcomed at the airport, how they introduce themselves and are introduced to others in a friendly and fairly informal manner.

Claudia Schneider from Germany and George Potts from America arrive in the United Kingdom on the same flight from Frankfurt and are met and welcomed at Manchester airport by Deborah Hargreaves before being driven to the firm's offices.

DH: = Deborah Hargreaves; GP: = George Potts; CS: = Claudia Schneider; DD: = David Duckham

DH: Welcome to Manchester. I´m Deborah Hargreaves from Personnel at *Joystix*. I hope you both had a good flight?

GP: Good morning. Sure, the flight was fine. Well, from Frankfurt anyway.

CS: A bit bumpy. But not too bad. It´s the first time I´ve travelled business class.

GP: It was lucky my flight from L.A. got in yesterday and I had a night's stopover in Frankfurt. The jet lag will catch up with me tomorrow though!

DH: It's good to meet you at last. If you'd like to follow me, we have transport waiting outside to take us to the office. We`ll do all the formalities there. Have you got all your luggage?

Both: Yes. Thank you.

GP: It´s great to be here again. We´ll follow you then.

Deborah leads the way to the minibus.

DH: Here we are. If you´d both like to pile in. It´ll take us about forty minutes into town to the office.

After about half an hour the minibus pulls into the firm´s car park. David Duckham, the Personnel Manager is waiting for them.

DD: Hello, George, good to see you again.

GP: Good to see you, too.

Bei der Ankunft

▲ In den folgenden kurzen Gesprächen hören wir, wie Geschäftskollegen vom Flughafen abgeholt werden, wie sie sich selbst vorstellen und wie sie anderen auf freundliche und relativ informelle Art vorgestellt werden.

Claudia Schneider aus Deutschland und George Davis aus Amerika kommen mit dem selben Flug aus Frankfurt in Manchester an. Deborah Hargreaves erwartet sie am Flughafen, begrüßt sie und fährt mit ihnen zum Büro der Firma.

DH: Herzlich willkommen in Manchester. Ich bin Deborah Hargreaves von der Personalabteilung bei *Joystix*. Ich hoffe, Sie hatten einen guten Flug?

GP: Guten Morgen. Ja, der Flug war okay. Zumindest von Frankfurt hierher.

CS: Ein bisschen unruhig. Aber nicht allzu schlimm. Das ist das erste Mal, dass ich in der Business Class geflogen bin.

GP: Ich hatte Glück, dass mein Flug von Los Angeles gestern ankam und ich eine Nacht in Frankfurt verbringen konnte. Aber morgen holt mich der Jetlag wahrscheinlich ein.

DH: Schön, Sie endlich kennen zu lernen. Wenn Sie mir folgen wollen, draußen steht ein Wagen, der uns ins Büro fahren wird. Alle Formalitäten erledigen wir dort. Haben Sie Ihr gesamtes Gepäck bereits ?

Beide: Ja.

GP: Sehr schön, wieder hier zu sein. Wir folgen Ihnen also.

Deborah führt die Gruppe zum Kleinbus.

DH: Da sind wir schon. Wenn Sie beide bitte einsteigen wollen. Die Fahrt in die Stadt zum Büro wird circa vierzig Minuten dauern.

Nach etwa einer halben Stunde biegt der Kleinbus in den Firmenparkplatz ein. David Duckham, der Personalchef, erwartet sie.

DD: Hallo, George, schön, Sie wiederzusehen.

GP: Ganz meinerseits.

DD: And you must be Claudia Schneider? Welcome.
CS: That´s right. How do you do.
DD: I´m David Duckham in charge of Personnel. I´ll be showing you later where you'll be working and we´ll be discussing all the various jobs lined up for you.
CS: I´m really looking forward to learning a lot while I´m here!
DD: We´re very pleased to have you here. Both of you. And we´re all looking forward to working together.
GP: It´s great to be back in England again. And it´s not raining this time!
DD: I think we ought to go upstairs now and meet the boss. He´s due to join us in our conference room shortly. Would you both just sign the visitors´ book and Deborah will give you your ID-badges.
CS: That´s fine by me. Is just my signature enough?
DD: Yes, that will do. Have you been to the UK before, Claudia ? I´m sure you´ll soon get used to things.
CS: Oh yes, I have. I've been to London on holiday a couple of times.
DD: Well, I think you´ll find we´re a pretty friendly lot up here in Manchester. Shall we go upstairs?

DD: Und Sie müssen Claudia Schneider sein. Willkommen.
CS: Richtig. Freut mich, Sie kennen zu lernen.
DD: Ich bin David Duckham, der Personalchef. Später zeige ich Ihnen Ihren Arbeitsplatz, und dann besprechen wir auch die verschiedenen Aufgaben, die Sie hier erwarten.
CS: Ich freue mich wirklich drauf, eine ganze Menge zu lernen, während ich hier bin.
DD: Wir freuen uns sehr, Sie hier begrüßen zu dürfen. Alle beide. Und wir freuen uns alle auf die Zusammenarbeit.
GP: Es ist schön, wieder in England zu sein. Und diesmal regnet es nicht einmal!
DD: Ich glaube, wir sollten jetzt nach oben gehen, damit Sie den Chef kennen lernen. Er wird sich uns gleich im Konferenzzimmer anschließen. Würden Sie sich bitte beide in das Gästebuch eintragen? Deborah besorgt Ihnen Ihre Namensschilder.
CS: Alles klar. Reicht eine Unterschrift?
DD: Ja, das genügt schon. Waren Sie schon mal in Großbritannien, Claudia? Sie werden sich bestimmt schnell eingewöhnen.
CS: Oh, ja. Ich habe einige Male in London Urlaub gemacht.
DD: Ich glaube, Sie werden feststellen, dass wir hier oben in Manchester ziemlich freundliche Leute sind. Wollen wir jetzt raufgehen?

Exercises

1 Please listen to the following sentences and repeat them.

1. Welcome to Manchester. I hope you had a good flight.
2. It´s good to meet you at last.
3. We´re very pleased to have you here.

2 Please listen to the following expressions and choose the correct explanation.

1. I´m in charge of Personnel.
   To be in charge of. *Does this mean:* to be responsible for *or:* to pay for?
   To be in charge of *means:* to be responsible for.
2. He´s due to join us in our conference room shortly.
   To be due to. *Does this mean:* to be obliged to *or:* to be about to do something?
   To be due to *means:* to be about to do something.
3. But I'm sure you´ll soon get used to things over here.
   To get used to. *Does this mean:* to work with something *or:* to become accustomed to something?
   To get used to *means:* to become accustomed to something.

3 Please listen to the following part of the dialogue again and pay close attention to what George Potts and Claudia Schneider say. First listen.

DD: I´m David Duckham in charge of Personnel. I´ll be showing you later where you'll be working and we´ll be discussing all the various jobs lined up for you.
CS: I´m really looking forward to learning a lot while I´m here!
DD: We´re very pleased to have you here. Both of you. And we´re all looking forward to working together.
GP: It´s great to be back in England again. And it´s not raining this time!
DD: I think we ought to go upstairs now and meet the boss. He´s due to join us in our conference room shortly. Would you both just sign the visitors´ book and Deborah will give you your ID-badges.
CS: That´s fine by me. Is just my signature enough?

Now it is your turn. Listen again and take the role of George Potts and Claudia Schneider. You'll hear one answer as a model. Other solutions are, of course, also possible.

1. I´m David Duckham in charge of Personnel. I´ll be showing you later where you will be working and we´ll be discussing all the various jobs lined up for you.
   Now it´s your turn. Take Claudia Schneider´s part and say that you are really looking forward to learning a lot while you are here.
   I´m really looking forward to learning a lot while I´m here!
2. We´re very pleased to have you here. Both of you. And we´re all looking forward to working together.
   Now it´s your turn. Take George Potts' part and say that it´s great to be back in England again and that it´s not raining this time.
   It´s great to be back in England again. And it´s not raining this time!
3. I think we ought to go upstairs now and meet the boss. He´s due to join us in our conference room shortly. Would you both just sign the visitors´ book and Deborah will give you your ID-badges.
   Now it´s your turn. Take Claudia Schneider´s part and say that that is fine by you. Ask if just your signature is enough.
   That´s fine by me. Is just my signature enough?

ℹ In the UK and the USA, people only shake hands with colleagues and friends when meeting them for the first time, when there is a formal goodbye, on special occasions or if they have not seen them for a long time.

Vocabulary

informal manner	informelle Art
sure (AE)	ja, sicher; klar
a bit bumpy	ein bisschen holprig
L.A.	*Kurzform für* Los Angeles
to catch up	einholen
It´s good to meet you.	Es ist schön, Sie kennen zu lernen.
It´s great to be here.	Sehr schön, hier zu sein.
to pile in ***(coll.)***	einsteigen
to pull into	hineinfahren in
Personnel Manager	Personalchef
in charge of personnel	für das Personal verantwortlich
the jobs lined up for you	die Aufgaben, die wir für Sie geplant haben
ID-badges	Namensschilder
to be due to do ***s.th.***	demnächst *etwas* tun sollen
to get used to ***s.th.***	sich an *etwas* gewöhnen
a pretty friendly lot	ziemlich freundliche Leute
to manage to	gelingen; es schaffen

2 Meeting the MD

▲ In this dialogue the visitors are introduced in a more formal way to a boss who is obviously pressed for time.

David Duckham and Deborah Hargreaves take Claudia Schneider and George Potts up to the conference room. Outside, David introduces them to the Managing Director, John Grisedale.

DD:= David Duckham; DH:= Deborah Hargreaves; JG:= John Grisedale; CS:= Claudia Schneider; GP:= George Potts

DD: Here we are. This is our main conference room. Before we go in we can say hello to John Grisedale, our MD. He'll be here in a moment. Deborah, did you let John know we're here?

DH: Of course, David.

At that moment the managing director arrives, obviously in a hurry.

JG: Well, hello there everyone. Very nice to see you. My name is John Grisedale. I'm *Joystix'* Managing Director.

(Shakes hands with the guests.)

DD: John, this is Claudia Schneider from Munich.

CS: How do you do.

JG: Hello, Claudia. Pleasure to meet you.

DD: And you remember George, don't you?

GP: Hello, there. Remember me? George Potts.

JG: Nice to see you again, George. How are things in Los Angeles?

GP: Busy as ever. I've brought the results of that last batch of tests you asked for with me.

JG: That's excellent, George. Well, welcome to both of you. May I say how much we are all looking forward to having you with us for the next six months. I wish you every success and we all hope to profit from the experience.

Den Firmenchef kennen lernen

▲ In diesem Gespräch werden die Besucher einem Chef, der offensichtlich unter Zeitdruck steht, auf etwas formellere Art vorgestellt.

David Duckham und Deborah Hargreaves führen Claudia Schneider und George Potts zum Konferenzraum. Vor der Tür stellt David die beiden dem Firmenchef John Grisedale vor.

DD: Da wären wir. Das ist unser Hauptkonferenzraum. Bevor wir reingehen, können Sie John Grisedale, unseren Firmenchef, begrüßen. Er wird jeden Moment hier sein. Deborah, Sie haben John doch Bescheid gesagt, nicht wahr?

DH: Selbstverständlich, David.

In dem Moment kommt der Chef, offensichtlich in großer Eile.

JG: Ja, guten Tag allerseits. Schön, Sie kennen zu lernen. Mein Name ist John Grisedale. Ich bin der Geschäftsführer von *Joystix.*

(Er gibt den Gästen die Hand.)

DD: John, das hier ist Claudia Schneider aus München.

CS: Guten Tag.

JG: Guten Tag, Claudia. Freut mich wirklich sehr, Sie kennen zu lernen.

DD: Und Sie erinnern sich sicherlich an George?

GP: Hallo. Sie erinnern sich an mich? George Potts.

JG: Schön, Sie wieder zu sehen, George. Wie stehen die Aktien in Los Angeles?

GP: Viel zu tun wie immer. Ich habe die Ergebnisse der letzten Testserie mitgebracht, um die Sie gebeten haben.

JG: Ausgezeichnet, George. Also, herzlich willkommen Sie beide. Darf ich sagen, wie sehr wir uns alle darauf freuen, Sie während der nächsten sechs Monate bei uns zu haben. Ich wünsche Ihnen viel Erfolg, und hoffentlich werden wir alle von der Erfahrung profitieren.

CS: Thank you, Mr Grisedale. We hope so, too.

JG: Oh, no need for that "Mister", Claudia! We all call each other by our first names here. Please call me John.

CS: Oh, yes, of course. Yes, fine. Thank you … er … John.

JG: If you have any problems, ask David and his highly competent staff. We have good people and we produce high quality products, as I´m sure you already know.

GP: That´s true, you have a neat little outfit here. But I think we have one or two good ideas in California, too!

JG: Well, I´m sure all your contributions will be greatly appreciated.

ALL: Thank you.

JG: Well, good luck everyone. Oh, just one small thing – my wife and I are having a small get-together tonight at our home and we´d be delighted if you could come. Seven for seven-thirty. Is that OK with everyone? See you there then. Must be off now. Next meeting! Over to you, David.

CS: Vielen Dank, Mr. Grisedale. Das hoffen wir auch.

JG: Oh, bitte, Claudia, lassen Sie das mit dem „Mister". Wir reden uns hier alle mit dem Vornamen an. Bitte nennen Sie mich John.

CS: Oh, ja, natürlich. Ja, schön. Danke schön … äh … John.

JG: Falls Sie irgendwelche Probleme haben, wenden Sie sich an David und sein überaus kompetentes Team. Wir haben wirklich gute Leute hier und wir stellen hochwertige Waren her, wie Sie bestimmt schon wissen.

GP: Stimmt. Sie haben einen ganz tollen Laden hier. Aber ich denke, wir in Kalifornien haben auch ein paar gute Ideen.

JG: Na ja, ich bin sicher, wir werden alle Beiträge von Ihnen zu schätzen wissen.

Alle: Danke schön.

JG: Also, viel Glück allerseits. Oh, eine Kleinigkeit noch … meine Frau und ich geben heute Abend bei uns zu Hause ein kleines Fest. Es wäre uns eine Freude, wenn Sie kommen könnten. So zwischen sieben und halb acht. Ist das okay für Sie alle? Dann sehen wir uns dort. Ich muss jetzt weiter. Die nächste Besprechung! David, übernehmen Sie.

Exercises

1 Please listen to the following sentences and then repeat them.

1. Well, hello there everyone. Very nice to see you.
2. Welcome to both of you.
3. May I say how much we´re looking forward to having you with us.

2 Please answer the following questions with "*yes*" or "*no*" and the correct form of the verb.

1. *Is John Grisedale the Managing Director of the firm Joystix?*
   Yes, John Grisedale is the Managing Director of *Joystix.*
2. *Has George Potts forgotten to bring the test results with him from Los Angeles?*
   No, George Potts hasn´t forgotten to bring the test results with him from Los Angeles.
3. *Does John ask Claudia to call him Mr Grisedale?*
   No, John doesn´t ask Claudia to call him Mr Grisedale.

3 Please listen again to the following extract from the dialogue and then take the appropiate parts. First listen.

DD: John, this is Claudia Schneider from Munich.

CS: How do you do.

JG: Hello, Claudia. Pleasure to meet you.
DD: And you remember George, don't you?
GP: Hello there. Remember me? George Potts.
JG: Nice to see you again, George. How are things in Los Angeles?
GP: Busy as ever. I've brought the results of that last batch of tests you asked for with me.

Now it's your turn. Listen again and then take the appropriate part. You'll hear one answer as a model. Other solutions are, of course, also possible.

1. John, this is Claudia Schneider from Munich. How do you do.
   Now take the role of John. Greet Claudia and say it's a pleasure to meet her.
   Hello, Claudia. Pleasure to meet you.

2. And you remember George, don't you?
   Now take George's part. Greet John, ask if he remembers you and say your name.
   Hello there. Remember me? George Potts.

3. Nice to see you again, George. How are things in Los Angeles?
   Now you take George's part again and say that you are as busy as ever. Say that you have brought the results of the last batch of tests that John has asked for with you.
   Busy as ever. I've brought the results of that last batch of tests you asked for with me.

ℹ It is usual in most modern companies in the UK and the USA for staff, including directors, to address each other by their first names. It is also common for people to be "on first name terms" from the very first meeting. This does not necessarily mean that people have a familiar or friendly relationship beyond the normal working environment.

Vocabulary

Managing Director (MD)	Firmenchef/in; Generaldirektor/in; leitende/r Direktor/in; Geschäftsführer/in
formal way	formelle Art
obviously	offensichtlich
to be pressed for time	es sehr eilig haben; in großer Eile sein; unter Zeitdruck stehen
in a hurry	in Eile
How do you do.	Guten Tag! Freut mich sehr!
Pleasure to meet you.	Sehr erfreut, Sie kennen zu lernen.
How are things?	Wie geht's? Wie steht's?
Busy as ever.	Viel zu tun wie immer.
batch	Serie; Quote; Reihe
first name	Vorname
staff	Mitarbeiter und Mitarbeiterinnen
high quality product	hochwertiges Produkt
neat little outfit (AE)	nettes, kleines Unternehmen
contribution	Beitrag
to appreciate	zu schätzen wissen; wert schätzen
get-together	kleine Feier; Party
to be delighted	sich freuen
seven for seven-thirty	so zwischen sieben und halb acht

3 Getting acquainted

▲ In this dialogue we hear how business colleagues talk about themselves and their personal histories.

David Duckham has a meeting with the two foreign guests with the aim of everyone getting to know each other.

DD:=David Duckham; CS:=Claudia Schneider; GD:=George Potts

DD: Well, now that everyone is here, why don´t we get to know each other a little better? As I said, my name is David Duckham. I´m the Personnel Manager here in Manchester.
CS: Have you been with *Joystix* long ?
DD: I´ve been with the firm just over five years now and this is the first time we´ve had a prolonged visit from someone in Germany who wants to learn from *us*.

CS: I´m very keen to see how you run things here and I´m very grateful to you, David, and to Mr Grisedale, ... er ... John, for giving me this opportunity to work with you. Are you a totally British firm?

DD: Yes, we are, but we have quite a number of partners throughout the world. As reflected by the fact that here today we have George with us from L.A. You'll notice that they speak English a bit differently up here in the north of England! But I´m sure we'll understand one another.

DD: But maybe you´d like to tell us something more about yourselves?
CS: My name is Claudia Schneider. I come from Augsburg, which is near Munich. I studied at Munich University and then went to America for a year. When I came back, I decided to start my own business. And for that I need to be computer literate.

DD: And what about you, George?

Sich näher kennen lernen

▲ In diesem Gespräch hören wir, wie Geschäftskollegen über sich selbst und ihren Lebenslauf sprechen.

David Duckham hat eine Besprechung mit den beiden ausländischen Gästen mit dem Ziel, dass alle sich näher kennen lernen.

DD: Also, jetzt wo alle da sind, sollten wir uns auch etwas näher kennen lernen. Wie gesagt, mein Name ist David Duckham. Ich bin der Personalchef hier in Manchester.
CS: Sind Sie schon lange bei *Joystix*?
DD: Ich bin jetzt bei der Firma seit etwas mehr als fünf Jahren und das ist das erste Mal, dass jemand aus Deutschland für längere Zeit zu uns kommt und von *uns* etwas lernen möchte.
CS: Ich will unbedingt sehen, wie Sie hier Ihre Geschäfte führen, und ich bin Ihnen, David und Mr. Grisedale, ... äh ... John, ... sehr dankbar für die Gelegenheit, mit Ihnen zusammen zu arbeiten. Sind Sie eine ausschließlich britische Firma?
DD: Ja, das sind wir, aber wir haben eine ganze Reihe von Partnern in aller Welt. Wie man schon daran sehen kann, dass wir heute George aus Los Angeles bei uns haben. Sie werden merken, dass das Englisch, das man hier oben in Nordengland spricht, ein bisschen anders klingt. Aber ich bin sicher, wir werden uns verstehen.
DD: Aber vielleicht möchten Sie uns etwas mehr über sich erzählen.
CS: Mein Name ist Claudia Schneider. Ich komme aus Augsburg, einer Stadt in der Nähe von München. Ich habe an der Universität in München studiert und dann bin ich für ein Jahr nach Amerika gegangen. Nach meiner Rückkehr habe ich beschlossen, meine eigene Firma zu gründen. Und deshalb muss ich mich mit EDV gut auskennen.
DD: Und wie ist es mit Ihnen, George?

GP: Oh, I'm just boring. When I left school I didn't really know what I wanted to do, so I set up my own software programming business – with some help from my father. And things have just developed from there. Oh, yeah and I'm forty-one years old. My name is George Potts and I come from Chicago originally. Now I live in L.A. But Manchester is just like a second home to me now.

GP: Oh, eigentlich eine ganz langweilige Sache. Nach der Schule wusste ich eigentlich nicht so recht, was ich machen sollte. Also gründete ich meine eigene Software-Programmierfirma – mit etwas Unterstützung von meinem Vater. Und seitdem haben sich die Dinge einfach weiterentwickelt. Oh, und ich bin einundvierzig Jahre alt. Mein Name ist George Potts und ich komme ursprünglich aus Chicago. Jetzt lebe ich in Los Angeles. Aber Manchester ist für mich schon fast ein zweites Zuhause geworden.

DD: Are you sure you don't mean you like the English rain? Or maybe it's the English golf courses?

DD: Sind Sie sicher, dass Sie nicht den englischen Regen meinen? Oder vielleicht die englischen Golfplätze?

GP: I like British ideas and the British way of thinking.

GP: Ich mag britischen Ideenreichtum und die britische Denkweise.

DD: Have you brought any good ideas with you, Claudia ?

DD: Haben Sie irgendwelche guten Ideen mitgebracht, Claudia?

CS: Well, as I said, now that I've done a degree in Economics and Business Studies at Munich University, I plan to start my own business next year. So actually I'm looking for ideas!

CS: Naja, wie schon gesagt, ich habe einen Abschluss in Volks- und Betriebswirtschaft an der Universität München und ich will nächstes Jahr meine eigene Firma gründen. Genaugenommen suche also *ich* Ideen!

DD: Well, we should be able to help you there. Particularly since we work closely with the whizz-kids in Silicon Valley.

DD: Da können wir Ihnen bestimmt helfen. Insbesondere weil wir mit den „Whizz-Kids" im Silicon Valley eng zusammen arbeiten.

CS: Are you a computer whizz-kid, George?

CS: Sind Sie ein „Computer Whizz-Kid", George?

GP: Well, *Joystix* and I are old friends – but we're certainly not kids any more! We go back a long way. I've been coming over here for about ten years now, but not since they moved to this new downtown office block. Very nice, David. Very nice. Not as big as back home in L.A. though!

GP: Naja, *Joystix* und ich sind alte Freunde – aber wir sind ganz sicher keine Kids mehr! Wir kennen uns schon sehr lange. Ich komme seit etwa zehn Jahren hierher nach England, aber nicht seitdem sie in dieses neue Bürohaus im Stadtzentrum umgezogen sind. Sehr schön, David. Wirklich schön. Wenn auch vielleicht nicht so groß wie bei uns zu Hause in Los Angeles!

CS: So you are a whizz-kid after all! A big whizz-kid!

CS: Also sind Sie doch ein „Whizz-Kid"! Ein großes „Whizz-Kid"!

DD: Right then, time for a tour of the building and we can stop off in the canteen for lunch on the way.

DD: Dann machen wir jetzt doch einen Rundgang durchs Haus, und zwischendurch können wir in der Kantine zu Mittag essen.

Exercises

1 Please listen to the following sentences and then repeat them.

1. I´ve been with the firm for just over five years now.
2. I´m very keen to see how you run things here.
3. We have quite a number of partners throughout the world.

2 Please listen to the following expressions and then choose the correct definition.

1. I´m very keen to see how you run things here.
   I´m very keen. *Does this mean:* I really want to *or:* I´m rather curious about it?
   I´m very keen *means:* I really want to.
2. So actually I´m looking for ideas.
   Actually. *Does it mean:* at the moment *or:* in reality?
   Actually *means:* in reality.

3 Please listen to the dialogue again and then answer the following questions.

1. *How long has David Duckham been with Joystix?*
   David Duckham has been with *Joystix* for just over five years.
2. *Where does George Potts live and work?*
   George Potts lives and works in Los Angeles.
3. *What did Claudia Schneider study at university?*
   Claudia Schneider studied Economics and Business Studies at university.

> ℹ There is a strong difference between accents in the North and South of England. In the North vowels are broader – much more like German! In particular the "a" and "u" sounds. As an example, you will now hear a short sentence first spoken in a northern accent and then in a southern one:
> *– Pleased to meet you. I understand that you come from Germany.*

Vocabulary

to get acquainted	sich näher kennen lernen
aim	Ziel; Absicht
to get to know each other	sich kennen lernen
prolonged	länger(fristig)
to be very keen to do *s.th.*	*etwas* unbedingt tun wollen
to run things	das Unternehmen führen
to give *s.o.* the opportunity to do *s.th.*	*j-m* die Gelegenheit geben, *etwas* zu tun
as reflected by	bestätigt durch; wie man an … sehen kann
to be computer literate	sich mit EDV auskennen
boring	langweilig
to set up	*hier:* gründen
I guess … (AE)	… glaube ich
degree	(akademischer) Grad
Economics and Business Studies	Volks- und Betriebwirtschaft
actually	eigentlich; genau genommen
particularly	insbesondere
whizz-kid	Senkrechtstarter; junges Talent
We go back a long way.	Wir kennen uns von früher/schon sehr lange.

4 At the boss's home

▲ Now we hear what kind of conversation may take place among colleagues after accepting a private invitation.

That evening Claudia, George, David and Deborah are invited to the house of John and Anne Grisedale. After introductions, the guests talk to their hosts about themselves.

JG: = John Grisedale; DD: = David Duckham; CS: = Claudia Schneider; AG: = Anne Grisedale; GP: = George Potts

JG: *(At the front door)*
Well, hello there. Come on in, won't you? Nice to see you again. Come and meet my wife. Anne, our guests have arrived. David, will you introduce everyone? I'm hopeless at names.

DD: Hi, Anne. How are you? Let me introduce you to our German and American colleagues. Ladies first. This is Claudia Schneider.

CS: Hello, Mrs Grisedale. Nice to meet you.

AG: *(Shakes hands)* Hello, Claudia. Please call me Anne. It's very nice to meet you, too.

CS: Hello, Anne. Thank you so much for inviting us.

AG: Not at all. Very nice to meet you. Do come on through.

DD: And this is George Potts from Los Angeles.

AG: *(Shakes hands)* Hello, George. Nice to see you. We met once last year, didn't we, when you were over here for a meeting?

GP: That's right. We went for a meal at that Indian restaurant.

AG: Yes, I remember. John is always talking about the success we've had in Los Angeles and that it's mostly down to you!

GP: Well, I'm flattered. Thank you. And thank you, too, for inviting us to your home tonight.

Beim Chef zu Hause

▲ Nun hören wir, welche Art von Gesprächen stattfinden kann, wenn Kollegen privat eingeladen werden.

Am selben Abend sind Claudia, George, David und Deborah bei John und Anne Grisedale zu Hause eingeladen. Nach der Begrüßung reden die Gäste mit ihren Gastgebern über sich selbst.

JG: *(An der Haustür)*
Guten Abend. Kommen Sie bitte herein. Schön, Sie wiederzusehen. Darf ich Ihnen meine Frau vorstellen? Anne, unsere Gäste sind da. David, machen Sie bitte alle miteinander bekannt. Ich kann mir einfach keine Namen merken.

DD: Hallo, Anne. Wie geht's? Darf ich Ihnen unsere deutschen und amerikanischen Kollegen vorstellen? Damen zuerst. Das ist Claudia Schneider.

CS: Guten Abend, Mrs. Grisedale. Freut mich sehr.

AG: *(Gibt ihr die Hand)* Guten Abend, Claudia. Bitte nennen Sie mich doch Anne. Ich bin ebenfalls sehr erfreut, Sie kennen zu lernen.

CS: Hallo, Anne. Ganz herzlichen Dank für die Einladung.

AG: Ich bitte Sie. Schön, Sie hier zu sehen. Aber kommen Sie doch bitte weiter.

DD: Und das hier ist George Potts aus Los Angeles.

AG: *(Gibt ihm die Hand)* Hallo, George. Schön Sie zu sehen. Wir haben uns letztes Jahr kurz kennen gelernt, als Sie zu einer Besprechung hier waren, nicht wahr?

GP: Richtig. Wir waren doch zusammen Indisch essen gegangen.

AG: Ja, ich erinnere mich. John erzählt unentwegt von unserem Erfolg in Los Angeles und dass das alles hauptsächlich Ihnen zu verdanken ist.

GP: Ich fühle mich geschmeichelt. Vielen Dank. Und danke auch, dass Sie uns heute Abend zu sich nach Hause eingeladen haben.

AG: Our pleasure. Now, please, come on through. There will be some food in a short while.
(All go into the living room.)
JG: Do sit down all of you and I'll get some drinks organised.
GP: That sounds a great idea, John. But a non-alcoholic one for me, please. I'm a Californian now. And very health-conscious.
AG: Good for you, George. Well, welcome everyone. I thought we could chat for a while before we eat. John, have you sorted those drinks out yet? Claudia, tell me something about yourself.

CS: Well, I live in Munich.
AG: Ah yes, the Oktoberfest! John and I went there once. A long time ago now. Tell me, Claudia, are you married ?
CS: No, I´m not married. And my boy-friend is in South Africa for two years.
AG: Is he in computers, too?
CS: Oh, no. He´s a doctor. He´s working at a big hospital in Pretoria.
JG: Sorry to butt in, ladies. But it's just occurred to me you could say we run a hospital for computers!

AG: Don´t listen to him, Claudia. To hear my husband talk, you´d think computers were the be all and end all of everything and we couldn´t live without them.

AG: Ist doch selbstverständlich. Aber jetzt kommen Sie doch bitte weiter. In Kürze gibt es auch etwas zu essen.
(Sie gehen alle in das Wohnzimmer.)
JG: Nehmen Sie doch bitte alle Platz. Ich kümmere mich um die Getränke.
GP: Keine schlechte Idee, John! Aber für mich etwas Alkoholfreies, bitte. Ich bin jetzt Kalifornier und daher sehr gesundheitsbewusst.
AG: Gut für Sie, George! Also dann, herzlich willkommen allerseits. Ich dachte, wir könnten ein bisschen miteinander plaudern, bevor wir essen. John, bist du mit den Getränken so weit? Claudia, erzählen Sie doch etwas über sich.
CS: Naja, also, ich lebe in München.
AG: Ach ja, das Oktoberfest! John und ich waren schon mal dort. Schon einige Zeit her. Sagen Sie, Claudia, sind Sie verheiratet?
CS: Nein, ich bin nicht verheiratet. Mein Freund ist für zwei Jahre in Südafrika.
AG: Arbeitet er auch in der Computerbranche?
CS: Nein. Er ist Arzt. Er arbeitet in einem großen Krankenhaus in Pretoria.
JG: Entschuldigung, wenn ich mich einmische, meine Damen. Aber mir fällt gerade ein, dass wir ja sozusagen ein Krankenhaus für Computer betreiben!
AG: Hören Sie nicht auf ihn, Claudia. Wenn es nach meinem Mann ginge, könnte man glauben, dass Computer das einzig Wichtige auf Erden sind und wir ohne sie gar nicht leben könnten.

Exercises

1 Please repeat the following sentences.

1. Let me introduce you to our German and American colleagues.
2. Welcome everyone. Do sit down.
3. Now, tell me something about yourself.

2 Please listen to the following sentences and then say whether they are true or false.

1. *George has met Anne Grisedale before.*
   This sentence is true. George Potts met Anne Grisedale once last year in an Indian restaurant.
2. *Claudia is married to a South African.*
   This sentence is false. Claudia has a boy-friend who works at a hospital in South-Africa.
3. *John Grisedale believes in computer technology.*

This sentence is true. John Grisedale thinks that computers are the be all and end all of everything and we can't live without them.

3 Please listen to the following questions and answer them with "*Yes, I …*" or "*Yes, we …*" and the correct form of the verb.

1. *We met once last year, didn't we?*
   Yes, we did meet once last year.
2. *Are you very health-conscious?*
   Yes, I am very health-conscious.
3. *Do we run a hospital for computers?*
   Yes, we do run a hospital for computers.

ℹ It is not considered either obligatory or usual when invited to someone's home to take a gift for the host unless it is a special occasion (a birthday for example). Coming from a foreign visitor, however, it would be thought of as a nice gesture.
To add extra politeness when asking people to do things, the auxiliary verb "do" is often used. For example: "Do come in", "Do sit down", "Do go on through".

Vocabulary

invitation	Einladung
introduction	Vorstellung
host	Gastgeber
I'm hopeless at names.	Ich kann mir keine Namen merken.
Thank you so much for inviting us.	Herzlichen Dank für die Einladung.
Not at all!	Ich bitte Sie!; Keine Ursache!
to go for a meal	essen gehen
It's mostly down to you.	Das haben wir hauptsächlich Ihnen zu verdanken.
I'm flattered.	Ich fühle mich geschmeichelt.
in a short while	gleich; in Kürze
non-alcoholic	alkoholfrei
health-conscious	gesundheitsbewusst
to sort out *s.th.*	*etwas* klären
Sorry to butt in.	Verzeihen Sie, wenn ich mich einmische/ wenn ich Sie unterbreche.
to hear *s.o.* talk	wenn es nach … ginge
the be all and end all	das einzig Wichtige

5 Meeting in the lunch break

▲ Here we listen as chance meetings during the working day are used to discuss personal views and to ask colleagues for advice.

George Potts and Claudia Schneider meet David Duckham and Deborah Hargreaves in the firm's canteen at lunchtime. They take separate tables as George needs to talk to David confidentially about problems at work and asks for his advice and help. Claudia and Deborah talk about British food.

Begegnung in der Mittagspause

▲ Hier hören wir, wie zufällige Begegnungen im Laufe des Arbeitstages genutzt werden, um persönliche Ansichten zu äußern und Kollegen um Rat zu bitten.

George und Claudia treffen David und Deborah während der Mittagspause in der Kantine. Sie setzen sich an getrennte Tische, weil George mit David ein vertrauliches Gespräch über Probleme bei seiner Arbeit führen und ihn um Rat und Hilfe bitten möchte. Claudia und Deborah reden über die britische Küche.

GP: = George Potts; DD: = David Duckham; CS: = Claudia Schneider; DH: = Deborah Hargreaves

GP: Hello, David. Glad I caught you. Can I talk to you about this new program for *Newsdesk International*? Strictly off the record. I'm a bit worried about it.

DD: Yeah, sure. Let's go over there. There's a table free.

They sit down. Seeing there's a seat free, Claudia comes over with her tray of food.

DD: Hello, Claudia. How are things?

CS: Fine. Do you two want to talk or can I join you ?

GP: Well, if you don't mind ... I did rather want ...

CS: No, sure. No problem. There's Deborah over there. I'll sit with her. Bye. See you later.

Claudia goes over to the other table.

CS: Hi, Deborah. Mind if I join you?

DH: Hi, Claudia. Not at all. How are you doing? Please take a seat.

CS: What have you got there?

DH: Fish and chips. I love fish and chips.

CS: With salt and vinegar? I'll never get used to English food.

DH: Well, it's pretty difficult to find good fish these days. Cod is the best but it's so expensive now. Not many cod left in the sea. Are George and David talking business?

CS: I think so. I didn't want to intrude.

Let's join David and George again at the other table:

DD: So what's the problem, George?

GP: Well, I really don't like the way *Newsdesk* are messing us around. We still haven't received an official order for the programming and at the same time it's all very urgent. Have you had any experience with them before?

DD: Oh yes. It sounds like par for the course. They always have problems getting a

GP: Tag, David. Gut, dass ich Sie treffe. Kann ich Sie wegen dieses neuen Programms für *Newsdesk International* sprechen? Unter uns: Ich mache mir Sorgen.

DD: Aber klar doch. Gehen wir doch da drüben hin. Da ist ein Tisch frei.

Sie setzen sich. Claudia, die gesehen hat, dass ein Platz frei ist, kommt rüber mit ihrem Tablett.

DD: Tag, Claudia. Wie geht's?

CS: Bestens. Wollen Sie beide alleine reden, oder darf ich mich zu Ihnen setzen?

GP: Wenn es Ihnen nichts ausmacht ... ich wollte eigentlich lieber ...

CS: Ja, sicher. Kein Problem. Da drüben sitzt Deborah. Ich setze mich zu ihr. Tschüs. Bis später.

Claudia geht zum anderen Tisch.

CS: Tag, Deborah. Darf ich mich zu Ihnen setzen?

DH: Hallo, Claudia. Aber klar doch. Wie geht es Ihnen denn? Bitte setzen Sie sich.

CS: Was haben Sie da?

DH: „Fish and Chips". Ich liebe „Fish and Chips".

CS: Mit Salz und Essig? Ich werde mich nie an die britische Küche gewöhnen.

DH: Naja, es ist schon ganz schön schwierig, heutzutage guten Fisch zu bekommen. Kabeljau ist am besten, aber der ist ja so teuer geworden. Es gibt nicht mehr viel Kabeljau im Meer. Reden George und David gerade übers Geschäft?

CS: Ich glaube schon. Ich wollte nicht stören.

Noch einmal zurück zu David und George an den anderen Tisch:

DD: Also, wo liegt das Problem, George?

GP: Ich komme überhaupt nicht klar mit der Art und Weise, wie *Newsdesk* mit uns umspringt. Wir haben immer noch keinen offiziellen Auftrag für die Programmierarbeit erhalten, und trotzden ist alles furchtbar eilig. Haben Sie schon früher Erfahrungen mit ihnen gemacht?

DD: Oh ja. Das hört sich alles ganz normal an. Die haben immer Probleme, wenn es um

signature under documents.

GP: You mean I can rely on their word and plan the programming work for next week without a contract? Later than that will mean I'll have problems getting a programmer.

DD: Do they know that?

GP: Sure they do. I told Simon on the phone yesterday.

DD: Well, you'll probably have the contract signed on your desk tomorrow then.

GP: And if not?

DD: Why don't you cross that bridge when you come to it? You've got a couple of days to pressure them, haven't you?

GP: Yeah, you're right. I just wanted to hear someone else say what I was thinking! Thanks, David.

eine Unterschrift auf irgendeinem Dokument geht.

GP: Sie meinen, ich kann mich auf die mündliche Abmachung verlassen und die Programmierarbeit für nächste Woche einplanen, ohne Vertrag? Wenn es später wird, werde ich Probleme haben, einen Programmierer zu finden.

DD: Wissen die das?

GP: Aber ja doch. Ich habe es Simon gestern am Telefon gesagt.

DD: Dann werden Sie den unterschriebenen Vertrag wahrscheinlich morgen auf Ihrem Schreibtisch haben.

GP: Und wenn nicht?

DD: Darüber würde ich mir erst Gedanken machen, wenn es soweit ist. Sie haben noch ein paar Tage Zeit, um sie unter Druck zu setzen, oder?

GP: Ja, Sie haben Recht. Ich wollte nur mal meine Meinung aus anderem Mund hören. Danke, David.

Exercises

1 Please listen to the following sentences and then repeat them.

1. I'm glad I caught you. Can I talk to you about this? Strictly off the record.
2. Do you two want to talk or can I join you?
3. Why don't you cross that bridge when you come to it?

2 Please listen to the following expressions and then choose the correct definition.

1. George Potts needs to talk to David Duckham confidentially.
   Confidentially. *Does this mean:* George Potts trusts David Duckham *or:* George Potts doesn't trust David Duckham?
   Confidentially *means:* George Potts trusts David Duckham.
2. Well, if you don't mind. I did rather want …
   If you don't mind. *Does this mean:* would you object *or:* what do you mean?
   If you don't mind *means:* would you object.
3. It sounds like par for the course.
   Par for the course. *Does this mean*: normal *or:* unusual?
   Par for the course *means:* normal.

3 Please listen to the first part of the dialogue again and pay close attention to what David Duckham and Claudia Schneider say.

GP: Hello, David. Glad I caught you. Can I talk to you about this new program for *Newsdesk International*? Strictly off the record. I'm a bit worried about it.

DD: Yeah, sure. Let's go over there. There's a table free.

They sit down. Seeing there's a seat free, Claudia comes over with her tray of food.

DD: Hello, Claudia. How are things?

CS: Fine. Do you two want to talk or can I join you?

GP: Well, if you don't mind … I did rather want …

CS: No, sure. No problem. There's Deborah over there. I'll sit with her. Bye. See you later.

Now it's your turn. Please listen and take the appropiate part. You'll hear one answer as a model. Other solutions are, of course, also possible.

1. Hello, David. Glad I caught you. Can I talk to you about this new program for *Newsdesk International*? Strictly off the record. I'm a bit worried about it.
   Now please take David's part. Accept George's request and suggest you both go over to a free table.
   Yeah, sure. Let's go over there. There's a table free.

2. Hello, Claudia. How are things?
   Now please take Claudia's part and say you're fine and then ask David and George if they want to talk or if you can join them.
   Fine. Do you two want to talk or can I join you?

3. Well, if you don't mind … I did rather want …
   Now please take Claudia's part again and say that it isn't a problem. Tell George that you can see Deborah and that you'll sit with her. Say a quick goodbye and that you'll see him later.
   No, sure. No problem. There's Deborah over there. I'll sit with her. 'Bye. See you later.

> ℹ Eating habits vary greatly from country to country. The British and American custom of putting vinegar on chips is as strange to the Germans, Swiss and Austrians, as putting mayonnaise on chips is to the British and Americans!
> Nowadays, however, there is such a wide range of international restaurants on both sides of the Atlantic and all over Europe, that the cultural divide with regard to eating habits is becoming ever smaller.

Vocabulary

lunch break	Mittagspause
confidentially	im Vertrauen; unter uns gesagt
Glad I caught you.	Ich bin froh, dass ich Sie erwischt habe.
strictly off the record	ganz unter uns; im Vertrauen
tray	Tablett
if you don't mind	wenn es Ihnen nichts ausmacht
I did rather want …	ich wollte eigentlich lieber …
Mind if I join you?	Darf ich mich zu Ihnen setzen?
How are you doing?	Wie geht's?
cod	Kabeljau
to talk business	über das Geschäft reden; fachsimpeln
to mess around	schikanieren; hinhalten; nicht geradlinig handeln
par for the course	völlig normal *(„par" ist der Platzstandard beim Golfspiel)*
to rely on *s.th.*	sich auf *etwas* verlassen
to pressure *s.o.*	auf *j-n* Druck ausüben
Cross that bridge when you come to it.	*(Sprichwort)* Lass doch die Dinge auf dich zukommen.

6 At the local pub

▲ Let's now hear how colleagues might talk amongst themselves in one of the most common social contexts.

David Duckham and Deborah Hargreaves invite Claudia Schneider and George Potts for a drink one evening at the local pub. David orders drinks in the British way. They talk about British customs, traditions and sport.

DD: = David Duckham; GP: = George Potts; CS: = Claudia Schneider; DH: = Deborah Hargreaves; T: = Tom, the Barman

DD: Welcome to the *Rose and Crown*!
GP: It's your round, isn't it, David? I seem to remember getting the last one in L.A.!
DD: Trust you to remember that, George.
DD: What are you having, ladies?
CS: A glass of white wine for me, please.
DH: I'll have a half of cider, David, please.
GP: I'll just have a tonic water, please.
DD: OK, George. I'll just have an ordinary pint. There are some seats over there in the corner, look. Grab them and I'll bring the drinks over.
Claudia, Deborah and George go over to the corner.
CS: Why don't they serve you at the table in the pubs over here? In Germany you don't have to queue at the bar and get the drinks yourself.
DH: Tradition, I suppose.
GP: And they save on staff and wages! …
DD: A pint of bitter, a tonic water, … er … a half of cider, and a glass of white wine, Tom, please.
T: Right you are, Mr Duckham.
David takes the drinks over to the others.
GP: Thanks, David.
DD: Well, cheers everyone. Here's to us and more successful projects.
ALL: Cheers!

In der Stammkneipe

▲ Hören wir jetzt, wie sich Kollegen und Kolleginnen privat in entspannter Atmosphäre unterhalten könnten.

Eines Abends laden David Duckham und Deborah Hargreaves Claudia Schneider und George Potts zu einem Drink in ihrer Stammkneipe ein. David bestellt die Getränke auf die übliche britische Art. Sie unterhalten sich über britische Sitten und Gebräuche.

DD: Willkommen im *Rose and Crown.*
GP: Sind Sie nicht dran mit der ersten Runde, David? Ich glaube, die letzte in Los Angeles ging auf mich.
DD: Das sieht Ihnen ähnlich, George, dass gerade Sie sich daran erinnern.
DD: Was darf es denn sein, meine Damen?
CS: Ein Glas Weißwein für mich, bitte.
DH: Ich nehme einen kleinen Cider, bitte, David.
GP: Ich nehme nur ein Tonicwater, bitte.
DD: Okay, George. Für mich ein gewöhnliches Pint. Da drüben in der Ecke sind einige Sitzplätze frei. Gehen Sie schon mal hin – ich bringe dann die Getränke mit.
Claudia, Deborah und George gehen zu dem Tisch in der Ecke.
CS: Warum gibt es hier in den Kneipen keine Bedienung am Tisch? In Deutschland muss man sich nicht an der Theke anstellen und die Getränke selber holen.
DH: Das ist wahrscheinlich Tradition.
GP: Und man spart Personal und Lohnkosten.
DD: Ein Helles, ein Tonicwater, … äh … ein Cider und ein Glas Weißwein, bitte, Tom.
T: Alles klar, Mr. Duckham.
David bringt die Getränke rüber zu den anderen.
GP: Danke, David.
DD: Prost allerseits. Auf uns und noch viele erfolgreiche Projekte!
Alle: Zum Wohl!

DD: Would anyone like anything to nibble?
DH: No, thanks. Too fattening!
CS: I'll have some chips, David, please.
GP: You mean crisps, don't you? I always make the same mistake. We call them chips in the States, too. But the British call them crisps. I mean potato chips, of course, not silicon chips!

DD: That's right. But we do have chips as well – as in fish and chips!
GP: We call *them* "french fries".
CS: And in Germany we call them what the French call them: "Pommes frites".
DH: Confusing, isn't it?
GP: Yeah, Britain sure is different! You know what George Bernard Shaw said: Britain and America are two countries divided by the same language!

David goes to the bar to get the crisps.
GP: Right, everyone. What about a game of good old English darts?

DD: Möchte jemand etwas zum Knabbern?
DH: Nein, danke. Das macht nur dick.
CS: Ein paar Chips für mich, bitte, David.
GP: Sie meinen bestimmt die englischen „Crisps". Ich mache immer den gleichen Fehler. Wir in den Staaten nennen sie auch „Chips". Aber bei den Briten heißen sie „Crisps". Ich meine natürlich Kartoffelchips und nicht Computer-Chips.
DD: Richtig. Aber „Chips" gibt es bei uns auch – wie in „Fish and Chips"!
GP: Ja, *die* heißen bei uns „French Fries".
CS: Und in Deutschland nennen wir sie genauso wie die Franzosen: „Pommes frites".
DH: Verwirrend, oder?
GP: Ja, Großbritannien ist eben anders. Sie kennen den Ausspruch von George Bernard Shaw: „Großbritannien und Amerika sind zwei Länder, die durch die gleiche Sprache voneinander getrennt sind!"
David geht zur Theke, um die Chips zu holen.
GP: Wie wär's – spielen wir eine Runde englisches „Darts"?

Exercises

1 Please listen to the following sentences and then repeat them.

1. It's your round, isn't it? I seem to remember getting the last one.
2. A pint of bitter and a glass of white wine, please.
3. Well, cheers everyone. Here's to us and more successful projects.

2 Please listen to the following sentences and then say which one is correct. Listen to the dialogue again if you need to.

1
a) *The pub is called the King's Head.*
b) *The pub's name is the Rose and Crown.*
c) *The name of the pub is the Bull.*
The correct answer is **b)**. The pub's name is the *Rose and Crown.*

2
a) *In British pubs you collect your drinks yourself from the bar.*
b) *The barman brings the drinks to your table in a British pub.*
c) *A waiter comes to your table in a British pub to take your order.*
The correct answer is **a)**. In British pubs you collect your drinks yourself from the bar.

3
a) *What Americans call "french fries", the British call "crisps".*
b) *What the British call "crisps", the Germans call "Chips".*
c) *What the Germans call "Pommes frites", the Americans call "chips".*
The correct answer is **b)**.What the British call "crisps", the Germans call "Chips".

3 Please listen to the following part of the dialogue again and pay close attention to what George Potts and Claudia Schneider say.

DD: Welcome to the *Rose and Crown*!
GP: It's your round, isn't it David? I seem to remember getting the last one in L.A.!
DD: Trust you to remember that, George.
DD: What are you having, ladies?
CS: A glass of white wine for me, please.
DH: I'll have a half of cider, David, please.
GP: I'll just have a tonic water, please.

Now it is your turn. Listen again and then take the role of George Potts and Claudia Schneider. You'll hear one answer as a model. Other solutions are, of course, also possible.

1. Welcome to the *Rose and Crown.*
   Now take George's part and tell David that it's his round and that you remember getting the last one in L.A.
   It's your round, isn't it, David? I seem to remember getting the last one in L.A.

2. Trust you to remember that, George.
   What are you having, ladies?
   Now take Claudia's part and say you'd like a glass of white wine.
   A glass of white wine for me, please.

3. I'll have a half of cider, David, please.
   Now take George's part and tell David what you would like to drink.
   I'll just have a tonic water, please.

ℹ Most pubs have two or three bars – the Public Bar, the Saloon Bar and maybe a Cocktail Bar to cater for different sets of customers. Drinks such as beer and cider are still served using old British measures: the pint and half-pint.
"Last orders, please" and "Time, please" are shouted by the landlord before closing time; alternatively, a bell may be rung. The "landlord" runs the pub, he may employ a "barman" or a "barmaid". "Barkeeper" is American English.

Vocabulary

local	örtlich; lokal; *hier:* nächstgelegen	**wage**	Lohn
customs	Bräuche; Gebräuche	**a pint**	*etwa:* ein halber Liter; eine Halbe
It's your round.	Sie sind an der Reihe (die Runde zu bezahlen)!; Die nächste Runde geht auf Sie!	**to grab (a seat)**	sich (einen Stuhl) „schnappen", ergattern
		bitter	englisches helles Bier
		Right you are!	Alles klar!
Trust you.	Das sieht Ihnen ähnlich.	**Cheers!**	Prost!
		Here's to us!	Auf uns!
What are you having?	Was möchten Sie denn trinken?	**to nibble**	knabbern
		crisps (BE)	Kartoffelchips
a half (pint)	*etwa:* ein Viertel (Liter)	**(potato) chips (AE)**	Kartoffelchips
cider	*etwa:* Apfelwein oder Cidre	**chips (BE)**	Pommes frites
		(french) fries (AE)	Pommes frites
ordinary	gewöhnlich; normal	**confusing**	verwirrend
to queue	Schlange stehen; sich anstellen	**darts**	Darts (Wurfpfeilspiel)

7 Getting there

▲ In this dialogue we hear how the visitors arrange to travel to a meeting.

George Potts and Claudia Schneider have an important meeting with their Newsdesk clients on the other side of town. They discuss preparations and how best to get there. George Potts is under pressure and unusually irritated.

GP: = George Potts; CS: = Claudia Schneider

GP: Claudia, Deborah has just reminded me. We have another meeting with the *Newsdesk* people this afternoon. You hadn't forgotten, had you?
CS: No, George. I hadn't forgotten. It's at two thirty in the *Royal Hotel*. Have you got the paperwork finished?
GP: Yes, of course I have. I've done the overall costing, but I need to get it signed off by John. I'm seeing him at eleven this morning.
CS: I've done the timetabling. Do we need anything else?
GP: No, I'm not doing any more calculations. Let's hope they accept the price and the delivery date.

CS: Shall we take a taxi? It's pouring down!
GP: OK. Well, you take care of that and I'll clear the budget details, OK? I really don't care how we get there, just as long as we do!

CS: Fine. OK. Calm down. There's no need to shout at me.
GP: I wasn't shouting. Look, sorry, I'm in a hurry and I really have to get these figures cleared first.
CS: OK – meet you downstairs at one thirty.

At one thirty Claudia and George meet in the reception hall.
GP: Hello, Claudia. Listen, sorry I was a bit short with you this morning. Nothing personal. These figures have been driving me crazy.

Ans Ziel gelangen

▲ In diesem Gespräch hören wir, wie sich die Besucher bezüglich der Fahrt zu einer Besprechung abstimmen.

George und Claudia müssen zu einer wichtigen Besprechung mit ihrem Kunden Newsdesk am anderen Ende der Stadt. Sie besprechen die nötigen Vorbereitungen und auch, wie man am besten hinfährt. George steht unter Druck und ist ungewöhnlich gereizt.

GP: Claudia, Deborah hat mich gerade daran erinnert. Wir haben heute Nachmittag noch eine Besprechung mit den Leuten von *Newsdesk*. Sie hatten es nicht vergessen, oder?
CS: Nein, George. Ich hatte es nicht vergessen. Sie findet um halb drei im *Hotel Royal* statt. Haben Sie die Papiere alle fertig?
GP: Ja, natürlich habe ich sie fertig. Ich habe die Gesamtkalkulation abgeschlossen, aber ich brauche noch Johns Unterschrift für die Freigabe. Ich treffe ihn heute Morgen um elf.
CS: Ich habe den Terminplan gemacht. Brauchen wir sonst noch was?
GP: Nein, und ich habe auch nicht vor, noch irgendwelche weiteren Kalkulationen zu machen. Hoffentlich akzeptieren sie den Kostenvoranschlag und den Liefertermin.
CS: Nehmen wir ein Taxi? Es gießt in Strömen.
GP: Okay. Sie kümmern sich darum und ich kläre die Einzelheiten das Budget betreffend, okay? Mir ist es völlig egal, wie wir hinkommen. Hauptsache, wir kommen hin!
CS: In Ordnung. Okay. Beruhigen Sie sich. Sie brauchen mich nicht anzuschreien.
GP: Ich habe Sie nicht angeschrien. Es tut mir Leid. Ich habe es sehr eilig und ich muss mir noch diese Zahlen absegnen lassen.
CS: Okay, wir treffen uns dann unten um halb zwei.
Um halb zwei treffen sich Claudia und George in der Empfangshalle.
GP: Hallo, Claudia. Hören Sie, es tut mir Leid, wenn ich heute Morgen ein bisschen kurz angebunden war. War nicht persönlich ge-

meint. Diese Zahlen machen mich wahnsinnig.

CS: Don't worry about it, George. Main thing is they've been approved. They have been approved now, haven't they?

CS: Machen Sie sich deshalb keine Sorgen, George. Hauptsache, sie wurden genehmigt. Sie sind doch genehmigt worden, oder?

GP: Yes, at last. I know we have to be careful, but some people – mentioning no names – never seem to be satisfied.

GP: Ja, endlich. Ich weiß, dass wir vorsichtig sein müssen, aber manche Menschen – ohne irgendwelche Namen nennen zu wollen – kann man anscheinend niemals zufrieden stellen.

CS: You wouldn't be referring to a certain J.G., would you ? I know he's got a reputation for being quite stubborn and – what do they call it here? – "pernickety"?

CS: Sie meinen nicht zufällig einen gewissen J.G., oder? Ich weiß, er hat den Ruf, ziemlich stur zu sein und ... wie nennen sie es hier? ... pingelig?

GP: "Pernickety" doesn't come into it! Some people just know everything better than anyone else. Know what I mean?

GP: Pingelig ist gar kein Ausdruck. Manche Menschen wissen einfach alles besser. Wissen Sie, was ich meine?

CS: Sure, George. I know what you mean. Oh, here comes our taxi!

CS: Aber sicher, George. Ich weiß, was Sie meinen. Oh, da ist unser Taxi!

Exercises

1 Please listen to the following sentences and then repeat them.

1. We have another meeting this afternoon. You hadn't forgotten, had you?
2. I've done the overall costing but I need to get it signed off.
3. Some people just know everything better than anyone else. Know what I mean?

2 Please listen to the following expressions and then choose the correct definition.

1. I've done the overall costing. I need to get it signed off by John.
   To sign off. *Does this mean:* to approve *or:* to regard as a loss?
   To sign off *means:* to approve.

2. Sorry I was a bit short with you this morning.
   To be short with someone. *Does this mean:* to talk quickly to someone *or:* to talk angrily to someone?
   To be short with someone *means:* to talk angrily to someone .

3. I know he's got a reputation for being quite stubborn.
   Stubborn. *Does this mean:* easy to please *or:* difficult to persuade?
   Stubborn *means:* difficult to persuade.

3 Please answer the following questions using "yes" or "no" and the correct form of the verb. Listen to the dialogue again first if you need to.

1. *Had Claudia forgotten about the meeting with Newsdesk?*
   No, Claudia hadn't forgotten about the meeting with *Newsdesk.*

2. *Does George want to revise all the calculations again?*
   No, George doesn't want to revise all the calculations again.

3. *Did John approve the figures?*
   Yes, John approved the figures.

Vocabulary

under pressure	unter Druck
irritated	ärgerlich; gereizt
paperwork	Papiere; Unterlagen
overall costing	Gesamtkosten; -kalkulation
signed off	genehmigt; freigegeben
timetabling	Terminplan, -gestaltung
delivery date	Liefertermin
It's pouring down.	Es gießt in Strömen.
to shout at *s.o.*	*j-n* anschreien
to go *s.th.* cleared	*etwas* absegnen lassen
to be short with *s.o.*	kurz angebunden sein zu *j-m*
to drive *s.o.* crazy	*j-n* wahnsinnig machen
mentioning no names	ohne irgendwelche Namen nennen zu wollen
to be never satisfied	niemals zufrieden sein
stubborn	stur; hartnäckig
pernickety	pingelig; kleinlich
doesn't come into it	ist gar kein Ausdruck

8 Eating out

▲ Here we listen in as our team meet in a restaurant and learn how to order food and drinks.

George, David, Claudia and Deborah have just finished another meeting with their Newsdesk clients. They go out together for a meal to an Indian restaurant and talk about food and British traditions.

CS: = Claudia Schneider; W: = Waiter; DD: = David Duckham; GP: = George Potts; DH: = Deborah Hargreaves

CS: Well, this is very nice. I hope the food is as good as the decor!

W: Would you all like an aperitif to start?

DD: That's a good idea. I think we deserve it, don't you? Now that we've sorted out that contract with Newsdesk.

GP: I couldn't agree more. That was some deal! Simon is a real tough cookie. …

DD: And what are we going to eat? Erm … what about some samosas and bhajis to start us off? With all the sauces.

Essen im Restaurant

▲ Unser Team trifft sich im Restaurant und bestellt Essen und Getränke.

George, David, Claudia und Deborah haben gerade eine weitere Besprechung mit ihren Kunden von Newsdesk hinter sich gebracht. Sie gehen jetzt gemeinsam zum Essen in ein indisches Restaurant und unterhalten sich über das Essen und über britische Traditionen.

CS: Das ist aber schön hier. Hoffentlich ist das Essen genauso toll wie die Inneneinrichtung!

W: Möchten die Herrschaften vielleicht einen Aperitif?

DD: Das ist eine gute Idee. Ich glaube, den haben wir auch verdient, nicht wahr? Nachdem wir den *Newsdesk*-Auftrag jetzt unter Dach und Fach haben.

GP: Ganz meine Meinung. Das war alles eine ziemlich knifflige Sache. Simon ist ein ganz schön harter Brocken. …

DD: Also, was wollen wir denn essen? Hm … wie wäre es mit ein paar Samosas und Bhajis als Vorspeise? Mit den verschiedenen Soßen.

CS: You're our "Good Food Guide", David. We'll follow your advice.
GP: Sounds good to me.
DH: Yes, they are very nice. For the main course I'm going for the chicken vindaloo.
DD: I didn't know you liked your curry that hot, Deborah.
DH: Oh, the hotter the better for me.
CS: Not for me though. David, what do you suggest?
DD: Well, what meat would you like? Chicken, lamb, beef?
CS: I like lamb.
DD: Well, have the lamb tikka, then. That's not hot.
CS: Fine.
GP: I'll join Deborah. Chicken vindaloo for me, too.
DD: I think I'll have the tandoori chicken.
The waiter comes and David orders the food.
DD: Oh, and some poppadums, some chappatis and a naan, too.
W: And to drink with your meal, sir?
GP: Oh, I'll take a mineral water.
DD: Well, I think we'll need some table water. A large bottle for all of us. And then what about a bottle of wine? OK by you, ladies?
DH: Yes, that's fine as long as it's white wine.
DD: White wine for you, Claudia?
CS: Yes, OK. Indian food has a great tradition in Britain, hasn't it? We don't have many Indian restaurants in Germany. More Turkish and Greek.
DD: Yes, well, we have a very large Indian population in Britain and you have a large Turkish population in Germany.
GP: It's certainly interesting dinner conversation, isn't it?! If you look at food and restaurants you can see the whole history and traditions of a country, can't you?

CS: Sie sind unser „Restaurant-Führer", David. Wir folgen Ihrem Rat.
GP: Ist mir auch ganz recht.
DH: Ja, die schmecken sehr gut. Als Hauptgericht nehme ich Hähnchen Vindaloo.
DD: Ich wusste gar nicht, dass Sie den ganz scharfen Curry mögen, Deborah.
DH: Oh, ich finde, je schärfer desto besser.
CS: Aber für mich bitte nicht. David, was schlagen Sie vor?
DD: Okay, welche Art Fleisch möchten Sie denn? Huhn, Lamm, Rind?
CS: Lammfleisch esse ich sehr gern.
DD: Ja, dann nehmen Sie Lamm Tikka. Das ist bestimmt nicht scharf.
CS: Fein.
GP: Ich schließe mich Deborah an. Hähnchen Vindaloo auch für mich.
DD: Ich glaube, ich nehme Hähnchen Tandoori.
Der Ober kommt, und David bestellt das Essen.
DD: Oh, und einige Poppadums und Chappatis und auch ein Naan, bitte.
W: Und was möchten Sie zum Essen trinken, Sir?
GP: Ich nehme ein Mineralwasser.
DD: Ich glaube, wir brauchen etwas Tafelwasser. Eine große Flasche für uns alle. Und dann – wie wäre es mit einer Flasche Wein? Ist das okay, meine Damen?
DH: Ja, schön, solange es ein Weißwein ist.
DD: Weißwein auch für Sie, Claudia?
CS: Ja, gerne. Die indische Küche hat eine lange Tradition in Großbritannien, nicht wahr? In Deutschland haben wir nicht sehr viele indische Restaurants. Dafür aber mehr türkische und griechische.
DD: Ja, klar, wir haben einen sehr hohen indischen Bevölkerungsanteil in Großbritannien, und Sie in Deutschland haben eben einen hohen türkischen Bevölkerungsanteil.
GP: Das ist wirklich ein interessantes Thema beim Essen. Wenn man sich das Essen und die Restaurants anschaut, sieht man die ganze Geschichte und alle Traditionen eines Landes vor sich.

Exercises

1 Please listen to the following sentences and then repeat them.

1. That's a good idea. I think we deserve it, don't you?
2. You're our "Good Food Guide", David. We'll follow your advice.
3. Indian food has a great tradition in Britain, hasn't it?

2 Please listen to the following sentences and say whether they are true or false. First listen to the dialogue again if you need to.

1. *Simon from Newsdesk is a difficult customer.*
   This sentence is true. Simon from *Newsdesk* is a difficult customer.
2. *Deborah hates hot curry.*
   This sentence is false. For Deborah the hotter the better.
3. *Deborah will have the lamb tikka for the main course.*
   This sentence is false. Deborah will have the chicken vindaloo for the main course.

3 Now listen to the following part of the dialogue and then take the role of Claudia Schneider and Deborah Hargreaves.

DD: And what are we going to eat? Erm … what about some samosas and bhajis to start us off? With all the sauces.

CS: You're our "Good Food Guide", David. We'll follow your advice.

GP: Sounds good to me.

DH: Yes, they are very nice. For the main course I'm going for the chicken vindaloo.

Now it's your turn. Listen again and take the role of Claudia Schneider and Deborah Hargreaves. You'll hear one answer as a model. Other solutions are, of course, also possible.

1. And what are we going to eat? Erm … what about some samosas and bhajis to start us off? With all the sauces.
   Now take Claudia's part and tell David that he is their "Good Food Guide" and that you will all follow his advice.
   You're our "Good Food Guide", David. We'll follow your advice.

2. Sounds good to me.
   Now take the role of Deborah and confirm that they taste nice and that for the main course you are going for the chicken vindaloo.
   Yes, they are very nice. For the main course I'm going for the chicken vindaloo.

ℹ Due to its colonial past the UK has now become a multicultural society. In any city there will be a number of shops and restaurants run by members of various ethnic groups. Indian and Chinese restaurants are particularly popular. Indian food is not all hot curry. There are dozens of other delicious aromatic dishes. The hotness of a curry dish can be judged by the name of the area of India from which it comes. The nearer the area or city to the equator the hotter the curry. Hottest of all is a vindaloo curry.

In the UK at the end of the meal you ask for the "bill", while in the USA you ask for the "check".

Vocabulary

decor Dekor; Ausstattung; Inneneinrichtung
to deserve verdienen
to sort out *s.th.* *etwas* klären; erledigen
I couldn't agree more. Ganz meine Meinung.
That was some deal. Das war eine ziemlich knifflige Sache.
a real tough cookie (AE *coll.*) ein wirklich schwieriger Verhandlungspartner; ein „harter Brocken"
Right then! Also!
samosas and bhajis *indische Vorspeisen*
guide Berater; Führer
vindaloo *die wohl schärfste Art, einen Curry zuzubereiten*
hot (spicy food) scharf
Not for me though! Aber nicht für mich!
tikka *aromatisches indisches Gericht*
tandoori *Bezeichnung für die Art der Zubereitung*
poppadums *indische Brotsorte, in Öl knusprig gebraten, in großen, sehr dünnen Scheiben*
chappatis *indische Brotsorte, weich gebacken, in kleineren Scheiben*
naan *größeres indisches Weißbrot*

9 At the theatre

▲ Here we listen in to what colleagues might discuss at a cultural event.

The four business colleagues discuss getting tickets for the theatre. On Saturday evening they meet at the theatre and then talk about the performance in the interval while having a drink at the bar.

DD: = David Duckham; GP: = George Potts; DH: = Deborah Hargreaves; CS: = Claudia Schneider

DD: I can get tickets for the "Complete Works of Shakespeare" next week. Anyone else interested?
GP: Is that still running? It's quite old now, isn't it?
DH: The complete works? You can't do them in sixth months let alone in one evening.

DD: No, this is a comedy version where they cut all the plays down to a few lines and then mix them up. It's supposed to be very funny.

Im Theater

▲ Hier können wir dabei zuhören, wie Kollegen über ein kulturelles Ereignis diskutieren.

Die vier Geschäftskollegen sprechen darüber, Theaterkarten zu besorgen. Am Samstag Abend treffen sie sich im Theater. In der Pause unterhalten sie sich dann über die Aufführung, während sie an der Bar zusammen etwas trinken.

DD: Ich kann für „Shakespeares gesammelte Werke" nächste Woche Karten kriegen. Hat noch jemand Interesse?
GP: Läuft das Stück immer noch? Es ist schon ziemlich alt, nicht wahr?
DH: Die gesammelten Werke? Das kann man nicht mal in sechs Monaten schaffen, geschweige denn an einem Abend.
DD: Nein, das hier ist eine Komödie. Alle Dramen werden auf ein paar Zeilen reduziert und dann durcheinander gemischt. Es soll sehr komisch sein.

CS: I wanted to go to that modern handicraft exhibition this weekend.
GP: I haven't been to the theatre for such a long time. Yes, I'll come. Good idea. Maybe I'll learn something about Shakespeare, too.
DH: I'd like a good laugh. It'll make a change from dealing with complaints from staff.

CS: I suppose I can go to the exhibition later. Are you sure you can get tickets for all of us, David?
DD: Yes, no problem. Great. I'll organise that then.
On the night of the performance they all meet at the theatre. In the interval after the first half they go into the bar.
DD: What did you think of that then?
DH: Oh, I enjoyed that. It's really funny, isn't it?

GP: I didn't know Shakespeare could be so entertaining.
CS: I thought it was a bit silly, really. And there was a lot of overacting.
GP: It is meant to be a comedy, you know! Lots of slapstick and silliness. That's the point.
CS: Not my style, I'm afraid.
DD: Well, maybe you'll like the second half more, Claudia. I must admit I was a bit disappointed. I thought the actors weren't particularly good. Maybe it's because I don't go to the theatre very often. Television spoils us a bit, I think, in that regard. You only get one chance to get it right on stage.

GP: That's what makes it unique … and live and vibrant and exciting. You're part of it all. Not like watching a film at all.

DD: Oh, I can see you're a theatre buff, George. Good for you.
GP: Yes, I admit it's one of my interests. Oh, come on, the second half is about to begin.

CS: Ich wollte dieses Wochenende in diese Ausstellung „Modernes Kunsthandwerk" gehen.
GP: Ich war seit ewigen Zeiten nicht mehr im Theater. Ja, ich komme mit. Gute Idee. Vielleicht lerne ich sogar noch etwas über Shakespeare.
DH: Ich möchte mal wieder richtig lachen. Das wird eine schöne Abwechslung sein, wo ich mich sonst nur um die Beschwerden von Mitarbeitern kümmern muss.
CS: Ich kann die Ausstellung ja später besuchen. Sind Sie sicher, dass Sie Karten für uns alle bekommen, David?
DD: Ja, kein Problem. Großartig. Ich kümmere mich dann darum.
Am Abend der Vorstellung treffen sie sich alle im Theater. In der Pause nach der ersten Hälfte gehen sie in die Bar.
DD: Wie hat es Ihnen bisher gefallen?
DH: Hat mir großen Spaß gemacht. Es ist wirklich lustig, nicht wahr?
GP: Ich wusste nicht, dass Shakespeare so unterhaltsam sein kann.
CS: Ich fand das alles eigentlich ein bisschen albern.
GP: Das ist doch eine Komödie! Viel Slapstick und Blödsinn. Gerade darum geht es ja!
CS: Tut mir Leid. Das ist nichts für mich.
DD: Na, vielleicht gefällt Ihnen die zweite Hälfte besser, Claudia. Ich muss zugeben, ich war ein bisschen enttäuscht. Die Schauspieler kommen mir nicht besonders gut vor. Vielleicht liegt es daran, dass ich nicht sehr oft ins Theater gehe. Das Fernsehen verwöhnt uns in dieser Hinsicht doch ein wenig, denke ich. Auf der Bühne hat man nur einmal die Chance, alles richtig zu machen.
GP: Aber gerade das macht das Theater doch so einmalig … und lebendig und voller Spannung und aufregend. Man ist selbst Teil davon. Überhaupt nicht wie bei einem Film.
DD: Oh, ich sehe schon. Sie sind Theaterkenner, George. Respekt!
GP: Ja, ich gebe zu, es ist eines meiner Interessengebiete. Aber kommen Sie jetzt, es geht gleich weiter.

Exercises

1 Please listen to the following sentences and then repeat them.

1. I can get tickets for the theatre next week. Is anyone else interested?
2. I haven't been to the theatre for such a long time.
3. I must admit I was a bit disappointed.

2 Please listen to the following expressions and then choose the right definition.

1. It'll make a change from dealing with complaints from staff.
   To deal with. *In this context does this mean:* to do business with someone *or:* to concern oneself with something?
   To deal with *here means:* to concern oneself with something.

2. That's what makes it unique.
   Unique. *Does this mean:* special and singular *or:* the same as everything else?
   Unique *means:* special and singular.

3. Oh I can see that you're a theatre buff, George.
   Theatre buff. *Does this mean:* an expert on the theatre *or:* someone ignorant of the theatre?
   A theatre buff *means:* an expert on the theatre.

3 Now listen to the dialogue again and then answer the following questions. Several answers are, of course, possible.

1. *What kind of play is "The Complete Works of Shakespeare"?*
   "The Complete Works of Shakespeare" is a comedy.

2. *What kind of exhibition did Claudia want to go to?*
   Claudia wanted to go to a modern handicraft exhibition.

3. *Why was David a little disappointed by the performance?*
   Because he thought the actors weren't particularly good.

Vocabulary

performance	Aufführung; Vorstellung
interval	Pause
let alone	geschweige denn
comedy	Komödie
to cut down	reduzieren
handicraft	Kunsthandwerk
I'd like a good laugh.	Ich möchte mal wieder richtig lachen.
It'll make a change.	Das wird eine schöne Abwechslung sein.; Mal was anderes.
to deal with *s.th.*	sich um *etwas* kümmern
complaints	Beschwerden
a bit silly	ein bisschen albern
overacting	Übertreibung
to overact *s.th.*	*etwas* überziehen/übertreiben
slapstick	Slapstick; Klamauk
silliness	Blödsinn; Albernheit(en)
That's the point!	Gerade darum geht es!
Not my style.	(Das ist) nichts für mich.
to spoil *s.o.*	*j-n* verwöhnen
unique	einmalig
vibrant	voller Spannung
theatre buff	Theaterkenner; Theaterfan
Good for you.	Respekt!

10 Saying goodbye

▲ In this dialogue we listen in as our team discuss their work experience before saying goodbye.

George and Claudia are invited with their Joystix colleagues to a planning conference. George and Claudia are in the hotel bar with David, Deborah and John Grisedale and use the occasion to describe their experiences over the past six months and to say thankyou and goodbye before leaving for the airport.

JG: = John Grisedale; GP: = George Potts; DD: = David Duckham; CS: = Claudia Schneider; DH: = Deborah Hargreaves

JG: Tell me, you two. How have you enjoyed your six months with *Joystix*? I know you've been a big help to us, especially in clinching that *Newsdesk* deal.

GP: Well, it's been a bit tougher this time – for me anyway. Time was short and decisions took a long time.

JG: Meaning me, I expect. Yes, David told me you weren't too happy with things at times. I'm sorry if it was my fault. If I've become a bottleneck, we'll have to do something about it. It's a cardinal sin in management.

GP: Well, you did take a long time to approve my figures on the *Newsdesk* deal.

JG: It was a big commitment, George. Your figures were OK, but I had to be certain we could deliver. You're leaving us tomorrow, remember, and a couple of our prospective new recruits have been head-hunted by the competition.

GP: So you need me to stay. Is that what you're saying?

Abschied nehmen

▲ Hier hören wir, wie unser Team vor dem Abschied seine Arbeitserfahrungen austauscht.

George und Claudia werden von ihren Kollegen von Joystix zu einer Planungskonferenz eingeladen. George und Claudia treffen sich mit David, Deborah und John Grisedale in der Hotelbar. Sie nehmen die Gelegenheit wahr, um über ihre Erfahrungen während der letzten sechs Monate zu berichten, sich vor ihrer Abreise für alles zu bedanken und sich zu verabschieden.

JG: Nun sagen Sie mal, Sie beide, wie haben Ihnen diese sechs Monate bei *Joystix* gefallen? Für uns waren Sie auf jeden Fall eine große Hilfe, insbesondere, als es darum ging, die Verhandlungen mit *Newsdesk* zum Abschluss zu bringen.

GP: Es war diesmal ein bisschen schwieriger – für mich jedenfalls. Die Zeit war knapp, und Entscheidungen haben eine Ewigkeit gebraucht.

JG: Damit meinen Sie wahrscheinlich mich. Ja, David hat mir schon erzählt, dass Sie manchmal nicht ganz zufrieden waren. Es tut mir Leid, wenn ich daran schuld war. Wenn ich zum Bremser geworden bin, dann müssen wir etwas dagegen unternehmen. Das ist ein Kardinalfehler im Management-Bereich.

GP: Na ja, Sie haben schon viel Zeit gebraucht, um meine Zahlen zum *Newsdesk*-Auftrag freizugeben.

JG: Da gingen wir eine große Verpflichtung ein, George. Ihre Zahlen waren völlig in Ordnung, aber ich musste ganz sicher sein, dass wir auch tatsächlich liefern können. Sie verlassen uns morgen – oder hatten Sie das vergessen? Und ein paar der vorgesehenen neuen Mitarbeiter wurden uns von den Headhuntern der Konkurrenz weggeschnappt.

GP: Also brauchen Sie mich noch. Ist es das, was Sie mir sagen wollen?

DD: No, it's OK, George. We've solved the problem. The new guy starts on Monday. Things will dovetail together nicely.

DD: Nein, George. Es ist alles in Ordnung. Wir haben das Problem gelöst. Der Neue fängt schon kommenden Montag an. Es wird schon alles glatt gehen.

GP: Well, that's good news for all of us. You know, I have enjoyed working with you all really. Honest!

GP: Na, dann können wir ja alle zufrieden sein. Wissen Sie, mir hat die Arbeit mit Ihnen allen wirklich Spaß gemacht. Ehrlich!

JG: What about you, Claudia? Any complaints or regrets?

JG: Und wie ist es bei Ihnen, Claudia? Irgendwelche Beschwerden? Oder bereuen Sie etwas?

CS: Oh no. Not really. I've enjoyed every minute of it. You've all been very kind and helpful and I've learnt such a lot. I feel very confident now about starting my own business back in Munich. What's impressed me most is how you all get on with each other despite the difficulties, the pressure and the occasional misunderstanding.

CS: Oh, nein. Eigentlich nicht. Ich habe jede Minute genossen. Sie sind alle sehr freundlich und hilfsbereit gewesen, und ich habe eine ganze Menge gelernt. Ich habe jetzt genug Selbstvertrauen, um mein eigenes Geschäft in München aufzubauen. Was mir am meisten imponiert hat, ist die Art, wie gut Sie alle miteinander auskommen trotz aller Schwierigkeiten, trotz Arbeitsdruck und gelegentlicher Missverständnisse.

DD: Well, we always try to cultivate a good working atmosphere. You need it when things start to go wrong. And they inevitably do!

DD: Wir bemühen uns immer um ein gutes Betriebsklima. Das ist wichtig, wenn Dinge beginnen schief zu laufen.

GP: Murphy's Law! If anything can go wrong, it will. And at the worst possible moment.

GP: Murphys Gesetz! Wenn etwas schief gehen kann, dann tut es das auch. Und immer im allerungünstigsten Augenblick!

The next day the conference takes place and plans are made for the next big project. At four thirty it's time to leave.

Am nächsten Tag findet die Konferenz statt. Pläne werden für das nächste große Projekt gemacht. Um halb fünf ist es dann Zeit zu fahren.

DH: Claudia, George, your taxi is here.

DH: Claudia, George. Ihr Taxi ist da.

GP: Well, this is it folks. Time to leave. Deborah, David, it's been great. See you again sometime. And if you're ever in L.A., promise to look me up.

GP: Okay, Leute. Es ist so weit. Zeit zum Adieusagen. Deborah, David, es war eine sehr schöne Zeit mit Ihnen. Wir sehen uns irgendwann wieder. Und wenn Sie zufällig mal in Los Angeles sein sollten, schauen Sie bei mir vorbei. Versprochen?

CS: Goodbye everyone. Thank you, David. Thank you, Deborah, for everything. If you come to Munich, let me know. I'd love to show you around.

CS: Auf Wiedersehen allerseits. Vielen Dank, David. Vielen Dank, Deborah, für alles. Wenn Sie mal nach München kommen, lassen Sie es mich wissen. Ich würde Ihnen sehr gerne die Stadt zeigen.

DD: Bye, Claudia. Bye, George. See you sometime.

DD: Wiedersehen, Claudia. Wiedersehen, George. Bis zum nächsten Mal.

Exercises

1 Please listen to the following sentences and then repeat them.

1. Your figures were OK, but I had to be certain we could deliver.
2. You've all been very kind and helpful and I've learnt such a lot.
3. We always try to cultivate a good working atmosphere.

2 Please listen to the following sentences and then say which is correct. Listen to the dialogue again if you need to.

1

a) *John Grisedale says to George that he didn't know he had been unhappy.*

b) *John Grisedale apologises to George for any slow decision-making.*

c) *George had told David that there was nothing to worry about.*

The correct answer is **b)**. John Grisedale apologises to George for any slow decision-making.

2

a) *John wants George to stay on longer to oversee the project.*

b) *David has already solved the problem with George's replacement.*

c) *George has hated every minute of his time at Joystix.*

The correct answer is **b)**. David has already solved the problem with George's replacement.

3

a) *Claudia is now very confident about going back to Munich.*

b) *Claudia has cultivated a good working atmosphere.*

c) *Claudia wants to forget all about Murphy's Law.*

The correct answer is **a)**. Claudia is now very confident about going back to Munich.

3 Please listen to the dialogue again and then answer the following questions. Of course, several solutions are possible.

1. *Why does George think that this time things have been tougher for him?*
   Because time was short and decisions took a long time.
2. *Why did John Grisedale take a long time to approve the figures George had compiled?*
   Because he thought it was a big commitment and George would not be there much longer.
3. *What impressed Claudia most about working at Joystix?*
   What impressed Claudia most was how everyone got on with each other despite the difficulties.

ℹ In the world of business a sense of humour always seems to aid progress – and is an essential ingredient of any small talk. Here are some of Murphy's "pearls of wisdom" particularly relevant to the world of business:
- The only way to discover the limits of the possible is to go beyond them into the impossible.
- You can't tell how deep a puddle is until you step in it!
- Asking dumb questions is easier than correcting dumb mistakes!
- Experience is something you don't get until just after you need it!

Vocabulary

to clinch a deal	eine Verhandlung zum Abschluss bringen
tough	hart; zäh
bottleneck	Flaschenhals; Engpass
cardinal sin	Kardinalfehler
commitment	Verpflichtung
prospective	voraussichtlich
recruit	Bewerber
to dovetail	koordinieren
confident	zuversichtlich
to get on with *s.o.*	mit *j-m* gut auskommen
Murphy's Law	Murphys Gesetz (*s. Info. oben*)
to look *s.o.* up	bei *j-m* vorbeischauen

Liste der ID-Nummern für CD 5: Small Talk

Inhalt der CD	ID-Nummer:		
Vorspann	**1**	**Dialogue 6**	**22**
Dialogue 1	**2**	Exercise 1	23
Exercise 1	3	Exercise 2	24
Exercise 2	4	Exercise 3	25
Exercise 3	5	**Dialogue 7**	**26**
Dialogue 2	**6**	Exercise 1	27
Exercise 1	7	Exercise 2	28
Exercise 2	8	Exercise 3	29
Exercise 3	9	**Dialogue 8**	**30**
Dialogue 3	**10**	Exercise 1	31
Exercise 1	11	Exercise 2	32
Exercise 2	12	Exercise 3	33
Exercise 3	13	**Dialogue 9**	**34**
Dialogue 4	**14**	Exercise 1	35
Exercise 1	15	Exercise 2	36
Exercise 2	16	Exercise 3	37
Exercise 3	17	**Dialogue 10**	**38**
Dialogue 5	**18**	Exercise1	39
Exercise 1	19	Exercise 2	40
Exercise 2	20	Exercise 3	41
Exercise 3	21	End	42